I'm in This for You

The Truth in Becoming a Great Leader

Dear David,
Your leadership will continue to flourish as you continue to learn and battle through the challenges that HE allows.
Godspeed,

Dr. Roger Kingston

Command Sergeant Major, U.S. Army (Retired)

ISBN 978-1-63844-391-9 (paperback)
ISBN 978-1-63844-392-6 (digital)

Christian Faith Publishing, Inc.
832 Park Avenue
Meadville, PA 16335
www.christianfaithpublishing.com

This book references over nine hundred verses from forty-seven different Books in the Bible. All Biblical scripture in this book is from the New Living Translation (NLT).

Printed in the United States of America

CONTENTS

THE LEADER'S PRAYER

Heavenly Father, thank you for the honor and privilege of serving and leading others this day. Please grant me the wisdom of King Solomon, King David's courage, and the heart of Jesus Christ as I serve and lead for Your glory.

In Jesus's name, I pray, amen.

INTRODUCTION

Show me a great team of individuals or show me a great organization, and you can bet that they are led by a great leader or hierarchy of great leaders. Great leaders who understand the real motive required to maximize people's abilities and efforts are their desire to serve those they lead. Leading others at any level of leadership requires technical and professional competencies. However, to achieve the status of being a great leader requires a leader motivated by something more significant than their success. Forming a group of random individuals, each with their unique talents, education, cultural backgrounds, beliefs, strengths, weaknesses, biases, and agenda into one cohesive and singularly oriented team or organization, requires a leader with the right motive.

So much is researched, written, and discussed about "leadership styles" as the answer to becoming an effective or great leader. Meanwhile, the singular motive for becoming a great leader is overlooked. Who are we leading for, ourselves or others? We lead for others. As a leader, our motive must always remain, "I'm in this for you!"

Before retiring from the military, people would ask me what I would like to do after the military. I would tell them that I would love to work again and in a place where I could be the link between the workforce and the organization's leadership. Being in such a position would allow me to make sure the workforce's needs were being heard and addressed by the leadership. I would also be able to make sure the workforce responded appropriately to the organization's leadership needs. I want to make people's lives better and more fulfilling in the workplace. Working for one organization would minimize the number of people affected by leading by the Truth. I sincerely believe every person deserves leaders who lead according to God's Truth; therefore, this book was written.

I loved being a soldier. There was not one minute in thirty-two years that I ever hated my job. Even during multiple deployments of combat, I never woke up hating my career. I would wake up already tired but loving my profession as a soldier. I use the New Living Translation Version of the Holy Bible in my daily Scripture reading. Second Timothy chapter 2 is titled "A Good Soldier for Christ Jesus." This introductory title caught my attention because I loved being a good soldier for this country. I thought to myself, *I don't have to stop being a good soldier. I need to change who I am soldiering for in life.* And then I read 2 Timothy 2:2, ***You have heard me teach things that have been confirmed by many reliable witnesses. Now teach these truths to other trustworthy people who will be able to pass them on to others.***

I pray that God will use this book to place His Truth in leading into the hearts, minds, tongues, and hands of leaders worldwide. If we lead as God's Word teaches, we will be God's hands and feet of love in this world and the lives of our fellow brothers and sisters. Life is so hard, and this world is dangerous right now because we have all forgotten how to be here for one another, not just ourselves. We need God's help and protection. It all starts with God's Truth. The "Truth" in becoming a great leader is God's Word. Apply it and follow it, and greatness will come.

PART 1

Leadership God's Way

All Scripture is inspired by God and is useful to teach us what is true and to make us realize what is wrong in our lives. It corrects us when we are wrong and teaches us to do what is right. God uses it to prepare and equip his people to do every good work.

—2 Timothy 3:16–17

WARNING! This book will **not** introduce some new-fangled or radically secret way to become a great leader. Ecclesiastes 1:9–10 let's all of us in on the truth, ***History merely repeats itself. It has all been done before. Nothing under the sun is truly new. Sometimes people say, "Here is something new!" But actually it is old; nothing is ever truly new.*** Sorry if that's what you were expecting. However, this book will spotlight the tested under fire, verified, and validated through years of leadership application, the psychological and sociological leadership perspectives established by God to promote greatness in life and leadership. Everything begins with God's Truth; His is the standard by which we serve and lead others. Truth is God's view on any subject matter, including leadership!

The study of leadership may leave a person with more questions than answers when attempting to find an agreed-upon leadership definition. After conducting an extensive search designed to identify the published variances of the definitions of leadership, leadership scholars concluded, "We reviewed 160 articles and books that contained a definition, a scale, or a construct of leadership."[1] Determining a "one size fits all" definition of leadership seems almost impossible, as leadership is defined differently throughout society. The study of leadership must move past defining it and shift its focus to identifying the elements found in good leadership, which will produce great leadership when cultivated with God's truth. The ultimate question in leadership studies is not "What is the definition of leadership?" The ultimate point of studying leadership is "What is *good* leadership?" The use of the word *good* here has two senses, morally good and technically good."[2]

This book will present the essential elements of "morally good," along with the central and significantly important motives and methods for great leadership. When applied correctly, these motives and methods will metamorphize into great leadership according to God's Truth. You may be asking yourself, "Where did this guy find these "not so secret" ingredients to becoming a great leader?" It all starts with the "Seed of Truth"! In Revelation 3:14, Jesus says, ***"This is the message from the one who is the Amen—the faithful and true witness, the beginning of God's new creation."*** *Amen* means "It is so; so be it." God is the final authority on everything that was, is, and will be.

The "Seed" is the Word of God. In the "Seed" is life. A seed by itself sitting in a jar is just a little seed; it can remain only a seed for hundreds of years if left in the jar. But place that single seed into the soil, feed it water, and surround it with a warm temperature. Now, that same single dead-looking seed will burst open and begin creeping up through the dark, moist soil searching for sunlight. That little seemingly dead seed burst into a new and grander creation of life. For an abundant and meaningful experience as a person, God's Word is our seed. Jesus told His disciples in Matthew 13:12, ***"To those who listen to my teaching, more understanding will be given, and they will have an abundance of knowledge."*** By studying the Word and applying the Word to our lives, we will burst into more abundant lives. We will burst forth into leading our lives and leading others with the greatness God created us to achieve.

The Seed of God is Truth; in other words, God's Word is Truth—it has always been true, is true, and will always be true. We are to base our lives and how we lead others on God's Truth. Jesus Christ came to reveal the Truth. In John 18:37, Jesus, when asked if he was a king, answered, saying, ***"I was born and came into the world to testify to the truth. All who love the truth recognize that what I say is true."*** Just before Jesus is to be betrayed and crucified, He speaks to the Father about His disciples and those that believe in him in John 17:16–17, ***"They do not belong to this world any more than I do. Make them holy by your truth; teach them your word, which is truth."*** Throughout the Bible, the Truth in God's Word has been validated time and time again:

> ***Every word of God proves true.*** (Proverbs 30:5)

> ***This truth gives them confidence that they have eternal life, which God—who does not lie—promised them before the world began.*** (Titus 1:2)

> ***So God has given both his promise and his oath. These two things are unchangeable because it is impossible for God to lie.*** (Hebrews 6:18)

> ***God is not man, so he does not lie. He is not human, so he does not change his mind.*** (Numbers 23:19)

> "***I, the LORD, speak only what is true and declare only what is right.***" (Isaiah 45:19)

> The LORD says, ***"I have sworn by my own name; I have spoken the truth, and I will never go back on my word."*** (Isaiah 45:23)

> ***All who invoke a blessing or take an oath will do so by the God of truth.*** (Isaiah 65:16)

God, who is Truth, and what He says is Truth, tells us as a person and as a leader how important it is that we follow the Words of His Truth. God told Joshua as he became the leader of millions of people.

> ***Be strong and very courageous. Be careful to obey all the instructions Moses gave you. Do not deviate from them, turning either to the right or left. Then you will be successful in everything you do. Study this Book of Instruction continually. Meditate on it day and night so you will be sure to obey everything written in it. Only then will you prosper and succeed in all you do. This is my command—be strong and courageous! Do not be afraid or discouraged. For the LORD your God is with you wherever you go.*** (Joshua 1:7–9)

Leaders are people leading other people, but we cannot humanize how we lead others. We cannot allow this world's culture of "man knows best" to minimize or override how God tells us to lead others. This logic of thought falls under the philosophy of secular humanism. Secular humanism follows the thought process that other people's ideas should tell a person how to live life. In other words, use man's self-taught ways of living life over how God's Word tells us to live our lives. How can man, created by God, overrule or claim to know better ways to lead other people than the creator himself? Technology has made drastic changes throughout the span of humanity's existence. Still, man himself is the same beast, with the same moral challenges encountered from the time of our creation. And leadership is all about how an individual, given the honor of leading others, addresses those same moral and ethical challenges today.

God's Word leaves no challenge of leadership without guidance and an example. Throughout God's Word, any use of the word *shepherd* represents calling the person a "leader." God's Word teaches leaders their role of serving and caring for people the way shepherds tended their sheep. Man has not created any new humanistic moral challenges within the leadership arena that was not present and addressed by God's Word. God's Word represents "The Truth." Man's word represents "my Truth," and "my Truth" is anything we want it to be, while God's "Truth" is always what he says it is, "The Truth."

I have never been mistakenly identified as being the brightest or smartest person you might meet. But even I understand that if everything God says is true, God's Word is Truth, and God's Word tells us repeatedly how we are to lead and serve others; this might be something worth exploring deeper.

Nonnegotiable Needs

Physically: Air
Water: ➢➢➢ To Sustain the Flesh
Food

Spiritually: God's Word ➢➢➢ For Life More Abundantly

> ***For the word of God is alive and powerful. It is sharper than the sharpest two-edged sword, cutting between soul and spirit, between joint and marrow. It exposes our innermost thoughts and desires. Nothing in all creation is hidden from God. Everything is naked and exposed before his eyes, and he is the one to whom we are accountable.*** (Hebrews 4:12–13)

God's Word presents the most truthful and absolute best way to lead. God's Word is filled with pinpoint instruction and beautiful examples of leadership. Let's look at an example of God telling us how to lead others:

> ***Care for the flock that God has entrusted to you. Watch over it willingly, not grudgingly—not for what you will get out of it, but because you are eager to serve God. Don't lord it over the people assigned to your care but lead them by your own good example.*** (1 Peter 5:2–3)

(In other words, leader, keep watch over those you lead because you genuinely care about them, lead ethically, lead selflessly, empower and encourage others, and lead by example.) Great stuff indeed!

Now you are thinking, "Okay, God's Word is true, but why learn to lead based on what God says and not on some secular leadership "guru's" latest "bestseller"? A "bestseller" is most likely written by some person that thinks they know how to lead because other "scholars" tell them they know what they are talking about. ***The LORD has given me a strong warning not to think like everyone else does*** (Isaiah 8:11). We are to think and act like God's Word so clearly and precisely tells us to.

The world is full of self-promoting, opinionated, and secularly (a way of thinking that God is not necessary, or we have this figured out on our own) educated leadership "experts/scholars." Still, they are not teaching leadership from the foundational Word of God. ***Those people belong to this world, so they speak from the world's viewpoint, and the world listens to them*** (1 John 4:5). This viewpoint equates to the blind leading the blind. Jesus addressed the absurdity of following someone that is not teaching leadership aligned with His truth in Luke 6:39–40, ***Then Jesus gave the following illustration: "Can one blind person lead another? Won't they both fall into a ditch? Students are not greater than their teacher. But the student who is fully trained will become like the teacher."***

God tells us to avoid the secular world's thoughts and ways in Colossians 2:8, ***Don't let anyone capture you with empty philosophies and high-sounding nonsense that come from human think-***

ing and from the spiritual powers of this world, rather than from Christ. Trusting in man's theories and mere speculations of how we lead others lend to following flawed advice and instruction from man's perspective. God's Word warns against following those who are "wise" in their own opinion or insight and not God's. ***These wise teachers will fall into the trap of their own foolishness, for they have rejected the word of the LORD. Are they so wise after all?*** (Jeremiah 8:9). God's Word warns us again in 1 Corinthians 3:18–19, ***Stop deceiving yourselves. If you think you are wise by this world's standards, you need to become a fool to be truly wise. For the wisdom of this world is foolishness to God.*** Instead, we are to follow God's instruction, who warns us in Isaiah 2:22, ***Don't put your trust in mere humans. They are as frail as breath. What good are they?*** Some may argue that we must lead as society tells us with a particular "leadership style." But God's Word tells us to avoid entertaining their desire to teach others down the wrong path in their leadership development. ***Guard what God has entrusted to you. Avoid godless, foolish discussions with those who oppose you with their so-called knowledge*** (1 Timothy 6:20). God's Word even tells us to listen to him, and His way in Hebrews 12:25, ***Be careful that you do not refuse to listen to the One who is speaking.***

I am certainly no one to say that man has no good motives and suggestions in their leadership teaching; many do. We are all seeking to find ways to better ourselves. Even God's Word asks us why wouldn't we want to learn how to lead from God? ***But shouldn't people ask God for guidance?*** (Isaiah 8:19). Scripture then instructs us in Isaiah 8:20, ***Look to God's instructions and teachings! People who contradict his word are completely in the dark.*** Yes, there is plenty to learn in becoming a great leader; we are clay being formed by the potter. **And yet, O LORD, you are our Father. *We are the clay, and you are the potter. We are all formed by your hand*** (Isaiah 64:8). The main point here is we should learn to lead as God instructs, for His ways are perfect. ***The instructions of the LORD are perfect, reviving the soul*** (Psalm 19:7). There is plenty to learn to become a great leader. God's Word should be the foundational basis of how we lead. Still, there is plenty to learn from people God has appointed to teach and strengthen our leadership abilities. We should seek leadership development founded on leadership principles reflecting God's Truth in leading others.

Much of the things we attempt to do in life flows from the process of trial and error. We stumble around in the dark of naivety, hoping to get things right. We do not have to lead in the dark, we can lead in the light provided by God's Word. John 8:12 Jesus said, ***"I am the light of the world. If you follow me, you won't have to walk in darkness, because you will have the light that leads to life."*** We try to think our way through life's challenges, hoping we're correct. God has already figured it all out for us. There has never been an instance of something surprising God. He has never said, "Whoa, where did that come from? I didn't see that one coming." Instead, God's Word tells us that if we listen to Him, and live and lead according to His Word, we will significantly benefit from it.

> ***My thoughts are nothing like your thoughts," says the LORD. "And my ways are far beyond anything you could imagine. For just as the heavens are higher than the earth, so my ways are higher than your ways and my thoughts higher than your thoughts. The rain and the snow come down from the heavens and stay on the ground to water the earth. They cause the grain to grow, producing seed for the farmer and bread for the hungry. It is the same with my word. I send it out, and it always produces fruit. It will accomplish all I want it to, and it will prosper everywhere I send it.*** (Isaiah 55:8–11)

The Apostle James tells us to do more than to listen to God's Word in James 1:22–25:

> ***But don't just listen to God's word. You must do what it says. Otherwise, you are only***

> ***fooling yourselves. For if you listen to the word and don't obey, it is like glancing at your face in a mirror. You see yourself, walk away, and forget what you look like. But if you look carefully into the perfect law that sets you free, and if you do what it says and don't forget what you heard, then God will bless you for doing it.***

The Apostle Paul reminds us that what Jesus said over two thousand years ago applied to man then, now, and forever. ***Jesus Christ is the same yesterday, today, and forever. So do not be attracted by strange new ideas*** (Hebrews 13:8–9). In the Book of Galatians, Paul reveals why we are to lead others as God's Word instructs us. ***Obviously, I'm not trying to win the approval of people, but of God. If pleasing people were my goal, I would not be Christ's servant*** (Galatians 1:10).

These statements present themselves as simple enough to understand, and simple is my middle name! Following thirty-two years as a leader in the US Army, a Doctorate in Strategic Leadership from Regent University (Christian Leadership to Change the World), and several years in the private sector as a leader and college professor I decided to identify and apply God's Word to the situations I have encountered as a leader. This book is founded on God's Truth and God's way we are to lead. Jesus tells us to listen to Him; in Matthew 7:24, Jesus says, "***Anyone who listens to my teaching and follows it is wise, like a person who builds a house on solid rock.***" We have the assurance that everything Jesus taught on how to serve and lead others is the absolute truth. Jesus tells us in John 8:26, ***"For I say only what I have heard from the one who sent me, and he is completely truthful."*** Jesus said this a while ago, but it remains valid forever, ***The grass withers and the flowers fade, but the word of God stands forever*** (Isaiah 40:8).

While I do/did not always hit the mark as a leader, my foundation is built on my family's Christian values instilled in me as a young person. I know I did not and still do not have it all down. I am always telling my beautiful wife Jenny, there is so much to learn.

The best way to work toward becoming the best leader you can be is to remember and practice:

> Leadership is activated by a *spirit of humility*,
> Leadership is saturated by *increased knowledge*,
> and
> Leadership is dedicated to *serving others*.

Humility, increased knowledge, and selfless service will open the door to becoming a great leader in your personal and professional life. Let's move forward and get into it.

We will set the stage for everything discussed with God's Word (***Work willingly at whatever you do, as though you were working for the Lord rather than for people*** [Colossians 3:23]), supportive writings, and real-world narratives that will provide practical application (in other words, experiences and observations from leaders that follow God.) At the end of each chapter are several "Reflection Questions" for you to spend time contemplating what was discussed before moving on to the next chapter. Don't measure yourself as a leader against what others say or how others around you lead. Measure yourself as a leader against God's Truth in leading, His is the approval we seek, not man's. ***Instead, let the Spirit renew your thoughts and attitudes*** (Ephesians 4:23).

Oh yeah, just in case you need another reason why understanding that leading others as God would have us to is **ABSOLUTELY ESSENTIAL**, remember what King David stated.

> ***Joyful are people of integrity, who follow the instructions of the LORD. Joyful are those who obey his laws and search for him with all their hearts. They do not compromise with evil, and they walk only in his paths. You have charged us to keep your commandments carefully. Oh, that my actions would consistently reflect your decrees! Then I will not be ashamed when I compare my life with your commands.***

> ***As I learn your righteous regulations, I will thank you by living as I should! I will obey your decrees. Please don't give up on me!*** (Psalm 119:1–8)

> ***Oh, how I love your instructions! I think about them all day long. Your commands make me wiser than my enemies, for they are my constant guide. Yes, I have more insight than my teachers, for I am always thinking of your laws. I am even wiser than my elders, for I have kept your commandments. I have refused to walk on any evil path, so that I may remain obedient to your word. I haven't turned away from your regulations, for you have taught me well. How sweet your words taste to me; they are sweeter than honey. Your commandments give me understanding; no wonder I hate every false way of life.*** (Psalm 119:97–104)

If God's Words of wisdom and methods for leading others were good enough for David, the Great Warrior and Anointed King, whom God said in Acts 13:22, ***"I have found David son of Jesse, a man after my own heart. He will do everything I want him to do,"*** well then, count me in. We will develop our leadership into greatness, keeping God's Word as our foundation for all motives and actions. Remembering that God's Word is a light revealing how we are to live and lead.

> ***You must pay close attention to what they wrote, for their words are like a lamp shining in a dark place. Above all, you must realize that no prophecy in Scripture ever came from the prophet's own understanding, or from human initiative. No, those prophets were moved by***

> ***the Holy Spirit, and they spoke from God.*** (2 Peter 1:19–20)

Come with me as we discover God's Truth in Leadership and apply His Truth to today's leadership environment and its multiple challenges. Come with me as we discover *The Truth in becoming a great leader*! ***Your word is a lamp to guide my feet and a light for my path*** (Psalm 119:105).

> *All the good from the Savior of the world is communicated through this book. All things desirable to man are contained in the Bible.* (US President Abraham Lincoln)

Reflection Time

Have you ever contemplated applying how God tells us to live our lives as a way to serve and lead others? Why?

Do you lead with your head, or do you lead with your heart? Do you lead with both your head and your heart?

Which did Jesus lead with? If it worked for Him, will it work for you?

When challenged in leading, have you ever sought God's answer for how to handle the challenge?

---

1 Bruce Winston and Kathleen Patterson, "An Integrative Definition of Leadership," International Journal of Leadership Studies, 1, no. 2 (2006): 6-66.

2 Joanne B. Ciulla, ed., Ethics, the Heart of Leadership (Santa Barbara: ABC-CLIO, LLC, 2014), 16.

PART 2

Starting Out or Finishing Strong

No one will be able to stand against you as long as you live. For I will be with you as I was with Moses. I will not fail you or abandon you.

—Joshua 1:5–6

The words found in Joshua 1 are the words of God speaking to Joshua. Moses, who had led millions out of bondage into the wilderness toward the promised land, has just died. God has appointed Joshua to be their leader. As God appointed Joshua to lead in Joshua chapter 1, three times, God says to Joshua, ***"be strong and courageous."*** Once God says ***"be strong and very courageous."*** As a leader, I encourage you the same, "Be strong and courageous."

Think about being Joshua. God has told you precisely how you are to lead His people (over 2 million people) into their promised land. What I love about chapter 1 is that God not only appoints Joshua, He tells him EXACTLY how to lead:

> ***"Be strong and very courageous. Be careful to obey all the instructions Moses gave you. Do not deviate from them, turning either to the right or left. Then you will be successful in everything you do. Study this Book of***

> ***Instruction continually. Meditate on it day and night so you will be sure to obey everything written in it. Only then will you prosper and succeed in all you do. This is my command—be strong and courageous! Do not be afraid or discouraged. For the LORD your God is with you wherever you go."*** (Joshua 1:7–9)

Before we dive off the deep end into the waters of leading others, I want you to ask yourself this question; who do I want to be as a leader? I don't know if you know this or not, but who you will be as a leader is who you are as a person. That's right, any and every leader, regardless of how many they lead, how grand their position or title is, is simply a person entrusted with greater responsibility. A leader's worth and motivation are revealed by magnifying their character and who they are as a person. Character, values, integrity, virtues, morals, and beliefs are magnified and exposed during leadership stressors. We are fortunate that God's Word is His way of telling us, just like He told Joshua, EXACTLY how we are to live as a person. The person we become by living by God's Word creates who He wants us to be as a leader of others.

Leaders are not extraordinary people among humanity; they are not invincible or hold some mystic powers. Leaders are simply people blessed to serve everyone they lead. Just like God stated that Moses, as a leader, was God's servant, so are we. We serve God as leaders by serving others. I did not say the leader is not in charge of others; they are. The leader is responsible for everything good, bad, right, or wrong in an organization. To lead, however, is a person positioned to serve others. Jesus tells us in Matthew 20:26, "***Whoever wants to be a leader among you must be your servant"*** and shows that He serves as an example in Matthew 20:28, Jesus states, "***For even the Son of Man came not to be served but to serve others and to give his life as a ransom for many."*** There is no more incredible honor than to be entrusted with the responsibility of leading others. Being trusted to serve as a leader positions a person into a calling of responsibility, not privileges of comfort and positional perks. Being allowed to lead others is from God's authority and appointment, not something you are entitled to be.

> God's Word, talking about making King David a leader, "***See how I used him to display power among the peoples. I made him a leader among the nations.***" (Isaiah 55:4)
>
> ***The LORD says, "For my people will serve the LORD their God and their king descended from David—the king I will raise up for them.*** (Jeremiah 30:9)
>
> ***For all authority comes from God, and those in positions of authority have been placed there by God.*** (Romans 13:1)
>
> ***The authorities are God's servants, sent for your good.*** (Romans 13:4)
>
> The LORD said, "***And I will set over them one shepherd, my servant David. He will feed them and be a shepherd to them. And I, the LORD will be their God, and my servant David will be a prince among my people. I, the LORD, have spoken!***" (Ezekiel 34:23–24)
>
> ***Long ago you spoke in a vision to your faithful people. You said, "I have raised up a warrior. I have selected him from the common people to be king. I have found my servant David. I have anointed him with my Holy oil. I will steady him with my hand; with my powerful arm I will make him strong. His enemies will not defeat him, nor will the wicked overpower him. I will beat down his adver-***

> ***saries before him and destroy those who hate him. My faithfulness and unfailing love will be with him, and by my authority he will grow in power."*** (Psalm 89:19–24)

Regardless of a person's level of responsibility at the beginning of their professional career, achieving success in the small things is required before earning the honor of leading others. God will use time and experiences to prepare a person to lead when He decides to appoint them into leadership.

Small streams don't choose to be mighty rivers. They just run in the direction they were created to move, and their Creator decides what they'll become.[1]

While pinning on Sergeant's rank for a newly promoted first-time leader in the Army, I would congratulate them and recognize their great achievement. Most importantly, I would point out the huge and nonnegotiable responsibility they were accepting with their promotion. With their hand still grasping my firm handshake, I would look them in the eyes and tell them, "No longer the words I, Me, or My exist in your vocabulary; you no longer exist for yourself. You now exist for them. They are everything and the reason you exist as a leader. Do not let them, their parents and family, the Army, or this nation down. Take care of them, train them, equip them, and be the leader for them that you want from those who lead you." Their promotion into leadership just became a very serious responsibility!

When I attended my first military leadership school, we were all placed in different leadership roles over a thirty-day leadership development course. Before attending, I always tried to blend in with my peers' crowd, trying not to get noticed (usually resulting from doing a bad thing). About two weeks into the course, my Cadre Leader called me over and told me for the next four days, I would be leading a platoon (group) of twenty-five of my peers. This leadership position required disseminating needed to know information, ensuring everyone knew where to be, when to be there, and what uniform or equipment was required for training. It also meant moving this formation of soldiers to where they were to go (chow hall, classrooms, fitness training area, or anywhere else we were told to go.)

For me, the scariest part came the first time I had to stand in front of them in a military formation and speak. You've probably watched those military movies where the leader is standing in front of the soldiers barking out orders. It's like they are possessed with a loud distinctive voice that booms out, leaving no doubt who is in charge. In my mind I was thinking; I'm a simple country boy from rural North Carolina, my dogs would not even respond appropriately to my voice; this is not going to be pretty. This was when I realized it's not about who Roger is; it's about the leader they need me to be. Be strong and courageous. When I opened my mouth, it was like an out-of-body experience. I heard this voice and these words coming out of my mouth and I subconsciously thought, *Where did that come from?* Later, one of my friends in the formation asked, "Where did that voice come from? Man, you took charge!"

Flash forward fourteen years, and I had that same high anxiety experience again. Over the years, I had been blessed to lead soldiers in several organizations up to 125 people in size. The call came that I was selected to lead a Company of 420 paratroopers in the 82nd Airborne Division. The first morning I stood in front of 420 of America's finest soldiers, I had that same thought as to when I stood in front of twenty-five peers years ago; can and how do I do this? Again I realized, be strong and courageous, and it's not about who Roger is; it's about the leader they need me to be.

Was I a natural-born leader? NO. I argue that there is no such thing as a natural-born leader. Even those great leader names we are all familiar with: Eisenhower, Lincoln, King Jr. Mandela, Churchill, and numerous others, which societies recognize as great leaders had to learn and develop into how they would lead. Some people are more inclined to ease into leading others. Still, there has never been a person outside of Jesus Christ born to lead with all of the attributes and competencies required of "great leaders." ***And it was only right that he should make Jesus, through his suffering, a perfect leader, fit to bring them into their salvation*** (Hebrews 2:10). All people honored and anointed to lead require development, growth, and experience to become the best leader others deserve to have to lead them. ***Don't think you are better than you really are. Be honest in your evaluation of yourselves, measuring yourselves by the faith God has given us*** (Romans 12:3). As a leader, the second you look at yourself in the mirror and think you are all that and a bag of chips, the only person you are fooling is the person you see in the mirror.

> ***Intelligent people are always ready to learn. Their ears are open for knowledge.*** (Proverbs 18:15)

> ***If God has given you leadership ability, take the responsibility seriously.*** (Romans 12:8)

All leaders must transform over time into the leader God calls us to be, or the mantle of leadership will slip from our grip. Just as a person changes from childhood into adulthood, we grow, and we learn that there is a right way to do things, and there are wrong ways to do things. Some leaders make it a while because their talent within a particular field is remarkable and extremely valuable to an organization. Do not make the mistake and think that talent alone can carry the day, who you are as a person will be tested in leadership. Eventually, the call to lead others requires the person you are, not the talent you embody. *The Leadership Secrets of Billy Graham* discusses how Billy Graham's success as a leader was much more attributed to Dr. Graham as a person than his gift/talent for teaching God's Word.

> *Talent can take a leader far, but the accomplishments that talent brings also produce great temptations. And talent is not sufficient to sustain a leader's effectiveness if the ever-present human flaws are not addressed.*[2]

Leaders must experience a developmental/transformational process to become the leader God made them be as a person. By identifying and embodying God's Word, you can fast forward your transformation to become a great leader. ***Get all the advice and instruction you can, so you will be wise the rest of your life*** (Proverbs 19:20). Whether it's your family you are leading or members within your organization, God's Truth in Leadership is essential to greatness in leading and serving others. Have no doubt; you have been directed to this book to become the leader God would have you to be, His hands and feet. Your previous style and motives of leading are in the rearview mirror of life, time to do it right, as God would have you to lead.

> ***But forget all that—it is nothing compared to what I am going to do. For I am about to do something new. See, I have already begun! Do you not see it? I will make a pathway through the wilderness. I will create rivers in the dry wasteland.*** (Isaiah 43:18–19)

Finishing Strong

But you say, "Hey Roger, I've been leading for a while now, I am not new at this leadership thing, what can this book offer me? Can this old dog learn a few new tricks?" Even after spending more than three decades leading others, I realize that there is so very much more to learn. ***A wise person is hungry for knowledge, while the fool feeds on trash*** (Proverbs 15:14). We are not to imitate man's self-promoting way of leading others, but God's way. We must apply His methods to our practice; we are to step boldly into God's ways provided in His Words of wisdom. God tells us in Proverbs 3:13–18,

> ***Joyful is the person who finds wisdom, the one who gains understanding. For wisdom is more profitable than silver, and her wages are better than gold. Wisdom is more precious than rubies; nothing you desire can compare with her. She offers you long life in her right hand, and riches and honor in her left. She will***

> ***guide you down delightful paths; all her ways are satisfying. Wisdom is a tree of life to those who embrace her; happy are those who hold her tightly.***

Let me ask you another question, "Have you been, or are you the person and leader God wants you to be for others? Has all of your intentions and methods of leading others always been honorable to God's ways of leading?" The Apostle Paul tells us there is always hope to become the person and leader God would have you to be. ***If you keep yourself pure, you will be a special utensil for honorable use. Your life will be clean, and you will be ready for the Master to use you for every good work*** (2 Timothy 2:21).

Until we take our last breath, we should be seeking wisdom and knowledge that will make us a better person, a better leader. Romans 12:2 reminds us, ***Don't copy the behavior and customs of this world, but let God transform you into a new person by changing the way you think.*** Regardless of our mistakes and failures along the way, we can pick ourselves back up, dust ourselves off, seek wisdom, and learn ways to improve ourselves. Then, we can get back in the fight of leading people and organizations to new and higher levels of achievement and success. Your internal and intrinsic desire to grow is what lead you to this book.

Once our minds are transformed to lead according to God's Truth in leadership, our hearts' complete transformation to lead in love becomes our character in Christ. Ephesians 4:14–15 tells us:

> ***Then we will no longer be immature like children. We won't be tossed and blown about by every wind of new teaching. We will not be influenced when people try to trick us with lies so clever they sound like the truth. Instead, we will speak the truth in love, growing in every way more and more like Christ, who is the head of his body, the church.***

I want to state upfront, I am not a trained theologian. I try every day to understand what God is saying in Scripture as I have worked to spend time each day in His Word. In no way have I achieved all of the right ways to lead according to God's Truth in leading others. My heart has always loved to serve, but pride and selfishness always lingered in the fringes of my efforts and when allowed would sneak in a jab or two into my humanistic nature. Thankfully, God's grace and mercy are more extraordinary than my iniquities. Like you, I strive to be the person, the leader, that God made me to become. I have found that if I lay down my humanistic ways of leading and focus on God's ways as a person and as a leader, not only is my life more enjoyable, so are the lives of those I serve and lead.

Have you ever worked a job and a "new" leader was coming in to take leadership reins? What did you hope for in this new leader? Have you ever been that "new" leader coming into a new group of people to lead? In the military, this was and is a prevalent practice. As an Adjunct Professor, I am experiencing a third new leader for our Department. Change is inevitable, and leaders come and go within organizations. Wouldn't you love it if those you were coming in to lead viewed you and your new leadership team as described in Isaiah 32:1–3,

> ***Look, a righteous king is coming! And honest princes will rule under him. Each one will be like a shelter from the wind and a refuge from the storm, like streams of water in the desert and the shadow of a great rock in a parched land. Then everyone who has eyes will be able to see the truth and everyone who has ears will be able to hear it.***

Whether you are the new leader or the one that has been around for a while, this is how we should strive to be seen by those we serve and lead. A leader should create a work environment and organizational climate that makes people want to work there. They want a great leader that can be trusted and believed in.

Let's move forward now into the areas of Leadership that God tells us in His Word are the way and the truth to becoming a great leader. If you don't know where you are going, any route will get you there. We are going toward becoming great leaders of our fellow man, and the only road that will take us there is the road built on God's Word. By traveling this road, we might find ourselves closer than ever to our Father, and that is just what He desires. God desires a relationship with each of us so that He can lead our lives into joy and peace. Before a leader can make a positive difference in the lives of those they lead (at home or in an organization), they must first establish the same thing God desires with us, a relationship.

> *In periods where there is no leadership, society stands still. Progress occurs when courageous, skillful leaders seize the opportunity to change things for the better.* (President Harry S. Truman)

Are you ready to seize this opportunity to lead in God's truthful way He would have us lead others? Are you prepared to be the unique and authentic leader God created you to be? The saying goes, "Be yourself. Everyone else is already taken." God created you and destined you to make the lives of others better. Your time for greatness in leadership is at hand; here we go!

Reflection Time

Before becoming a leader, did you ever think about how you would serve and lead others?

What are your greatest challenges in serving and leading others? (For example: Communication, Disciplinary Actions, Relationships)

What are you willing to change in yourself to be the leader others deserve?

---

1 Bob Goff, Live in Grace, Walk in Love, A 365-Day Journey (Nashville: Nelson Books, 2019), 238.

2 Harold Myra and Marshall Shelley, The Leadership Secrets of Billy Graham (Grand Rapids: Zondervan, 2005), 58.

PART 3

Relationships Role in Leadership, It's More Than a Theory

Always be humble and gentle. Be patient with each other, making allowance for each other's faults because of your love. Make every effort to keep yourselves united in the Spirit, binding yourselves together with peace.

—Ephesians 4:2–3

Why Relationships?

Psychology is the mental characteristics or attitude of a person or group. As a young leader, I realized that a large part of leading others often requires having to reorient others' perspectives or attitudes toward specific ones of the leader. This may sometimes even include the reorientation of large groups of people's perspective or attitude toward the vision and objectives needed to move an organization toward success. I call this the Psychology of Leadership.

In other words, part of leading others will require that the leader influence a change in people's perspective of how they see an issue or challenge. The leader must affect a person's ability to reframe the way they view or feel about something. Let me provide you with an example of the Psychology of Leadership, as witnessed in history. As summer arrived in 1940, the Nazi German Army was sitting on the shores of a defeated France ready to launch Operation Sea Lion to invade and conquer the United Kingdom. The Nazi German Army seemed unstoppable in their evil quest. The only thing between them and the United Kingdom was the narrow English Channel. Faced with a life-threatening challenge the United Kingdom people had to decide whether to fight or ultimately concede their nation to the Germans. Enter Prime Minister Winston Churchill, who established a mind-set for all in the United Kingdom of fighting the fight. Prime Minister Churchill stated, "This is the lesson: never give in, never give in, never, never, never, never—in nothing, great or small, large or petty—never give in except to convictions of honor and good sense." Where doubt and fear may have lay in the mind-sets of some before, their leader changed their doubts and fears to resilience and determination. Without a leader helping his people in the United Kingdom believe in themselves, history may have had a world-changing event.

Influence is the capacity to affect the character, development, or behavior of someone or something. Not all forms of influence are the same, and not all situations require the same type or method of influence. Let me give you an example of one kind of influence I experienced as a young civilian meeting my Army Drill Sergeant for the first time. My Army Drill Sergeant would quickly influence what would become my new life behaviors, my physical and mental development, and what would evolve into my moral values as a soldier.

I had taken Junior ROTC classes in high school and had entered the Army knowing how to march (drill and ceremonies), but very little else in the soldierly skills required to become a Soldier. A group of Drill Sergeant's arrived to receive us recruits (several hundred naïve civilians) at the reception center. We were all sitting down in a large covered area outside in the South Carolina humid July heat, nervously and anxiously awaiting their arrival. As a recruit at the reception center, we had received our military stylish hair buzz cut, uniforms, and what seemed like a million immunizations. By this time, we had "in-processed (on-boarded)" and were ready to begin Basic Training (Boot Camp) for the next ten weeks. We now belonged to the Drill Sergeants who would take us civilians and "influence" us into becoming Soldiers.

The Drill Sergeants yelled for anyone that had any prior military or Junior ROTC experience to come up front and form a line for them to speak to each person. When it came my time to move forward, the Drill Sergeants just stood there looking at this scared country boy (who knew nothing of what was to come.) I executed a sharp move to Parade Rest (hands behind your back and feet shoulder width apart,) hoping to impress them (it didn't). My Drill Sergeant, a man who had fought in Vietnam, was a Combat Expert Infantryman, and Airborne Jumpmaster approached me. With his round, brown Drill Sergeant hat cantered intimidatingly forward and just above his eyes, he stepped to within inches of my sweating face. He looked down at my name tag and asked, "Kingston, where are you from, son?"

I nervously replied, "Eden, North Carolina, Sergeant."

The Drill Sergeant said, "I'm from Raleigh, North Carolina. Do you know where that is, son?"

I answered, "Yes, Sergeant, that is our state capital."

The Drill Sergeant said, "I could walk out of my house in Raleigh and throw a rock and hit your house in Eden, do you believe me son?"

I was thinking, it's over seventy-five miles as the crow flies from Eden to Raleigh, but this was no time to explain geographical distances to this scary man. I replied, "I'm not sure, Sergeant." Enter the Drill Sergeant's method of influencing me quickly into understanding he was in charge of me and my every second of life for the next ten grueling weeks. The Drill Sergeant leaned forward, placing the brim of his Drill Sergeant's hat on the bridge of my nose right between my eyes. With his chewing tobacco breath and spit all over my face, he said, "Well, here is something you can be sure of son, you are mine (there were a few expletives added at the time), now go back and sit down." I quickly returned to where I had been seated, and the guy sitting next to me had witnessed me talking to the Drill Sergeant from afar but did not hear what was spoken.

He asked me, "What did he say?"

I nervously replied, "I'm dead!"

The type and style of influence required by a Drill Sergeant to morph civilians into soldiers are unique and very authoritative based on the Drill Sergeant's position of power. Thankfully, outside of the military in today's private and public work sectors, leadership influence looks very different. Please allow me to ask you a question. Are you more aptly to be influenced by someone you know and trust, or by someone you are unfamiliar with and do not know their intentions and motives? It is always easier to create the needed buy-in required for influencing someone to follow your ideas when the person being influenced trusts your methods and reasoning. This is why relationships are crucial and essential for great leadership to be achieved. ***Let us think of ways to motivate one another to acts of love and good works*** (Hebrews 10:24).

How meaningful are relationships to leading our family or others professionally? Relationships are everything; without them, we find ourselves all alone in life and in the workplace. In reality, relationships are the cornerstone of the foundation of leadership. A cornerstone is an important quality or feature on which a particular thing depends or is based. To maximize our effectiveness in leadership, we must establish relationships with those we lead. Pastor Tom Holladay wrote a beautiful book titled *The Relationship Principles of Jesus.* Pastor Holladay reveals how our relationships are to be prioritized.

> *Place the highest value on relationships! Not on money, but on relationships—first with God and then with others. Not on time, but on relationships—first with God and then with others. Not on things, but on relationships—first with God and then with others. Not on your work, but on relationships—first with God and then with others.*[1]

Relationships are the nonnegotiable ingredient required to build the essential foundation of trust for a successful leader. When God tells us in Colossians 3:12, "***You must clothe yourselves with tenderhearted mercy, kindness, humility, gentleness, and*** **patience,**" we are not being told this to act this way toward ourselves, but toward everyone else. These attributes propel relationships forward and nurture their existence. They are intended to establish and build relationships, not merely as a prescriptive method for leaders searching for ways to grow and maximize their effectiveness. Relationships are what society thrives on and what professionals in the workplace have identified as their preferred leadership methodology theory of application for the last two decades.

That's right, the Relational Theory of Leading others has been considered as the preferred method of leading for the past twenty years. Leadership theory's ebb and flow with the societal needs of their moment in time. A Theory is a supposition or a system of ideas man uses to explain something, especially one based on general principles independent of the thing to be explained. This pushes the study of leadership into the sociological realms of application. Sociology is defined as the study of the development, structure, and functioning of human society. Many of the leadership needs a society identifies as their preferred method of being led are dictated by external social environmental conditions.

How's this work? Let's look at several of the past Leadership Theories and see how society's external environment created them. From 1950 to 1960, society identified *The Great Man Theory* as their preferred method of leading. The Great Man Theory was represented by having the right "great leader" in place as the societal situation required. For example, in Great Britain, they had Winston Churchill, who would lead them in peace after leading them to victory in World War II (WWII). During this same period in the United States, General (Five-Star) Dwight Eisenhower served first as Supreme Allied Commander for all allied fighting forces in Europe in WWII, leading to a great victory. He was then voted into office for two terms as the United States President in the peaceful years following the war. Great leaders were required for great challenges in this decade.

The Behavior/Contingency Theories existed from 1960 to 1980. Their primary focus was actionable to accommodate what the social environment dictated as the prevalent leadership style for the particular situation an organization or society was encountering. In the behavioral theory leaders could grow and evolve into greater leadership roles and responsibilities utilizing leadership development and collegiate education to gradually prepare for greater responsibilities. Chains of command were established, and societies used a vertical hierarchy/bureaucratic command and control methodology for leading, especially in the American Business Sector. Successors were groomed and prepared for future leadership roles based on their behavioral attributes and their anticipated future organizational success needs.

The Influence Theory existed from 1980 to 2000. The Influence Theory is just as it sounds. Look around and see if someone has a system or style that works within their industry and become influenced to imitate (copy) their style or way. This period introduced global influencers into an ever-increasing globalized economy. Horizontal/Cross Teams influenced by leadership theories found in Japanese automakers soon found their way into industries in the US and the world. The Influence Theory introduced leading methods that created greater efficiencies for organizations, which significantly hinged on a leader's ability to build teams. Peer's or teammates were levied as influencers for fellow teammates. If they failed in the team building piece, other efficiencies gained by production systems like the assembly line would suffer as machines only operate as well as those running them.

The Relational Theory, 2000 to present, is inspired by a shared vision of society members and is easily adaptable to change if needed. The Relational Theory was greatly influenced by the Information Technology Revolution and today's Globalized Society and Economy. Technology provides multiple platforms for personal and professional relationships to be established and nurtured through social media platforms, online dating, virtual meeting platforms, and technologies' ever-increasing capabilities. Relationships are incredibly vital to societies' psychological need to have multiple personal and professional relationships. Here's where we go back to the beginning of man; man has always sought/needed relationships for a better life. ***Then the LORD God said, "It is not good for the man to be alone. I will make a helper who is just right for him"*** (Genesis 2:18).

But a theory is made by man, and this book seeks to apply God's Laws of leadership, not man's theories. God's Laws are the Kingdom of God's rules and His way of life for all humanity, and they are divine and perfect in intent, equity, and administration. God has designed man to desire and seek long-lasting relationships in the form of family, friends, and even those with whom we work. The humanistic nature of man is a longing for relationships; this has never changed. Humanity has titled periodical eras of time with differing "leadership theories" to meet society's leadership needs. In reality, however, God established that humanity from creation needs a relationship with others; this includes leaders and those they serve.

Relationships Are Essential

As I am writing this book, we are enduring many long months of the Coronavirus Pandemic. Everywhere you look on television or the internet, people talk about how they miss their former social life and relationships. Social Service and medical agencies have reported a spike in reported depression cases as people are restricted from interaction and engaging in normal social relationships to bolster their security and self-worth feelings. A globalized society went on quarantine lockdown almost overnight. In the first few weeks, people suffered from relationship withdrawal pains from being disconnected from many of their usual social life elements.

Everyone began practicing social (physical) distancing. Workplaces were closed unless they were deemed "essential." The nonstop news networks showed on our television screens the horrific scenes of hundreds of thousands of deaths globally from the pandemic. Relationships became interrupted with their extended family, classmates, workmates, and Church congregations. At the same time, sports and public entertainment venues were shuttered closed. Any place you were allowed to go to as an essential business requires a face mask to be worn. People began secluding themselves, not only socially distancing themselves but keeping entirely away from personal contact with others. Relationships matter, and the worldwide

Coronavirus Pandemic of 2020 has reminded us of just how much we require relationships to make our lives better and more fulfilling.

As a college professor, we were told to switch overnight from classroom settings to virtual classrooms. Over the semester, as the weeks rolled on, I could see the emotional toll on the faces of the students who needed more than just an online classroom relationship. Students sought to be in the presence of others again, to have access to establishing new connections with classmates and others on campus. Whether we are at home, at work, or at school, we all seek a place that allows for meaningful relationships.

Leadership's success or failure hinges on relationships. Leadership requires the establishment, time investment, and cultivation of close relationships to maximize leadership effectiveness. For leaders, a relationship creates a bridge for the gaps found in leading a globalized society of individuals. These "gaps" are represented by different value systems, belief systems, cultural norms, and individual goals. Relationships for leaders do not discount our differences but encourages the exploration of our commonalities. Commonalities form the foundation and starting point for building and enhancing our relationships with those we serve and lead. Later in this book, we will expound on methods to identify commonalities when discussing *Know Those You Lead.*

But before we discuss ways to create and enhance our relationships with those we serve and lead, we need to lay a cornerstone for this relationship foundation. We need the one key ingredient required in any relationship for it to have a chance at success. Whether it's a relationship with your significant other in life, your children, your friends, or those with whom you work every day, we need to trust one another. If there is no trust, there can be no relationship.

Reflection Time

In your family life, which relationships mean the most to you? What do you do to strengthen those relationships?

In your professional life, which relationships mean the most to you? What do you do to strengthen those relationships?

Which relationships have you found yourself taking for granted?

Which relationship requires your focus and undivided attention? What are you going to do about it?

---

[1] Tom Holladay, The Relationship Principles of Jesus (Grand Rapids: Zondervan, 2008), 29.

PART 4

Trust: The Cornerstone of Relationships

How meaningful are relationships? As stated earlier, God desires a relationship with every person. God knows the essential element required for us to have a personal relationship with Him is for us to believe in Him, and trust Him. God's Word deliberately seeks to convey to us that Trusting in Him bolsters a relationship that allows God to serve our needs as His people. Let's look at God's guidance on trusting Him, and then see how it relates to trust between a leader and those they serve and lead.

Let us hold tightly without wavering to the hope we affirm, for God can be trusted to keep his promise (Hebrews 10:23). (Those you serve and lead must know without doubt or hesitation they can trust you. No matter what comes against them or the organization, they have a leader they can trust to do right by everyone involved. A leader's word is everything. People must know that you will keep your word, and that your actions will reinforce them and be trusted regardless of the dilemma or the challenge.)

Trust in the LORD with all your heart; do not depend on your own understanding (Proverbs 3:5). (So to should those you serve and lead faithfully believe in your decisions and guidance. Once people trust and understand that as a leader, you see the big picture and have insights they may not be privy to, they find it easier to follow your lead. We have all been there with our trust in God's promises. In John 16:23 Jesus says, ***"You will ask the Father directly, and he will grant your request because you use my name."*** Something is going on around us, or to us, and we don't understand why God is allowing it to happen, even when we have asked for His help. We say, and sometimes yell at God, "How is this helping me? Why won't you take this from me? If I were the one in charge, I would fix it right away!" We ask ourselves, why should we still trust God?

Then we read God telling us in Isaiah 55:8–9, ***"My thoughts are nothing like your thoughts," says the LORD. "And my ways are far beyond anything you could imagine. For just as the heavens are higher than the earth, so my ways are higher than your ways and my thoughts higher than your thoughts."*** A leader's thoughts contemplate many potential residual effects that may occur from their decisions before making them. Leaders are always looking up and out, seeing the obstacles and the opportunities the future presents. When a leader's decision-making proves wise over time, those they serve and lead will grow more trusting of the leader. People will learn that even though they may doubt their leader has a greater understanding and situational awareness, they can be trusted. And so can God's decisions for our lives be trusted; we simply need to believe that He knows more than we do. He does!)

O, my people, trust in him at all times. Pour out your heart to him, for God is our refuge (Psalm 62:8). (Trust between a leader and those they serve and lead creates a place of safe shelter needed in every workplace. Life is going to happen to everyone. When it does, people need a leader they can trust with their circumstances and challenges. A leader must be a person trusted at all times, so others feel safe to reveal their burdens without being judged. A leader is their shelter in the storm of life.)

But I trust in your unfailing love. I will rejoice because you have rescued me (Psalm 13:5). (What a wonderful feeling it is to know that someone is always there for you. We have this in our Heavenly Father for life's times of distress. Those you serve and lead must have this same wonderful feeling in the workplace. How reassuring it is when the workplace is filled with leaders who genuinely care for those they serve and lead. Everyone wants to work in this trusting environment.)

You will keep in perfect peace all who trust in you, all whose thoughts are fixed on you! Trust in the LORD always, for the LORD GOD is the eternal Rock (Isaiah 26:3–4). (When people go to a workplace where peace and harmony are not only encouraged but are ensured by caring and trustworthy leaders, success is unavoidable! Leaders must be trusted to promote peace in the workplace and enforce standards of conduct conducive to a peaceful work environment. We trust God for peace in our lives when we obey His laws and commands. Those you serve and lead should trust that their leader will provide a peaceful workplace where everyone thrives and enjoys peace and harmony.)

Those who know your name trust in you (Psalm 9:10). (My father taught me as a young man, "Your name is made by your actions, which reflect your character." Let your name be one established by the trustworthy actions your walk-in life and leading makes you. When your name represents a leader that automatically evokes a sense of trust from others, your ability to influence their perspective and attitude is significantly enhanced.)

But blessed are those who trust in the LORD and have made the LORD their hope and confidence (Jeremiah 17:7). (We trust in the LORD and are blessed by receiving His peace. Jesus tells us in John 14:27 that because we are His, and He is ours, ***"I am leaving you with a gift—peace of mind and heart. And the peace I give is a gift the world cannot give. So don't be troubled or afraid."*** The people you serve and lead should consider themselves blessed to have a leader they can trust. From this trust, people can be hopeful and confident that their leader will always be available for their needs. People can remain hopeful and confident that they will always be told the truth, be kept informed, provided opportunities to shine, and always be respected. Being led by a leader that can be trusted is a great blessing, and people seek this kind of leader in their lives and the workplace.)

They do not fear bad news; they confidently trust the LORD to care for them (Psalm 112:7). (Trust is never more needed than when things look grim up ahead. When challenging economic times are forecasted, it is only natural for people to fear possible workplace layoffs. These layoffs represent so much more to them than not having a job to come to each day. Their potential loss of health insurance and reduction in income creates nights of unrest and significant stress. Everyone is seeking hope for their future; they need someone to reassure them that we will all make it together. It is never more vital for them to have a leader that they can trust. A leader not only speaks words of encouragement to them, but the leader provides them options being entertained to avoid severe economic impacts. People must trust that their leadership will make sure their jobs are safe and that contingency plans are in place to weather the oncoming economic storm. Life may bring uncertainties but having a leader we can trust to take care of us provides emotional confidence that fear cannot overtake.)

But when I am afraid, I put my trust in you (Psalm 56:3). (Have you heard the saying, "Trust me, I got this?" When people trust their leader, they know that their leaders' "got this." Trust now allows those you serve and lead to get back to the organization's work. Trust is crucial in a leaders' relationship with others; it is critical to an organization's ability to overcome challenges and succeed.)

The LORD is my strength and shield, I trust in him with all my heart. He helps me, and my heart is filled with joy. I burst out in songs of thanksgiving (Psalm 28:7). (Leaders are meant to be a source of strength for those in need. Leaders are meant to shield those they serve and lead from the bureaucratic distractors that today's globalized workplace presents. A sense of having a leader who is a person's strength and shield, which can always be trusted in word and deed, is what every person deserves. This kind of trust promotes a peace that results in greater work productivity and job satisfaction.)

Trust in the LORD and do good. Then you will live safely in the land and prosper (Psalm 37:3). ("Do your part, and I will do mine." This is what God is saying to us. Our part is trusting Him, obeying His commands, and in return, we have His promise for a safe and provisioned life. This is all any leader can ask of those they serve and lead. "Trust me, do what you are supposed to do, and I will make sure you are always taken great care of." This is an agreement every leader should make with those they serve and lead. Now, this is every person's dream, "I will do my part, and they will do theirs for me." Everyone, the employee, the leader, and the organization win in a workplace with a trusting environment.)

Commit everything you do to the LORD. Trust him, and he will help you (Psalm 37:5). (One of the significant by-products of our trust in God's Word is the sense of knowing that if we do what God tells us to do, we will always have Him to call on as needed in life. The workplace relationship between leaders and those they serve and lead should mirror this analogy. People need a feeling of trust in their leaders. I knew as a soldier, that if I did my very best and cared about my work, I would be helped along the way when needed. I knew this because the military culture was one where they always took care of those doing right by their organization. This is the culture and climate every leader and every organization should promote. It is okay to sit with those you serve and lead and promise them, "If you give our organization your all, we will give you all of the support and help you need when you face challenges and trials in the workplace." Trust is a two-way street; we trust you to do your best work, and you can trust us to take good care of you.)

Many sorrows come to the wicked, but unfailing love surrounds those who trust in the LORD (Psalm 32:10). (Have you ever had someone come to you after a situation in their life has reached a point of no return? Our first reaction is to ask them, Why didn't you come to me sooner so I could have helped you find the proper solution to your situation?" Most of the time, they might say that they "were too embarrassed to ask for help." Or they might say, "I thought I could handle it myself." When a person knows with certainty that you can be trusted to jump in with both hands and feet to help them, they are much more likely to approach you early on in their situation. Throughout this book, we will discuss love's role in leading others. Love is only available when trust is present. When sorrow strikes one of those you serve and lead (deserved or not), your establishment of trust with them opens the door for them to lay their burdens on your heart. They know that you are not there to judge them; you are there to love and help them. Where love resides, trust already existed.)

Our ancestors trusted in you, and you rescued them (Psalm 22:4). (A leader's example of being trustworthy is one that is broadcasted not only on today's audience but on tomorrow's newcomers in the workplace. What an excellent reputation to have as a leader, one of being trustworthy when you serve and lead others in need.)

See, God has come to save me. I will trust in him and not be afraid. The LORD GOD is my strength and my song; he has given me victory (Isaiah 12:2). (When a leader walks in the door, they should create an atmosphere of hope and care. When a leader is made aware of a challenge in the lives of those they serve and lead, their words and actions should promote assurance that everything will be okay. It is no different than a child's fear of the noises at night that makes them cry out for mom or dad. As soon as mom or dad enters their bedroom, sits beside them on the bed, and reassures them that there is nothing to be afraid of, and we are just down the hall if you need us, the child's fears subside. The child realizes they are not alone, and they trust their parents to protect them if needed. Those you serve and lead are not alone; they have you as their leader to protect them. What a great role to have in the lives of others!)

Building trust between yourself and those you lead empowers your ability to simultaneously serve their individual needs and achieve organizational successes. Trust allows those you lead to tell you the truth, even when it is bad news. People know they can trust your reaction to be respectfully consistent with your relationship's responsible bonds. Trusting you, the leader is also a wise and discerning investment in the future of those you lead. The adage, "Help me, help you," is exactly what trusting relationship allows.

Trust in a leader allows the leader to make the best decisions in the care and development of those being led. Trust is based on the leader's experience, education, training, and knowledge of the organizations strategic plan for the organization's future. Why is establishing trust paramount to relationships in leadership? What are the potential consequences of failing to establish trust as a leader? In

Isaiah 30:12–13, God reveals the outcome for those who did not trust Him, ***"Because you despise what I tell you and trust instead in oppression and lies, calamity will come upon you suddenly—like a bulging wall that bursts and falls. In an instant, it will collapse and come crashing down."***

Building trust is no simple task, whether it's in a personal relationship or a professional one. Building trust requires time, consistency between word and deed, and sustained repetition of reliability at all times. For each person, gaining their trust requires meeting their prerequisites for trusting you. Some people are always leery and suspect of a person's motives; gaining their trust requires a more extended time and more significant effort to assure them you are trustworthy. Meanwhile, some people will trust you from the beginning, until and unless you prove yourself untrustworthy.

Either way, trust must be earned and kept by our truthful words and our promised actions. In the world of Leadership, trust is crucial to success. When superiors lose their trust and confidence in a subordinate leader in the military, they are removed from their leadership position. In personal relationships, when someone commits an act that breaches the other person's trust, the association is fractured and sometimes to the point of disrepair. While a great amount of time and effort is required to establish and maintain trust, it only takes an act of seconds or minutes or a single word to dismantle and destroy the fragility of trust.

Trust is established and maintained through a complex assortment of leadership methods. No one method can singularly build and maintain trust. Still, through a combined and continued application of multiple processes, trust can evolve into the relationships needed for people to move forward in a unified effort. The mixture or application of various methods is not a "one size fits all" endeavor. Still, if you employ and practice them all, you will locate and fill the psychological "trust groove" for each person you lead. Remember to be consistent and genuine in your methods and let these methodologies become natural to how you lead. These methods are reflective of how God would have us to lead others as great leaders.

Trust is **EXTREMELY CRITICAL** and **ESSENTIAL** for establishing and reinforcing the foundation of any meaningful relationship. This includes our personal and family relationships, along with our professional work relationships. So before we go any further in building a great leader's structure based on God's Truth, we need to lay in place a foundation of trust. If you have ever built a house, you know that you have to go down before you can go up. Whenever you see a tall building, underneath it, deep in the ground is its foundation. The foundation for great leadership is relationships. Once we go deep and lay a foundation of relationships, we need to set our cornerstone of trust. From this perfectly placed cornerstone of trust, we can strengthen its support with parallel stones of leadership methods and attributes that no force brought against it can ever tear down. We will use an assortment of tools and strategies in emplacing God's instructions (stones) for building trust as a leader. This goes a bit deep at times, but it works…trust me (pun intended ☺).

> *Leadership is stirring people, so they are moved from inside themselves.* (Frederick R. Kappel, former chairman of AT&T)

Reflection Time

Test time: Would you feel confident in their reply if you asked your family and those you work with, "Do you see me as a trustworthy person?" Should others trust you?

Can you be trusted to follow through with the promises you make to others?

Are you faithful in word and deed to all that do trust you? Think about the damages and consequences of unfaithfulness.

PART 5

Methods for Building Trust in Leadership

O people, the LORD has told you what is good, and this is what he requires of you: to do what is right, to love mercy, and to walk humbly with your God.

—Micah 6:8

Let Them Know Your Method to the Madness

One definition for the word *madness* is a state of frenzied or chaotic activity. I just wanted to get that definition out of the way up front because I know you are probably asking, "What is he talking about?" The method to your madness is a specific, rational purpose in what one is doing or planning, even though it may seem crazy or absurd to another person. In this case, the word *madness* is used in place of the word *leadership*. Leadership, at least for me, was often represented by situations of *frenzied or chaotic activity.* That may be the reason I love it so much. Think about it, leadership day in and day out is never the same. Anytime you have two competing entities (people and the organizational mission), you will have a frantic itinerary and chaotic events to navigate as a leader. Letting them know your *Method to the Madness* of leading is a crucial first step in establishing their trust in you. You are now going to let them behind the curtain to see how you operate as a leader. You are going to let them know who you are and what made you. Before they can trust you, they have to know you, not your title or position, you the person.

Letting them know you is not about exposing your sensitive side. This is not telling them of your faults and failures. You are only letting them know things that allow them to relate to you, or more importantly, to let them know you can relate to them and where they are. It is NOT to establish or convey your differences and your position of authority over them. It is a time to share your leadership philosophy, how you lead, and what is important to you. It is a time to share your tolerances for essential things like honesty, loyalty, trust, respectfulness, and family as a group of people working together.

In the senior years of my military career, I never forgot the early years and what life was like as a junior soldier. As a junior soldier and then later as a new leader, I always viewed the older, senior leaders as different than me. I could not imagine that at one time, they had the doubts, fears, and dislikes that I sometimes felt. When I reached my senior leader years, I wanted to let the younger soldiers and leaders know that I could relate to them. I would tell them how I became a soldier because I wanted them to know I started the journey of being a soldier much like they had.

I told them that high school was not my favorite place to be. The only reason I volunteered to take the Armed Services Vocational Aptitude Battery test was that the teacher said we could go home after the test. I scored well enough, and weeks later was invited to breakfast at a local restaurant by the Army Recruiter. I would tell the listening soldiers I grew up as a rural country boy. We grew and harvested most of everything we ate (meat, pork, poultry, and vegetables); the milkman delivered dairy products to our home. If I had been well behaved, my mom would purchase me a pint of chocolate milk from the milkman. Unfortunately, I did not get many pints of chocolate milk, so chocolate milk carried great value with me.

The restaurant waitress asked what I would like to eat, the Army Recruiter said, “Get whatever you like.”

I looked at the menu and saw the word *waffle*. Now, I had heard of *waffles*, but I had never had one (we only had pancakes, not fancy food). So I said to the waitress, "Can I have one of those waffles?"

And she said, "Sure, what would you like to drink?"

I asked, "Do you have chocolate milk?"

And she said, "Yes, we do. Would you like a large or a small glass of chocolate milk?"

Before I could answer, the Army Recruiter told her, "Bring him a large glass." That waffle and a large glass of chocolate milk hit the table. Sixty seconds later, both were in my belly. The Army Recruiter laughed at me and asked, "You want another of both?"

In disbelief and with great joy, I answered, "Yes, sir!"

I would then tell the soldiers I was to lead that I stood before them because of two waffles and two glasses of chocolate milk. I must admit, there are some days as a person who is a soldier, "I hate waffles and chocolate milk." I wanted them to know that there is more to me than what a position or title implies. I wanted them to know that while their work as soldiers was necessary, I knew there was an individual behind the uniform. We were all in this together as people first.

When it came time to allow them into my leadership philosophy, it was not about my dos and don'ts; it was about how we would work and lead together. I called it the *Golden Rule of Leadership*. Most everyone has heard of the "Golden Rule." When Jesus was teaching crowds of people, he told them in Matthew 7:12, ***"Do to others whatever you would like them to do to you."*** The Golden Rule methodology can apply to many individual and organizational operating philosophies.

My father started his own construction company when I was in high school, *Golden Rule Builders Incorporated*. My dad's application of the Golden Rule for his company was *We will build the house for you, that we would have someone build for us*. In leadership, the Golden Rule provides a picture of the true nature of leadership. Lead others in the way you would like to be led. When I was faced with making decisions and taking action as a leader, I would subconsciously ask myself, *What would I want my leaders to decide and what actions would I expect them to make?* In other words, *How would I want to be led in this situation?*

It wasn't about me; instead, I contemplated how my decisions and actions were going to affect/impact those I led? Applying this Golden Rule in Leadership is making yourself a leader vulnerable to allowing the needs and care of those you lead to always be at the forefront of your decision-making process. Let me ask you something, would applying the Golden Rule of leadership represent a significant pivot in your current leadership decision-making process? Deep contemplation represents the kind of self-analysis we must take when identifying where/who we are as a leader.

Self-analyzation allows us to identify where we need to "pivot" in our leadership style/philosophy and behavior. Seeking to become the leader we would prefer to have leading ourselves. Ultimately when a leader's methodology and motive for leading applies the Golden Rule, becoming a more selfless leader materializes. The Golden Rule methodology/style of leading worked for me as a leader in the highly challenging and highly demanding US military. I applied this method in intensely demanding leadership positions in the 82nd Airborne, 101st Airborne, and the 25th Infantry Divisions, both in peacetime and multiple tours in combat operations.

Telling those you lead your *Method to the Madness* serves as a method for building trust in your relationship with those you lead by establishing the truth based on what you say about who you are, not what they have heard around the water cooler gossip network. The Apostle Paul worked hard as a Church leader to build followers' trust in their relationship with God.

> ***I want you to know how much I have agonized for you and for the church at Laodicea, and for many other believers who have never met me personally. I want them to be encouraged and knit together by strong ties of love. I want them to have complete confidence that they understand God's mysterious plan which is Christ himself. I am telling you this so no one will deceive you with well-crafted arguments.*** (Colossians 2:1–2 and 4)

In Colossians 2:1–2, and 4, we observe the Apostle Paul's revealing of his *Method to the Madness* for strategically emplacing defensive countermeasures against the attacks of "well-crafted arguments" by nonbelievers against the Church. Paul was upfront in explaining to the followers of Christ in the new Church that he empathizes with them. He is with them in Spirit. He encourages them to stand together, bonded by love against those opposing their beliefs in Christ. Paul was using encouragement and relationships founded on the love for one another to strengthen their confidence in God's way for them to live their lives.

The Apostle Paul was a very well-educated and intelligent man even before meeting Jesus on the Road to Damascus as his former self Saul. While Paul's religious belief system was askew before meeting Jesus, Saul was a man that knew how to inspire others with his perspectives and beliefs. Saul was apt at influencing others, even those he reported to and who had authority over his actions. As in Acts 9:1–2, ***Meanwhile, Saul was uttering threats with every breath and was eager to kill the Lord's followers. So he went to the high priest. He requested letters addressed to the synagogues in Damascus, asking for their cooperation in the arrest of any followers of the Way he found there.*** These spiritual gifts of influence that Saul/Paul possessed are within each of us. For some leaders, the ability to influence others into new perspectives is as natural to them as breathing. For others, it takes time to observe others and understand how they need to be approached to begin the influential process (Psychology of Leadership).

Telling others your *Method to the Madness* builds the confidence of those you lead in that they now know what matters to you, how you see things, and what is expected of them. I would tell soldiers, "There are four thousand of us in this organization. That means I have 3,999 employers, and I am your employee. Allow my position and authority to help you do your jobs. We are all the same here. We have different levels of responsibility, and I am responsible for you and this organization. I do not intend to let either one fail. You deserve leaders that will train you, care for you and your family, and make sure you have what you need to do your jobs. If you are not getting these things, let me know, and I will provide you a new leader that does do these things."

I wanted them to know my *Method to the Madness* of leadership was one to place them and the organization first. I would let those that served in administrative staff departments know that their number one priority of service was to meet the needs of the Soldiers they support. I would let every leader at every level know, "We as the leadership of the organization exist for the Soldier, and our responsibility is an honor to have." After conveying to others, your *Method to the Madness* of leading, the real work in building trust for stronger relationships begins. Telling those you serve and lead your *Method to the Madness* is a one-time endeavor. Now, the real work starts in leadership; talk is required, but those you serve and lead want to see your actions and be heard. It is time for effective communication with those you lead!

Reflection Time

Do those you serve and lead know your way of doing things (your method to the madness)?

Do others know your method by having to figure your ways out, or have you shared your ways so that they can adapt to your methods?

In your relationships, have you explained to others what is important to you? In other words, have you told others what makes you feel heard and valued?

Communication Is a Two-Way Street

We can make a large horse go wherever we want by means of a small bit in its mouth. And a small rudder makes a huge ship turn wherever the pilot chooses to go, even though the winds are strong. In the same way, the tongue is a small thing that makes grand speeches.

—James 3:3–5

Nothing surprising in that we are talking about communication as a critical tool in creating trust within our leadership relationship with others. Communication in leadership should be designed and implemented to invite those you lead toward you. Communication must not push others away, not alienate others, or create workplace divisions. Every relationship, personal or professional, requires communication, two-way communication that is. People pay lots of money to therapists in an attempt to communicate more effectively with someone they have chosen to spend their life with. Pastor Tom Holladay believes,

> *You cannot have high-quality communication without high-level trust. With great trust there can be great communication. With little trust there is little communication, and with no trust there is no*

communication. Whether we're working at establishing a relationship or rebuilding channels of communication, it has to begin with trust.[1]

How much harder do leaders need to pursue effective communication with someone they lead, when the person did not voluntarily choose them to be their leader? Instead, those you serve and lead had you (their leader) issued into their life? Two-way communication allows commonalities to be expressed and identified while inviting differences to be explored and learned from. In leadership, communication is a two-way street, meant to provoke thoughts and paint a picture for others to see and understand your perspective. Communication allows the leader and those they lead to ask questions, challenge assumptions, and engage in active and attentive listening to others' thoughts and ideas.

But don't we all know these things about communication already. I don't even know how many "effective communication" books I have sitting on a shelf in my study right now. According to my wife, I should either re-read them or get some more. Still, you know what I am talking about; it is a never-ending challenge in every relationship. We know man tells us we need to communicate effectively, but what I would like for us to do now is look at what God's Word tells us as leaders, how to communicate. God's Word tells us how to both talk and listen to communicate effectively.

Speak According to God's Word

Avoid worthless, foolish talk that only leads to more godless behavior. This kind of talk spreads like cancer (2 Timothy 2:16–17). (One of the repeated themes in God's guidance in communication is His warning against foolish talk. In God's Word, the repetition of certain words or themes is present to reveal God's WARNING against the action. In the area of communication, we find that God disapproves of foolish talk. Foolish talk many times serves as a precursor to poor behavior. Let the words you speak reflect your character of respect, love, and consideration for others.)

Don't get involved in foolish, ignorant arguments that only start fights. A servant of the Lord must not quarrel but must be kind to everyone, be able to teach, and be patient with difficult people (2 Timothy 2:23–24). (Later, as a prescribed method for building trust, we will discuss *Be Humble.* Being humble is the opposite of being proud. And have no doubt, the evilness of pride fuels foolish and ignorant arguments. A leader's words in communication must be oriented toward creating unity, synergy, camaraderie, and the close bonds needed in any trusting relationship.)

So get rid of all evil behavior. Be done with all deceit, hypocrisy, jealousy, and all unkind speech (1 Peter 2:1). (I remember my mom telling me as a young boy, "If you don't have something nice to say about someone, then don't say anything." Mom was right. We should never allow our unkind words to hurt people's hearts. As a leader intent on uplifting those you serve and lead, you MUST void your speech of any unkind words or innuendos. Why would anyone want to trust a leader that speaks unkindly of or toward them? Unkindness in speech demolishes the bridge of trust a leader must cross to establish and maintain a positive relationship with others.)

In Matthew 15:18 Jesus says, ***"The words you speak come from the heart—that's what defiles you."*** (Do your words unite or divide? If you want to know who a person is, sit and listen to them speak for a few minutes. Spoken words reveal the nature of their heart—good or bad, selfless or selfish, humble or proud, kind or unkind, and encouraging or discouraging. A person's words are a window into their heart, through which their level of righteousness or evil within can be seen.)

The words of the wise are like cattle prods—painful but helpful (Ecclesiastes 12:11). (Don't tell me what I want to hear; tell me the truth. Many times as I read God's Word, my conscience feels like cattle prods are poking me. I hear God's wisdom and realize that my life is far from where He would have it be. Wise words are meant to prod us toward growth. A person appointed to lead has achieved success in part due to their professional wisdom. A leader's knowledge is one that can encourage those they serve and lead toward more significant learning, development, and professional growth. Kindly and gently nudging others in the right direction may hurt their pride a little. Still, anything worth having usually requires a sacrifice and growth.)

In Luke 6:45 Jesus says, "***What you say flows from what is in your heart.***" (Allow words of love, encouragement, respect, kindness, gentleness, and selflessness to flow from your heart into the ears of those that you want to trust you. Trust flourishes or diminishes by the words which pass from your heart.)

Don't use foul or abusive language. Let everything you say be good and helpful, so that your words will be an encouragement to those who hear them (Ephesians 4:29). (Foul and abusive speech from anyone, especially a leader, is NEVER okay. Foul and abusive speech is bullying tactics and have no place in our personal or professional lives. Offensive and abusive language represents a vulgar and mean person. Is that how any leader should want to be viewed by others? Unfortunately, we all have witnessed those people/leaders whose mouths spew out ignorance in the form of foul or abusive language. Remember how you viewed them, how you could never respect them? Realize, if you speak the same way, you will be viewed by others in that same disrespecting way. Who could trust a leader that speaks this way? Instead, be a leader that encourages and promotes positivity with fair and uplifting words.)

Let your conversations be gracious and attractive (seasoned with salt) so that you will have the right response for everyone (Colossians 4:6). (People overhear what you may be saying to someone else in a conversation. People may read a comment you make in an email that was forwarded around to different offices. Today's smartphones, allow people to record both audio and video; everyone is subject to being "overheard." Never has it been more essential to adhere to God's guidance of letting your conversations be gracious and attractive. There should not be one way of communicating as a person and then another way as a leader.

Remember, we discussed that who you are as a leader is who you are as a person first. I have failed in this arena. While serving as a leader in the 82nd Airborne Division, I found myself embarrassed by how the leader in me spoke to others. My sister had stopped by my headquarters for a surprise hello (she had never done this before since she lived several hours away.) I spoke to soldiers behind the headquarters building, chastising their sub-standard training performance earlier that day. As I turned to go back into the building, there stood my sister with eyes wide open and a look of disbelief on her face. I said, "Hello," but she said, "Oh my goodness, if our mom and dad heard you talking that way to someone, they would not believe it was you." I laughed and said, "That was not me. That was their leader. He is not a nice guy when they mess up. I'm not that guy. I'm Roger." My response was a pitiful excuse. My sister's surprise visit reminded me that someone is always listening. My parents would not have liked or approved of my poor choice of words. My words revealed who I was as a person and as a leader at the time. I still had a lot to learn!)

Some people make cutting remarks, but the words of the wise bring healing (Proverbs 12:18). (Please know as a leader that your words are powerful and impactful. A leader's words and comments go deep. Let your words and comments go deep into building others up. You never know when a quick word of encouragement may just be the words that make a positive and healing difference in an otherwise bad day for someone. No promotion or salary increase can ever help a hurting heart like a wise leader's words of empathy, compassion, and encouragement.)

A gentle answer deflects anger, but harsh words make tempers flare (Proverbs 15:1). (In communication, it's not always *what* you say, but it is about *how* you say it. Another critical point to consider also is how the other person hears what you have to say. A method for disarming your words' emotional impact from an already emotional person asking a question is to provide them with gentle answer responses. A leader is responsible for promoting and keeping the conversation nonconfrontational. Critical or insulting responses only stoke the anger of the recipient.)

The tongue of the wise make's knowledge appealing, but the mouth of a fool belches out foolishness (Proverbs 15:2). (When I joined the Army, I did so because my only other known option was to work for my dad's construction company. No one in my family had been to college, and I stumbled into a life in the Army by luck.

My first platoon leader was a West Point graduate. I saw something different in him; he was intelligent and disciplined. He made me want to find out more about a college education. I wanted to be as smart and disciplined as this officer. What you say and how you conduct yourself as a leader should inspire others to seek more knowledge. Belching out foolishness dulls the cerebral senses of everyone in earshot. Those that gain wisdom from your words today are tomorrow's leaders.)

Gentle words are a tree of life; a deceitful tongue crushes the spirit (Proverbs 15:4). (A deceitful tongue is simply a lying person. As a sixteen-year-old country boy driving my truck with my yelling friends riding in the bed of the truck, I remember as we drove recklessly and blindly through fields of tall corn stalks. It was exhilarating and fun in our simple country lifestyle. But on Sunday morning at Church, when the farmer warned my dad that we better not do it again, I tried to deceive them both and denied any part in the mischievous act. When we returned home from Church, my dad told me to come with him to where I had parked my pickup truck. As he slid under my vehicle, I feared the worst. Sure enough, when he came from underneath my truck, he had removed pieces of corn stalks from my undercarriage. The look of disappointment on my dad's face for the lie he had caught me in was worse than any hurtful words or punishment he could have given. At that moment and for a while afterward, I lost my dad's trust in me. NEVER, NEVER, NEVER lie as a leader. When the truth comes out; and it will, you will never again gain their full trust in you. Once you can no longer trust a leader's words, they are only a leader in title alone. (I am still sorry, dad.))

The LORD detests evil plans, but he delights in pure words (Proverbs 15:26). (Pure hearts generate pure words. Pure words create trust and joy. ***Everything is pure to those whose hearts are pure. But nothing is pure to those who are corrupt and unbelieving, because their minds and consciences are corrupted*** (Titus 1:15). (Let your purity in motives of leading others create a trusting workplace environment of peace and harmony. People have enough evil going on around them outside of the workplace. Give them a place where evil is unwelcome, and goodness thrives.)

The heart of the godly thinks carefully before speaking; the mouth of the wicked overflows with evil words (Proverbs 15:28). (Let your comments be well crafted, respectful, and meant for good. By this, people will know you to be wise and of a good heart.)

A truly wise person uses few words (Proverbs 17:27). (Yes!)

Wise words are like deep waters; wisdom flows from the wise like a bubbling brook (Proverbs 18:4). (Be a Well of Knowledge and insight for those you serve and lead to drink from. Invite them to come and drink from the depths of your understanding. At the same time, seek a more bottomless well of knowledge for your own learning needs. There is so much to learn; never stop deepening your well of wisdom for others to drink from.)

The tongue can bring death or life; those who love to talk will reap the consequences (Proverbs 18:21). (Words of truth, encouragement, and love bring life to others. Babbling words of lies, deceit, and evil brings death to the one saying them.)

Watch your tongue and keep your mouth shut, and you will stay out of trouble (Proverbs 21:23). (This is excellent advice for a leader. They cannot hold words against you that were never said.)

Those who control their tongue will have a long life; opening your mouth can ruin everything (Proverbs 13:3). (Wise counsel for all!)

The wise are glad to be instructed, but babbling fools fall flat on their faces (Proverbs 10:8). (A leader is always seeking to learn. Wisdom allows a leader to say more with fewer words.)

Fools have no interest in understanding; they only want to air their own opinions (Proverbs 18:2). (When you find a leader who only wants to be heard and is unwilling to listen to what others have to say, you have a selfish person, not a leader. How will a leader ever listen to others' needs if they can't shut up long enough for others to speak?)

Better to hear the quiet words of a wise person than the shouts of a foolish king (Ecclesiastes 9:17). (Quite words of wisdom resonate louder than those of a fool shouting.)

Wise words bring approval, but fools are destroyed by their own words (Ecclesiastes 10:12). (Wise words get more than acceptance. Wise words allow trust to blossom and grow in the relationship between the leader and those they serve and lead.)

From God's Word, we learn that when leaders communicate, their words should be kind, provide instruction, and come from the heart. A leader's words are helpful, encouraging, full of grace, and gentle. A leader's words provide wisdom, are pure and wholesome, they create healing, are thoughtful, and when possible, as few as needed to convey the message.

> Encouraging words come from a happy heart.
> Gentle words come from a loving heart.
> Controlled words come from a peaceful heart.

> ***May the words of my mouth and the meditation of my heart be pleasing to you, O LORD, my rock and my redeemer*** (Psalm 19:14).

From God's Word, we learn how leaders should communicate. But just as importantly, we also know from God to refrain from; foolish talk, argumentative words, abusive talk, harsh words, deceitful vocabulary, evil suggestions, worthless words, or talking excessively. Nothing speaks lowlier of a leader than when they express themselves in one of these noted ways. In leadership, one of the quickest ways to kill trust and lose respect from those you serve and lead is expressing yourself with a vocabulary contrary to God's guidance.

> Harsh words come from an angry heart.
> Negative words come from a fearful heart.
> Boastful words come from an insecure heart.
> Judgmental words come from a guilty heart.
> Critical words come from a bitter heart.
> Filthy words come from an impure heart.

Matthew 12:37 Jesus says, ***"The words you say will either acquit you or condemn you."***

Hurtful words come from a person with an evil heart. No matter how well kept and attractive they may be, a person's outward appearance is not necessarily who they are. Making the outside look beautiful does no good in building trust if a leader has an evil heart. You still have a leader with an evil spirit. Nothing good will follow from hurtful words in establishing and maintaining a relationship of trust with those they lead.

> *The foolish and wicked practice of profane cursing and swearing is a vice so mean and low that every person of sense and character detests and despises it.* (US President George Washington)

Directive words by a leader can force people to reluctantly do things the leader's way. This method does not lend well to building relationships based on trust. However, a leader who listens and hears the thoughts and ideas of those they lead establishes a relationship of trust. A leader willing to listen has recognized the value in what others have to say. Regardless of the final decision a leader makes, others know their input and opinions were heard and contemplated in the decision-making process. This creates and supports a culture of people being valued and heard.

Listen According to God's Word

You must all be quick to listen, slow to speak (James 1:19). (God created man with two ears and one mouth. I think he was telling us to listen twice as much as we talk (at least that is what my beautiful wife tells me.) Listening allows a leader to weigh through all of the information and determine the truth. I love Jesus's guidance to us in John 8:32, ***"And you will know the truth, and the truth will set you free."*** Quick to listen, is quick to identify the truth. Don't you want to know all of the truthful facts before making decisions that will eventually affect a person or an organization's future opportunities for success?)

Let the wise listen to these proverbs and become even wiser. Let those with understanding receive guidance (Proverbs 1:5). (King Solomon, the wisest man to ever live, had counselors and advisors. He knew that he still needed to listen and hear the thoughts and ideas of others. Any person unwilling to listen to others only has the arrogant fool in the mirror to blame when their decisions lead to failure. A leader knows a lot, but no leader knows everything. We don't even know what we don't know. When we are willing to listen to others, we can be on a path to learning the truth.)

Even fools are thought wise when they keep silent; with their mouth shut, they seem intelligent (Proverbs 17:28). (Being a person of mystery means people don't know who you are. A leader must let those they serve and lead know who they are to begin a relationship and incubate trust in the relationship. However, a leader should be more intent on listening and hearing others than others hearing them. Let your walk of love and integrity do your talking, not your words.)

Spouting off before listening to the facts is both shameful and foolish (Proverbs 18:13). (Have you ever figuratively put your foot in your mouth? This saying indicates the action of speaking before you know the facts. This is followed many times by the person having to walk back their words shamefully. As a leader, we lose trust and respect when we speak without knowing the facts. A leader should listen and hear other's insights, information, and facts before speaking.)

Intelligent people are always ready to learn. Their ears are open for knowledge (Proverbs 18:15). (No person has never expanded their knowledge by merely relying on what they think. Listening to or reading the words of knowledgeable people arm's us with insights and wisdom needed to learn and grow as a person and as a leader. Learning is intaking, and the only way to intake is to listen.)

In Matthew 11:15 Jesus says, ***"Anyone with ears to hear should listen and understand."*** (These are words of truth spoken by the most excellent leader ever to walk this earth. If we are to understand anything, we must listen first.)

To one who listens, valid criticism is like a gold earring or other gold jewelry (Proverbs 25:12). (A leader may not always hear what they want to hear, especially when others provide legitimate criticism of something the leader has said or done. However, a wise leader will listen to the words and then search them for the truth that lies within. This is part of the refining process every leader requires to grow.)

If you stop listening to instruction, my child, you will turn your back on knowledge (Proverbs 19:27). (When we learn, we grow. The only way to learn is by listening. If we stop listening to others, we are saying, in reality; I don't need to know anything else. This is also a description of a foolish person.)

But all who listen to me will live in peace, untroubled by fear of harm (Proverbs 1:33). (Listen to God's Word, seek God's guidance in every decision you must make. God's Word leads us to a life of peace and joy. A leader's words should resonate the same with those they serve and lead. When those you serve and lead listen to your comments, they should become infused with stories that promote a sense of peace and harmony in the workplace.)

Anyone who listens to my teaching and follows it is wise, like a person who builds a house on solid rock (Matthew 7:24). (Listening to God's Word is the first step in establishing a firm foundation for life. When we are willing to listen to others, we can form a firm foundation of the truth.)

Fools think their own way is right, but the wise listen to others (Proverbs 12:15). (Be wise!)

An so my children, listen to me, for all who follow my ways are joyful. Listen to my instruction and be wise. Don't ignore it. Joyful are those who listen to me (Proverbs 8:32–34). (Leaders listen to be informed. When leaders speak, they are doing more than informing others. Leaders' words influence emotions, attitudes, and perspectives for those listening to them. When others hear you, let your words create joy, positivity, and hope.)

I love the LORD because he hears my voice and my prayer for mercy. Because he bends down to listen (Psalm 116:1–2). (I remember as a small child spending days at my grandparents while my parents were working. I had a special bond with my grandmother. Whenever she and I talked, grandma would bend down to my eye level to hear what I had to say. Usually, her hand was on my shoulder or softly gripping my arm as I spoke to her. She made me feel valued, loved, and that what I had to say was important to her.

The thing I loved most was that when she listened, I felt my words mattered. We all know that feeling. We know when someone genuinely believes that we and our words, thoughts, and opinions matter. We can read it in their eyes and their body language. The act of bending down to listen in the workplace may not be appropriate with fellow adults, but leaning in with interest represents the same method. When those you serve and lead learn to read you, they will know if you are listening or only acting like you are hearing them. When a leader listens, others feel that what they say matters. When a person feels that they matter in the workplace, they are more committed, loyal, and responsive to the organization's needs. Lean in, or if they are sitting, be like our Heavenly Father and bend down to hear what those you serve and lead have to say.)

From God's Word we see that when leaders listen to those they serve and lead, they acquire a greater understanding. They increase their wisdom. They promote an appearance of intelligence, and an ability to learn new things. They gain greater clarity of the issue or situation. They promote peace and joy in other's lives. They reinforce their foundation for better decision-making. Listening is a valuable investment in building trust in their relationships with others. Listening is an act of caring and an action of love.

From God's Word we learn that when leaders don't listen to those they lead, the leader displays foolishness and shamefulness. They present a refusal to learn from other people. They fear the unknown. They greatly diminish their decision-making effectiveness. They present a selfish attitude of believing they know it all. When a leader doesn't listen to others, they don't know what they don't know. How can a leader make proper decisions without considering all the facts and contemplating the valuable insights and viewpoints gained from listening to others? They can't!

Effective communication is the process of both speaking and listening before acting. Every word and action represent a communication seed being broadcast across a field of followers and the organization. These communication seeds impact a leader's ability to communicate their trust value in their relationship with others.

> *For good or ill, they are sowing seeds everywhere they go, in everything they do. A kind word, a clear insight, a visit to the hospital, a bold stance on a murky issue. A leader's every action has consequences both intended and unintended. People are like plowed ground; seeds find the soil of minds and emotions, sprouting powerful changes.*[2]

Let's plant some seeds through our communication skills as leaders. Seeds that will grow and produce the trust required in a leader's relationship with those they serve and lead. Seeds that inspire, encourage, teach, bless, reassure, support, and invite others into a relationship. These seeds create a workplace where individuals are valued. Everyone seeks relationships with people that listen to them. Listening is caring.

> ***A good person produces good things from the treasury of a good heart, and an evil person produces evil things from the treasury of an evil heart. What you say flows from what is in your heart.*** (Luke 6:45)

> ***For the Scriptures say, "If you want to enjoy life and see many happy days, keep your tongue from speaking evil and your lips from telling lies."*** (1 Peter 3:10)

How a leader communicates tells us most everything we need to know about who they are as a person and as a leader. If the leader has to be heard, and loves hearing themselves speak, they have a selfish and self-absorbed heart. If a leader patiently listens and hears everything a person has to say, they have a selfless and inviting heart. Let your speech be gracious, honest, and uplifting, while listening with compassion and empathy. This is God's way to two-way communication. Two-way communication supports the next critical and essential step in building a trusting relationship; you must *Know Those You Serve and Lead.*

Reflection Time

Do you hear others to listen to what they have to say, or do you hear others to speak back to them? Listen until they have finished speaking.

Do you give a person a solution or answer before they can even finish describing their problem or asking their question? If so, you may not be listening to the person, only their issue.

Do you speak more or listen more?

---

1 Tom Holladay, The Relationship Principles of Jesus (Grand Rapids: Zondervan, 2008), 145.

2 Harold Myra and Marshall Shelley, The Leadership Secrets of Billy Graham (Grand Rapids: Zondervan, 2005), 257.

Know Those You Serve and Lead

But God's truth stands firm like a foundation stone with this inscription: "The LORD knows those who are his."

—2 Timothy 2:19

Knowing those you serve and lead may be the very best part in the honor of leading others. The process of getting to know those you serve and lead creates value-added in everyone's life in the relationships developed. I firmly believe when He speaks about knowing those He leads, Jesus, reveals to us that as leaders, we should know those we lead. In John 10:14, Jesus states, ***"I am the good shepherd. I know my own, and my own know me."*** If you want to experience one of the best parts of leading, you have to know those you lead, and they should know you.

Knowing them requires work on the leader's part, and it requires that the leader let others know more about themselves. A relationship requires giving part of oneself to someone else, and this requires trust. Knowing those you lead provides the leader with a deeper understanding of who they are underneath their physical presence. A person's physical presence or appearance allows for speculation and guessing about the person. We think we know someone by their external persona; in reality, we don't know them. An organization may not require everyone to wear identical clothing like the uniforms needed for the military. There are plenty of workplaces where people wear what is acceptable and appropriate to their particular workplace. This does not necessarily reflect what those you serve and lead wear while in their private life. When a person is away from the workplace, they are more inclined to dress according to their personal beliefs.

Allow me to share a couple of examples that I experienced, which taught me to get past their exterior presence and get to the person underneath. It's no secret that the military has some extreme standards for things, like how clean and neat soldier's must keep their living space. In the Army, we called these places the barracks. A barracks room for junior enlisted soldiers usually houses anywhere from two to four soldiers. Each soldier's living space consists of a bed, a wall locker, and a desk with a chair. There is nothing unique or special about the furniture or the living area until a soldier makes it their home away from home.

In the soldiers "home away from home," just like anyone does in their home or apartment, they make it their own. Soldiers would place photos of family, friends, or that special someone in their life on their desk. Leaning in the corner might be a guitar, a baseball equipment bag, a surfboard (I was stationed in Hawaii once), or maybe a set of golf clubs. On their walls might be more family photos or posters of the things that captured their imagination, interest in life, and desires. These items used to set up "home away from home" speak loudly about the soldier/person who cherishes them.

It was one of my responsibilities to ensure soldiers maintained the cleanliness and functionality of their assigned "home" in the barracks. Army junior leaders' days are spent with the people they are responsible for from morning till the end of the workday. As their first line leader, it was my job to know them as a person and as a soldier. I made extra effort to see the person underneath the uniform of being a soldier. If a soldier was married, they and their family resided in a home on or off the military base.

I knew their spouse's names, children, and I knew where they lived. Leaders were required to go to each soldier's residence if they rented housing off the military installation to inspect the safety and structural soundness of where they lived. Leaders were not going to their soldier's homes to check how clean they were. Leaders were responsible for ensuring that landlords provided safe and sound living accommodations for the rent the soldier was paying.

In the beginning, I conducted the "visits" and "checks" because that was what generations of leaders in the Army had always done. For years, I did this repeatedly for every soldier I was responsible for because they told me to. I do not know about you, but I prefer not to be told to do something. I like to understand the bigger picture of something to be done to see where it is taking me; this is how I am best influenced or lead. No one ever did this for me when it came to these "visits."

One day God opened my eyes to the method of the madness in knowing those I was responsible for. All those visits to the barracks room or the rented off-post living place of the soldiers and their families were a valuable method for knowing them. What originated as an Army tradition became an excellent tool in teaching me to know those I led. Suddenly, it all made sense. I no longer would tell leaders to inspect their soldiers' living space because the Army said we had to. But that they would do so as a method for them to learn more about those they lead. I would teach this mind-set to up and coming young leaders to understand how important it was to know their people.

I made a point of taking inexperienced leaders to visit the living spaces of their soldiers. I wanted them to see the person behind the uniform. I wanted them to see the life outside of the uniform of their soldiers. I wanted them to see how tight their monthly budgets were. At this point in their career, most of the leaders made a decent wage and lived in a nice well-furnished home or apartment. Their soldiers did not.

The junior soldiers living room furniture was not from an upscale furniture store but the local twenty-four-hour low-cost and low-quality department store. The junior soldier could not afford the luxury of a dining room set. They were living at a standard well below what the leader had become accustomed to. The leader needed to be reminded of this. Why? Because the leader needed to know their decisions affected a soldier/person and the things important to them in life. Yes, they were leading a soldier, but I wanted them to see past the uniform and know the day-to-day life challenges of those they led. The people you serve and lead require the same understanding from you.

I wish someone would have pointed out that "visiting and checking" was more a way for me to learn more about those I served and lead. I understand that visiting someone's home as military leaders do is not logical in the "real" world. This is simply an example of finding a way to know those you lead. Leaders must be innovative in their methods to get to know others. Look for places and ways to learn about who people are. What about the work cubicle or the area they work in? Any opportunity available is worth taking to see what motivates and stimulates those you serve and lead. Worse case, and there are no physical representations to indicate these things, strike up a conversation, and pry a little. The fact that you took the time to try and get to know them better makes a relationship of trust more attainable.

If you lead a large organization or a large number of people, it requires a committed effort to know those you lead. Often this task is too grand. A leader is forced to focus their efforts on learning to know those within their closest circle of influence. Those you serve and lead are challenged to "know you." It's not easy or comfortable to initiate a conversation about life outside of the workplace with the boss. Not everyone is extrovert and willing to strike up a conversation with their leader. Assumptions about who a leader is as a person is veiled by an exterior of professionalism, which deters engagement. As a leader, I have encountered this and realized I had a lot to learn in knowing and being known.

By knowing the person behind their uniform or work attire, the leader has an avenue to communicate and build on their relationship with others. Revealing those common interests discovered in getting to know them opens huge doors of access for a leader to step into the trust required in leadership relationships. By learning what is important to others, the leader can reveal their similar interest and what you share in common with the person. They see you from an alternative viewpoint. It is not just a "boss" telling me what to do, but a person who understands how I feel and what I care about. A leader who knows and understands where others are coming from can better gauge how much they can be trusted. If the person is deemed trustworthy, the leader can now allow the person to see a little of who the leader is as a person.

The decisions made by a leader affecting people's lives requires the use of both head and heart. A leader weighs their knowledge of the organizational rules and standards and what they know about their people in their decision-making process. A leader's decisions must come from that gray area between the head and the leader's heart. To do this effectively, you must know those you lead. This becomes harder for the leader as they move higher in leadership positions. The increased distance between the leader and their people requires extra effort on the part of the leader. As a leader, you must capture every opportunity to know better those you lead; and to allow them to get to learn more about you. ***"Know well the condition of your flocks and give attention to your herds"*** (Proverbs 27:23).

As a leader, sometimes you have to create opportunities to spend time in the company of those you serve and lead. I would do so by self-inviting myself to sit at the table of a group of people as they ate lunch. We would sit and talk about anything and everything except the Army and the combat operations we were currently engaged in. It was nice to escape for a moment from the "organizational hierarchy" structure and be a person getting to know those I worked with. It was an enjoyable lunch, not scripted, and it was an informal conversation. It was genuine in that we communicated and learned about one another. Over lunch and discussion, I learned the hometowns representing cultures, values, and beliefs associated with peoples' geographical origins. I learned about their hobbies, favorite sports teams, and even about their families.

I learned from the simple act of sharing a meal that they were eager to learn more about me. They asked about my family, favorite sports, and things about our organization they wanted to know. When our mealtime had ended, and we were all heading out the door, I thanked them for letting me sit and eat with them. One of the soldiers felt comfortable enough with me now to come over and say, "Please don't take this the wrong way, but you are much nicer than I thought you would be. Seeing you from afar, and when you are out and about, you always look serious and maybe not very nice, but I was mistaken. Please sit with us anytime you see us here eating together." I thought I made myself approachable and that they knew I loved working for them and taking care of their needs. I had not done a very good job of letting them know me and realized the best way for them to know me was by making more effort to know them. The farther your leadership positions place you from the daily interaction of those you lead, the more action you must take in getting to know them.

Since retiring from the military and entering the private job sector, I have found that everyone, no matter the organization, wants to be known and wants to know their leader. Stopping by a person's work cubicle or self-inviting myself to sit with them on a bench or at a table as they ate their lunch opened terrific and insightful conversations. Assisting others with a weekend house project that some extra manual labor would greatly help, were great learning opportunities. These methods tore down many of the barriers that organizational hierarchies emplace, preventing leaders from knowing those they lead. Getting to know them is NOT fraternization. It is creating a bond that fortifies the trust value essential in a leader's relationship with others.

Notice, nothing has been said about going out drinking or socializing with those you lead; this is NOT how we know them. Enjoying time in these settings when your organization sponsors an event and everyone is appropriately respected is a whole different environment. You are not attempting to become their best friend or buddy. You are letting them know you are interested in learning about them in a way that allows them to trust you. You are revealing your heart of serving and caring for them and their needs, both in and outside the workplace. Caring is an action; you let them hear and see who you are as a leader and a person. No one can lead from behind a desk; a leader must get up, get out, and get about knowing those they lead. Every leader needs to get up and get out more often. ***The LORD replied to Moses, "I will indeed do what you***

have asked, for I look favorably on you, and I know you by name" (Exodus 33:17).

Knowing those you lead provides critical insight. Insight is required to learn how those you lead see things. This allows you to better influence their perspective in alignment with your perspective of the issue or challenge at hand. Perspective is defined as the interrelation in which a subject or its parts are mentally viewed; or, the capacity to view things in their true relations or relative importance. The root word for *psychology* is *psyche.* A person's psyche signifies what drives a person, what represents their passions in life, or what they are naturally drawn to and gifted in. Psychology is the scientific study of the human mind and its functions, especially those affecting how a person will behave in certain situations. Psychology is represented in the mental characteristics or attitude of a person or people created by the emotional factors presiding over a problem or activity.

In its most simple form, leadership is the process of influencing others by providing purpose, motivation, and resources for others to accomplish a goal or task. For a leader to influence others, the leader must know the individual and how they are best influenced, how do they hear you. The Psychology of Leadership requires leaders to understand that theirs and the organization's successes rely on the proper attitude, emotional soundness, and behaviors of those they lead. When a leader understands the psyche of an individual (what drives a person, what represents their passions in life, or what is the thing they are naturally drawn to and gifted in), the leader now has an avenue of approach in which they can influence others to want to do something rather than having to be told to do something.

Knowing them requires leaders to go deeper. Knowing those you lead creates more than a relationship based on trust. It creates a bond founded on personal interaction and personal revelation to another person. I have spent a bit of time talking about methods I encountered to help me get to know those I led in an organization. However, a military organization is a well-structured hierarchy that has been in place for over 244 years. The US Army has had plenty of time and experience figuring out how to maximize leadership effectiveness by leaders knowing those they lead. Everyone in the US military enters an established culture and value system ingrained into civilians beginning in basic training.

One-third of all people who enter the military do not complete their first enlistment contract (usually three to four years). The majority of these people don't make it because they cannot adapt to the military culture and values required in the military. Why? Because they have entered a culture with established values that they are so unfamiliar with and counter to their former culture and values that it exceeds their ability to adapt and overcome. The leader plays a significant role in helping others adapt to an organization's culture. To do this successfully, a leader must understand and respect the culture of each individual they lead.

Today, leaders lead in a globalized society. Every organization is filled with a special and unique blend of people from all over the world. For each of these individuals, their culture and values have made them and the way they see the world and the workplace differently. Cultures are represented by differing geographical locations, beliefs, customs, rituals, food, religions, values, and many times, different languages. These significant cultural differences create a considerable challenge in knowing those you lead. This significance is represented in the way they hear you and understand your words and motives. How important is it for you as their leader to learn and embrace these cultural differences?

> ***At one time all the people of the world spoke the same language and used the same words.*** (Genesis 11:1)

> The LORD said, ***"Look! The people are united, and they all speak the same language. After this nothing they set out to do will be impossible for them!"*** (Genesis 11:6)

Getting everyone aligned with your vision and guidance is why getting to know those you lead is very important in building trust. If a leader does not understand how others hear them and understand them, unity and faith will not occur. Understanding the cultural differences between yourself and those you lead is extremely important. This is why the leadership development of "global" leaders is a multibillion-dollar industry around the globe. Ensuring global leaders increase their Cultural Intelligence (CQ) is a nonnegotiable quest for those that want to make certain their leaders understand and respect different cultural societies. Cultural differences can be learned, respected, and considered even more if you know the person who has them. Others understand where you are coming from and how you see things.

In John 10:27, Jesus states, ***"My sheep listen to my voice; I know them, and they follow me."***

The average person spends one-third of their day at work, one-third of their day asleep, and one-third of their day being with the people and doing the things they hope will bring them joy in life. As a leader, why can't we make the one-third of their day at work more joyful and fulfilling? In John 10:10 Jesus says, ***"The thief's purpose is to steal and kill and destroy. My purpose is to give them a rich and satisfying life."***

When a leader knows the person and sees them for who they are, they have stepped the right way toward leadership greatness, on their way to where the heart of a great leader beats to a different drum. Bob Goff tells us something very significant, "People can't receive our love if they think we don't see them for who they really are."[1] I know what you are thinking, *What's love got to do with it?* No, I'm not talking about the song, although I do love that song. Let's go deeper now. This next part hurts to discuss, but it made me who I became as a leader. It alone is possibly the single most important quality of being a great leader. Jesus Christ had it, how about you?

Reflection Time

What methods do you use to get to know those you serve and lead in life?

When is the last time you made it a priority to get to know a family member or work relationship in a more profound sense?

What mannerism or characteristic about you may deter others from letting you know them better?

---

[1] Bob Goff, Live in Grace, Walk in Love, A 365-Day Journey (Nashville: Nelson Books, 2019), 266.

Love Those You Serve and Lead

If I could speak all the languages of earth and of angels, but didn't love others, I would only be a noisy gong or a clanging cymbal. If I had the gift of prophecy, and if I understood all of God's secret plans and possessed all knowledge, and if I had such faith that I could move mountains, but didn't love others, I would be nothing. If I gave everything I have to the poor and even sacrificed my body, I could boast about it; but if I didn't love others, I would have gained nothing.

—1 Corinthians 13:1–3

In leadership, love is an action fueled by a leader's emotion of caring for those they lead. I wanted to make this statement upfront because leadership "gurus" in today's secular leadership methodology world tend to get riled up when the word *love* is introduced in leadership. We are not talking about the level of love where intimacy or a touch reveals love. We are talking about love in the sense of support and understanding when caring for others. It is essential in leadership that we are motivated by a call of caring for those we serve and lead. Caring about others in leadership is to act from love. Second John verse 6 says, ***Love means doing what God has commanded us, and he has commanded us to love one another, just as you heard from***

the beginning. Our caring acts of love reveal our willingness to place other's needs first. A leader's love actions are revealed in how well they care for those they serve and lead. Love from a leader can be demonstrated in many ways, but mostly from the attributes associated with loving someone. God's description of love simultaneously reveals the qualities we should espouse in leading.

> ***Love is patient and kind. Love is not jealous or boastful or proud or rude. It does not demand its own way. It is not irritable, and it keeps no record of being wronged. It does not rejoice about injustice but rejoices whenever the truth wins out. Love never gives up, never loses faith, is always hopeful, and endures through every circumstance.*** (1 Corinthians 13:4–7)

I propose that 1 Corinthians 13:4–7 represents everything God requires of a great leader:

> A leader is patient and kind. A leader is not jealous or boastful or proud or rude. A leader does not demand their own way. A leader is not irritable and keeps no record of being wronged. A leader does not rejoice about injustice but rejoices whenever the truth wins out. A leader never gives up, never loses faith, is always hopeful, and endures through every circumstance.

In the beginning, we discussed who you are as a leader is who you are as a person. How you love as a person is how you will love as a leader. Love defeats societies attempt to convey a person's worth based on how they look. Love places an aesthetic filter over the eyes and heart of a leader. A filter that allows a leader to see into the core being of those they serve and lead. Love allows a leader to see with their heart, not their eyes. God, as the leader of mankind, showed everyone what love as a leader looks like.

> ***This is real love—not that we loved God, but that he loved us and sent his Son as a sacrifice to take away our sins. Dear friends, since God loved us that much, we surely ought to love each other. No one has ever seen God. But if we love each other, God lives in us, and his love is brought to full expression in us.*** (1 John 4:10–12)

God's word repeatedly reveals the significance of loving others: ***Don't just pretend to love others. Really love them. Hate what is wrong. Hold tightly to what is good. Love each other with genuine affection and take delight in honoring each other*** (Romans 12:9–10). (Get past the world's take on love, and love as God has told us to. Love does not indicate weakness; love is the most significant character attribute a leader can possess. Love opens doors to relationships founded on trust. These relationships represent a powerful formation that can overcome any challenge, endure any tests, and bring fulfillment to a person's life more generous than any gift of money.)

> ***Dear friends, let us continue to love one another, for love comes from God.*** (1 John 4:7)

> ***Above all, clothe yourselves with love, which binds us all together in perfect harmony.*** (Colossians 3:14)

> ***This is what the LORD says: "Don't let the wise boast in their wisdom, or the powerful boast in their power, or the rich boast in their riches. But those who wish to boast should boast in this alone: that they truly know me***

> ***and understand that I am the LORD who demonstrates unfailing love and who brings justice and righteousness to the earth, and that I delight in these things. I, the LORD, have spoken!*** (Jeremiah 9:23–24)

(God's love in our lives brings a sense of peace and joy beyond understanding. A leader's love brings peace and joy to the workplace. A leader's love can change people's lives for the better.)

God demonstrated his love for mankind by the sacrifice of His precious son, Jesus. God has never asked for this type of ultimate sacrifice of anyone else. Instead, we are to show a leader's love by our sacrificial and selfless actions of caring for those we serve and lead. While many actions can convey care and love for others, we will focus on two vital and critical actions of love. Actions that will build stronger relationships with those we serve and lead, encouragement and compassion.

Encouragement

> ***So encourage each other and build each other up.*** (1 Thessalonians 5:11)

> ***Let us think of ways to motivate one another to acts of love and good works.*** (Hebrews 10:24)

A leader looks not at what a person is but what they can become. A leader sees people's potential. A leader sees their growth and what they are intended to be. A leader brings out the best in others, not by labeling them but by encouraging them. A leader lets people know they are believed in, and the leader is confident they will be successful, whatever the endeavor. Before we go further into encouragement, we should discuss something essential; understanding your words' impact on those you serve and lead.

At the beginning of a person's leadership role, they will often find themselves situated side-by-side or in close and constant contact with those they lead. This close and constant contact leader is the leader that thoroughly knows their people, their strengths, weaknesses, and their needs. This leader communicates all day long with those they serve and lead, both in the good and bad times. Because of the natural propensity for first-line leaders to have a tighter relationship with those they lead, communication may, at times, be frank and direct. When things are going wrong, and a first-line leader has to use words that "bite" into those they lead, people know that their leader is just doing their job. Everyone refocuses and gets things done correctly; everyone moves on without it bothering them.

However, what if a senior leader from the organization comes around and observes things going wrong, and the senior leader begins using "biting" words toward that same person or group of individuals? ***But if you are always biting and devouring one another, watch out! Beware of destroying one another*** (Galatians 5:15). People become tolerable of the little bites received from their first line leader, but the senior leaders bite, well, those bites are going to leave a mark. Marks of discouragement, a sense of failure, and a sense that the senior leader sees them as less than they really are. While the senior leader goes on about their day, they are not thinking about what just occurred; they are focused on what's next on their schedule. Meanwhile, they have left a person or group of people reeling in emotions, none of which are encouraging.

I once observed my senior leader verbally berating a group of soldiers I was responsible for. While the senior leader had every right to exercise their authority, their position of responsibility was held in high regard. Their words of criticism and chastisement represented a mighty punch. The higher up the leadership chain one ascends, the more potent their words become as they fall upon hearing ears. I respectfully observed and waited for the senior leader to finish. I knew this leader well, and I understood he only wanted the best out of the soldiers. I felt comfortable enough with the senior leader to later approach him and ask if I could respectfully speak frankly with him; he said, "Yes, of course, you can."

I reminded him that these soldiers hold him and his position in high regard. I reminded him, when he spoke to them, the soldiers absorbed his words as either a source of great encouragement or debilitating discouragement (in other words, they would take his words personally). On the other hand, if those same words spoken came from me, they would know I was just doing my job in their development and correct themselves and move on. I witnessed the soldiers' demeanor after the senior leader had "bitten" into them, and I could see their feelings of low self-worthiness written all over their faces. The senior leaders' bite left a big gash in their sense of value to the organization and created deep despondency feelings.

While inspecting what he expected, he discovered something wrong, and because he was a leader, he addressed it. The senior leader was an honorable man and a great listener. The senior leader said to me, "You are right, and I did not mean to discourage them that way; I just wanted the problem fixed." He said I was correct and that he should have found me to let me "do my job." Later that same day, the soldiers said to me that the senior leader had stopped by and let them know he still loved and believed in them, now that's a great leader. He may not have apologized in words, "I am sorry," he didn't have to. Saying he believed in them was better than any apology. Yes, even as a senior leader in the challenging and mighty 82nd Airborne Division, we used the word *love* toward those in our care.

What am I saying with all this? Simply, you see yourself as just a person with the responsibility of leading. But the higher you go in leadership, the deeper your words penetrate the psyche of those you lead. ***Encourage each other*** (2 Corinthians 13:11). Allow subordinate leaders to do their job, and let them grow as they do the hard work of junior leaders. One of the best parts of rising higher in leadership positions is the tremendous opportunity to encourage others. Opportunities to make their day better, just by a few words and maybe a pat on the back. It's not how you see it; it is how they receive it that matters.

Taking just a moment to pat someone on the back or shake their hand as you tell them how much you appreciate them and thank them for all they do is powerful. Understand what your actions and words represent to others. First-line leaders exist to get others where the organization needs them to be. Don't handicap junior leaders by communicating discouraging words to those they are responsible for. If something is wrong, allow first-line leaders to fix it, others expect this from them. Words of encouragement from any leader at every level are powerful. Still, when those encouraging words come from someone at the top, now those are some words that create wonderful lifetime memories. ***So encourage each other with these words*** (1 Thessalonians 4:18).

Tell people who they are becoming, not who they used to be. Move others forward with your words and actions of encouragement, inspire them to reach their full potential. The success of those you lead takes nothing away from you. Seeing them achieve success means you have done your job in enabling their growth. Say the words "You can do it. I believe in you." "I know you can do this." Encouragement creates an extremely positive invisible force field that propels others forward with confidence by your belief in them. People start to believe in themselves and become more determined than ever to achieve success.

> ***As iron sharpens iron, so a friend sharpens a friend.*** (Proverbs 27:17)

> ***I want them to be encouraged and knit together by strong ties of love.*** (Colossians 2:2)

A leader's encouragement quells self-doubt, bolsters confidence, and lifts a person from feelings of anxiety. The stress created by today's fast-paced and highly competitive work environment can be calmed by encouraging and supportive comments. ***Worry weighs a person down; an encouraging word cheers a person up*** (Proverbs 12:25).

Encouragement promotes and sustains a positive work environment and organizational climate. Encouragement lifts people; it produces hope, perseverance, determination, and, most importantly, self-belief in a person's abilities. ***Don't use foul or abusive language.***

Let everything you say be good and helpful, so that your words will be an encouragement to those who hear them (Ephesians 4:29).

Kay Ash, the founder of Mary Kay Cosmetics, stated, "Everyone has an invisible sign hanging from his neck saying, 'Make Me Feel Important!' Never forget this message when working with people." She understood the emotional dynamics of leadership. People need reassurance and a regular flow of encouragement. Criticize the act, not the person.[1] Mary Kay Ash reminds us that we are leading people. People who will make honest mistakes, just like you and I have made and will continue to make as we live. These are people who need your encouragement to overcome failures, struggles, and challenges. ***Brothers and sisters, we urge you to warn those who are lazy. Encourage those who are timid. Take tender care of those who are weak. Be patient with everyone*** (1 Thessalonians 5:14).

I thank God that he provided leaders in my military career that encouraged me, even when my efforts fail short of success. These encouraging leaders helped me believe in myself and to challenge myself. At one point late in my career, I was contemplating serving twenty years and not a day more before retiring. While on an early morning run with one of my senior leaders, I shared this with him. He encouraged me to consider staying in the military longer. He advised me to weigh the retirement income difference of retiring at twenty years versus thirty years. The difference turned out to be one of having to work another job to assist a twenty-year pension versus not working unless I wanted to perform another job with a thirty-year retirement pension (which became thirty-two years). That leader's encouragement was more valuable than I ever imagined; I am so thankful for his encouragement and counsel. A leader's encouragement potentially represents a very long-term effect on those you speak into; know the power of your words. Bob Goff asks, "Do you realize the power you possess to strengthen another person with the simple words, "Good job." Through the words you speak, God has given you more power to build faith, hope, and love into others' lives than you can possibly imagine."[2]

Compassion

> ***You must be compassionate, just as your Father is compassionate.*** (Luke 6:36)

> ***He comforts us in all our troubles so that we can comfort others. When they are troubled, we will be able to give them the same comfort God has given us.*** (2 Corinthians 1:4)

The weaknesses, troubles, and needs of those we lead should stir up our compassion, our desire to help them. Compassion is an act of love that allows a leader to communicate that they understand and care about the difficulty being encountered by others. Not only to say they understand and care but to use their position of authority to introduce and support acts of compassion. Compassion is a sympathetic consciousness of others› distress together with a desire to alleviate it. Compassion is displayed by leaders when they show mercy and tenderhearted concern for the troubles of those they lead. As a leader, how would you answer Paul and Timothy's question in Philippians 2:1, ***Are your hearts tender and compassionate?***

We see Jesus's compassion in His emotions and actions. ***When the Lord saw her, his heart overflowed with compassion. "Don't cry!" he said*** (Luke 7:13). Following His words, Jesus then brought the woman's dead son back to life. In Luke 8 Jesus encounters a man named Jarius whose daughter dies from an illness just as the man is preparing to ask Jesus to help her. ***But when Jesus heard what had happened, he said to Jarius, "Don't be afraid. Just have faith and she will be healed"*** (Luke 8:50). From Verse 54, ***Then Jesus took her by the hand and said in a loud voice, "My child, get up!" And at that moment her life returned, and she immediately stood up!*** Jesus, the perfect leader, was on a mission to teach, but stopped when others needed help. He not only stopped what He was doing for others in need, He embraced their pain and had compassion on their circumstance.

Let's look at compassion throughout Jesus's ministry and leadership of His Church:

> ***When he saw the crowds, he had compassion on them because they were confused and helpless, like sheep without a shepherd.*** (Matthew 9:36)

> ***Jesus saw the huge crowd as he stepped from the boat, and he had compassion on them because they were like sheep without a shepherd. So he began teaching them many things.*** (Mark 6:34)

> ***Then Jesus said, "Come to me, all of you who are weary and carry heavy burdens, and I will give you rest. Take my yoke upon you. Let me teach you, because I am humble and gentle at heart, and you will find rest for your souls. For my yoke is easy to bear, and the burden I give you is light."*** (Matthew 11:28–30)

> ***Then Jesus wept. The people who were standing nearby said, "See how much he loved him!"*** (John 11:35–36)

> ***You can see how the LORD was kind to him at the end, for the LORD is full of tenderness and mercy.*** (James 5:11)

> ***A man with leprosy came and knelt in front of Jesus, begging to be healed. "If you are willing, you can heal me and make me clean," he said. Moved with compassion, Jesus reached out and touched him. "I am willing," he said.***

> ***"Be healed!" Instantly the leprosy disappeared, and the man was healed.*** (Mark 1:40–42)
>
> ***The LORD is merciful and compassionate, slow to get angry and filled with unfailing love. The LORD is good to everyone. He showers his compassion on all his creation.*** (Psalm 145:8–9)
>
> ***For the LORD has comforted his people and will have compassion on them in their suffering.*** (Isaiah 49:13)

Compassion from a leader changed my purpose in life and in leading others. At the very darkest moment in my life, love, by way of compassion, carried me through a dark and painful period in life. My beautiful four-year-old daughter Amber was diagnosed with cancer (brain tumor). We lived in the Vanderbilt University Hospital Pediatric Ward for seven weeks after her initial diagnosis. During those seven weeks, Amber went through a twelve-hour operation to remove the tumor and multiple setbacks in her health. When we were eventually allowed to return home before beginning her thirty radiation treatments and eight chemotherapy sessions, I was mentally, physically, and spiritually exhausted.

The first evening back home, a knock came on the front door. I opened the door to find our organization's senior leader standing there; he asked if he could enter and talk. He sat on the edge of a small table in front of the sofa, which Amber was resting on and looked at her with wonderful compassion in his eyes. He asked what he could do for us? I did not even know what to ask for; I was still in devastating shock of what Amber was enduring. He said to me, "You have given the Army everything it has asked of you, and now I am going to make sure the Army gives Amber everything you need to help in this life-battle she is in. Your number one priority and concern until this fight is complete is Amber. You are to take as much time as she needs you to take care of her. You will not be charged one day of leave (vacation time) while caring for her. If anyone in your chain-of-command says one negative word to you about being away from work, you let me know. Everyone at work answers to me, and I will make sure everyone knows what your priority is, and that is Amber."

Over the next fourteen months, which included multiple surgical operations, radiation, and chemotherapy sessions, we spent a total of 134 nights in the hospital. Then, on a bright sunny Sunday morning, following three nights in the Pediatric Intensive Care Unit, Amber went home to be with the LORD. I felt destroyed in a way that only a parent can understand. Her loss is as painful today as it was that Sunday morning. My senior leader was true to his word. We received the most loving and caring compassion from my entire chain of command throughout the whole time of Amber's illness. ***When the LORD saw her, his heart overflowed with compassion. "Don't cry!" he said*** (Luke 7:13).

After taking Amber home to North Carolina to be laid to rest, I mourned and contemplated the future. When I returned to the Army, I was embraced with tears and comforting compassion. It was then that I knew my calling in life. From the compassion given to me, I witnessed the greatest leadership attribute I had ever seen in a leader, the leadership attribute of compassion. My senior leader used his position of authority to help me when I could not help myself. This is what I wanted to do as a leader for others in the future. As God richly blessed my career with promotions and positions of greater authority, I was there for others when life threw a curveball into the lives of those I led.

As I would sit in the hospital or the home of an Army family dealing with life's cruel circumstances, I would promise them that the Army will take care of them through their ordeal. When those hurting would thank me, I would tell them, "I am here because God placed me here to help you, to be his hands and feet of compassion, thank God for allowing me to help you. God's word in Isaiah 58:6 tells all of us that lead, ***Lighten the burdens of those who work for you.*** It is my honor to serve you and help you in your time of need." For more than twenty years after Amber went to be with the LORD, my former senior leader's compassionate acts were still serving others, now through me as a leader.

This is what your compassion as a leader does for many more than you will ever know. It was absolutely the most awesome part of leading for me, and it will also be for you. God's word tells us how vital compassion is:

> ***You must clothe yourselves with tenderhearted mercy, kindness, humility, gentleness, and patience.*** (Colossians 3:12)
>
> ***All of you should be of one mind. Sympathize with each other. Love each other as brothers and sisters. Be tenderhearted and keep a humble attitude.*** (1 Peter 4:8)
>
> ***Then this message came to Zechariah from the LORD: This is what the LORD of Heaven's Armies says: Judge fairly and show mercy and kindness to one another.*** (Zechariah 7:8–9)
>
> ***Be happy with those who are happy, and weep with those who weep.*** (Romans 12:15)
>
> ***He comforts us in all our troubles so that we can comfort others. When they are troubled, we will be able to give them the same comfort God has given us.*** (2 Corinthians 1:4)
>
> ***So the LORD must wait for you to come to him so he can show you his love and compassion. For the LORD is a faithful God. Blessed are those who wait for his help.*** (Isaiah 30:18)

> ***Unfailing love and faithfulness protect the king; his throne is made secure through love.*** (Proverbs 20:28)

> ***Never let loyalty and kindness leave you! Tie them around your neck as a reminder. Write them deep within your heart. Then you find favor with both God and people, and you will earn a good reputation.*** (Proverbs 3:3–4)

> ***They do not fear bad news; they confidently trust the LORD to care for them.*** (Psalm 112:7)

> ***"For the mountains may move and the hills disappear, but even then my faithful love for you will remain. My covenant of blessing will never be broken," says the LORD, who has mercy on you.*** (Isaiah 54:10)

The wonderful senior leader who allowed me to see his heart showed me everything great in leadership. He did not reveal a weakness, but he revealed his strength through an act of compassion. I will never forget him for the compassion he gave to us. He changed my life; that is what compassion from a leader does. Compassion gets past titles and hierarchies and makes our fellow man the priority. Listen to how God, our creator and compassionate leader, described himself to Moses in Exodus 34:6–7, ***"Yahweh! The LORD! The God of compassion and mercy! I am slow to anger and filled with unfailing love and faithfulness. I lavish unfailing love to a thousand generations. I forgive iniquity, rebellion, and sin.*** Under every work uniform, suit, work coveralls, or whatever clothing defines a work position is a person; this is who you lead. As Christ our Savior is the leader we go to, to be led by love, which is fueled by his encouragement and compassion, so should those we serve be able to find the same in us. Hebrews 4:16, ***So let us come boldly to the throne of our***

gracious God. There we will receive his mercy, and we will find grace to help us when we need it most. Love them!

> ***Teacher, which is the most important commandment in the law of Moses? Jesus replied, "You must love the LORD your God with all your heart, all your soul, and all your mind. This is the first and greatest commandment. A second is equally important: Love your neighbor as yourself."*** (Matthew 22:36–39)

When we love those we are honored to lead, I believe we are doing what God intended us to do when leading others. "God didn't give you influence so you'd lead people better. He gave it to you, so you'd love people more."[3] God has always shown humanity that compassion is one of his most beautiful ways of loving us. ***Remember, O LORD, your compassion and unfailing love, which you have shown from long ages past*** (Psalm 25:6). What if society approached leading others in the workplace with the same emotions of love, care, and compassion society believes essential in guiding our families? What if leaders in the workplace assumed the Apostle Paul's mindset when writing to the Philippians? ***Every time I think of you, I give thanks to my God.*** Verse 7, **So it is right that I should feel as I do about all of you, for you have a special place in my heart.** Verse 8, ***God knows how much I love you and long for you with the tender compassion of Christ Jesus*** (Philippians 1:3).

When our motive for leading others is founded on the bedrock of our love for serving our fellow man, our leadership is fortified by the invaluable and precious leadership attribute of selflessness. A selfish leader is an oxymoron, as selfishness leads no one except the person in the mirror. Let's explore and compare, onward!

Reflection Time

Do you tell people what they are becoming instead of who they used to be?

How would others describe your demeanor? Is your behavior patient, kind, and considerate of other's needs?

How do you reveal to those you serve and lead that you care about them and their needs?

---

1 Harold Myra and Marshall Shelley, The Leadership Secrets of Billy Graham (Grand Rapids: Zondervan, 2005), 134.

2 Bob Goff, Live in Grace, Walk in Love, A 365-Day Journey (Nashville: Nelson Books, 2019), 190.

3 Ibid., 87.

Selflessness Over Selfishness

Don't be concerned for your own good but for the good of others.

—1 Corinthians 10:24

But watch out, you who live in your own light and warm yourselves by your own fires. This is the reward you will receive from me: You will soon fall down in great torment.

—Isaiah 50:11

It almost seems crazy when discussing leadership that we would need to pause and present a comparison/contrast between Selflessness and Selfishness. Whenever I have heard someone describe a leader as selfish, I say the term "selfish leader" is an oxymoron. A leader requires a selfless motive, which is contradictory to selfishness. I am also a realist and understand many in leadership positions appear to be mostly for themselves. Selfish leaders represent the doctrine of many fallen leaders, egoism. Their self-interest is their motive for all of their intentional actions.

When selecting others to lead, one of the keys and significant factors to consider is the person's motive. In other words, which need or desire do the person's behaviors and actions represent? Do they serve the organization and others, or are they focused on primarily benefiting themselves? Selflessness and selfishness are two-character traits in humanity that have not changed since man's creation (Cain and Abel, for example, Genesis 4:1–15). Selflessness is promoted throughout Scripture as an external focus of serving others. Selfishness is represented throughout Scripture as ways of using and deceiving others for self-gain and self-promotion.

The Right Way: Selflessness Revealed in Scripture

And don't forget to do good and to share with those in need. These are the sacrifices that please God (Hebrews 13:16). (A sure sign that a leader is selfless and focused on others' needs is their willingness to give and share with those in need. Giving comes from a good heart, a heart for serving those in need.)

In Mark 10:45 Jesus said, "***For even the Son of Man came not to be served but to serve others and to give his life as a ransom for many.***" (Jesus, who the Word says in Hebrews 2:10 was ***a perfect leader***, gave two primary reasons for His existence as a person, and as a leader. As **a perfect leader,** Jesus said he came to ***serve others and to give.*** Serving and giving is everything that being selfless represents. So you want to be a great leader (there was only one perfect leader). To be great, you must take an attitude of wanting to serve the needs of those you lead and give them your sacrifice of time and energy for their benefit.)

If you try to hang on to your life, you will lose it. But if you give up your life for my sake, you will save it (Matthew 16:25). (Professional athletes returning from a serious injury that required surgical repair have said that the worst way to play when returning to their sport is by guarding against reinjuring the old injury. In other words, these athletes say they have to go all out and play aggressive. In the same way, a leader cannot serve and lead others timidly. Being risk-averse is prudent in dangerous occupations, but leading people requires taking risks. The most significant risk for those you serve and lead is the risk of trusting you. Give everything you are to the organization and those you serve and lead. Like a great athlete returning from an injury, don't hold back; leave everything you have to give on the playing field. If you want to take care of your life and career as a leader, trust your selfless motive, and lay it all on the line for those who trust you.)

Dear children, let's not merely say that we love each other; let us show the truth by our actions. Our actions will show that we belong to the truth (1 John 3:18–19). (Talk is cheap when it comes to love and caring for others. Let your walk reveal a heart for serving others.)

For God loved the world so much that he gave his one and only Son, so that everyone who believes in him will not perish but have eternal life (John 3:16). (Are you willing to get over and past the things vital to you for the good of others? Selflessness requires sacrifice. How much are you ready to sacrifice for those you serve and lead? God sacrificed the life of His perfect Son for you and me, that if we choose to believe in Him, we have eternal life. As a leader, we are required to sacrifice our interest and needs for the interest and needs of those we serve and lead.)

He must become greater and greater, and I must become less and less (John 3:30). (John the Baptist realized his role in serving Jesus's ministry. John selflessly placed man's need for a Savior over the desires and needs of his calling. ***He is a voice shouting in the wilderness, "Prepare the way for the LORD's coming! Clear the road for him!"*** (Mark 1:3). John was willing to get out of the way of Jesus because he knew he lived to serve Jesus and no one else. Are you ready to step into the shadows for those you serve and lead, allowing them to stand in the spotlight of recognition and success? Clear the road for others!)

Give freely and become more wealthy; be stingy and lose everything. The generous will prosper; those who refresh others will themselves be refreshed (Proverbs 11:24–25). (The efforts a leader takes to ensure the success of those they serve and lead becomes an investment into creating their real value and worth as a leader. Success and wealth are so much more than who you are and what you have; success and wealth are what you did for others and what you gave away.)

We must not just please ourselves. We should help others do what is right and build them up in the Lord (Romans 15:1–2). (Self-pleasure is momentary and fleeting, becoming stagnant like a lifeless body of water. Serving others generates movements toward their success and is a flowing stream of hope and encouragement in their lives. Any person can look after only themselves, but only a selfless leader serves to please others.)

In Luke 22:42 Jesus says, ***"Yet I want your will to be done, not mine."*** (It takes a bold leader to commit their ways for the needs of those they serve and lead. Take a stand for others, not yourself!)

In John 5:30 Jesus says, ***"I carry out the will of the one who sent me, not my own will."*** (A leader carries out their work focused on others' work and needs. It's not about what you want, it's all about what others need. This is a recipe for greatness in leading!)

Use your freedom to serve one another in love (Galatians 5:13). (Use your role as a leader to help one another. As a leader, you are empowered with authority to make the lives of those you serve and lead more peaceful and enjoyable. Don't look at the power and authority of your leadership position as a tool for your benefit. See it as a tool to build up the lives of those you serve and lead.)

In John 5:30 Jesus says, **"I can do nothing on my own. I judge as God tells me. Therefore, my judgment is just, because I carry out the will of the one who sent me, not my own will."** (Do nothing for yourself but do everything for those you serve and lead. This is what God requires of you and what those you serve and lead deserve.)

The Wrong Way: Selfishness Revealed in Scripture

For wherever there is jealousy and selfish ambition, there you will find disorder and evil of every kind (James 3:16). (A leader longing for their success has ingested a motive willing to risk everything and everyone else for notoriety and promotion. These are people who practice deceit, corruption, debauchery, depravity, viciousness, and wrongdoing for their self-gain.)

Don't be selfish; don't try to impress others. Be humble, thinking of others as better than yourselves. Don't look out only for your own interests, but take an interest in others, too (Philippians 2:3–4). (Self is all about ME. Leading is all about OTHERS!)

> ***What is causing the quarrels and fights among you? Don't they come from the evil desires at war within you? You want what you don't have, so you scheme and kill to get it. You are jealous of what others have, but you can't get it, so you fight and wage war to take it away from them. Yet you don't have what you want because you don't ask God for it. And even when you ask, you don't get it because your motives are all wrong—you want only what will give you pleasure.*** (James 4:1–3)

(A leader's motives represent either peace and harmony or grief and chaos. Before placing any person in a leadership position, regardless of their talent, identify their motive for leading. Is it to help others thrive or serve their own needs?)

> ***Do not love this world nor the things it offers you, for when you love the world, you do not have the love of the Father in you. For the world offers only a craving for physical pleasure, a craving for everything we see, and pride in our achievements and possessions. These are not from the Father but are from this world.*** (1 John 2:15–16)

(Serve and lead as God's Truth tells us to, not as this world entices us to.)

See that no one pays back evil for evil, but always try to do good to each other and to all people (1 Thessalonians 5:15). Revenge is this world's selfish way of justice. ***Dear friends, never***

take revenge. Leave that to the righteous anger of God. For the Scriptures say, "I will take revenge; I will pay them back," says the Lord (Romans 12:19). Leaders take the high road of selflessness, not the world's low road of selfishness.)

Unfriendly people care only about themselves; they lash out at common sense (Proverbs 18:1). (Unkindness toward others reveals a dark, selfish person.)

He will give eternal life to those who keep on doing good, seeking after the glory and honor and immortality that God offers. But he will pour out his anger and wrath on those who live for themselves, who refuse to obey the truth and instead live lives of wickedness (Romans 2:7–8). (Selfishness is a one-way road to destruction, especially in leading.)

> ***In the last days, there will be very difficult times. For people will love only themselves and their money. They will be boastful and proud, scoffing at God, disobedient to their parents, and ungrateful. They will consider nothing sacred. They will be unloving and unforgiving; they will slander others and have no self-control. They will be cruel and hate what is good. They will betray their friends, be reckless, be puffed up with pride, and love pleasure rather than God. They will act religious, but they will reject the power that could make them godly. Stay away from people like that!*** (2 Timothy 3:1–5)

(This world already has enough selfish people. Let your leadership be a beacon of selflessness and righteous living. It is easy to find people who will take from others. The challenge in today's world is to find people willing to give for others. Great leaders humbly provide and serve.)

Your kindness will reward you, but your cruelty will destroy you (Proverbs 11:17). (Kindness in leading promotes hope; cruelty in leading promotes guaranteed failure.)

You say, "I am rich. I have everything I want. I don't need a thing!" And you don't realize that you are wretched and miserable and poor and blind and naked (Revelation 3:17). (Selfishness leaves people, even wealthy people, all alone. What good are the world's treasures if they leave a person without what represents real wealth, family, friends, and good health? Wealth is not what is seen in the idols around a person; wealth is what is inside a person and having peace and love in their life.)

A selfless leader serves to GIVE, while a selfish leader serves to GET. Before looking at how Scripture differentiates between selflessness and selfishness, we should look at words used today to describe/define the two opposites of a person's intentions.

Selflessness is represented by the following:

altruistic	charitable	generous	humanitarian
loving	magnanimous	noble	self-effacing
benevolent	chivalrous	denying	devoted
disinterested	extroverted	helpful	incorruptible
indulgent	liberal	open-handed	self-denying
self-forgetful	self-forgetting	self-sacrificing	

The mind and motive of Great Leaders is represented by those who are selfless, serving, and willing to sacrifice for those they lead.

Selfishness is represented by the following:

egotistical	greedy	narcissistic	self-centered
egocentric	egoistic	egoistical	egomaniacal
egotistic	hoggish	mean	mercenary
miserly	narrow	narrow-minded	parsimonious
prejudiced	out for number one	self-indulgent	self-interested
self-seeking	wrapped up in oneself	stingy	ungenerous

Selfishness is represented in a leader in many "self" ways:

Self-will: not anyone else's way, but my way.
Self-seeking: it is always about I, Me, or Mine.
Self-pity: always groaning, grieving, and complaining about their lot in life.
Self-conscious: always worried about how others view them.
Self-exalting: praise of self.
Self-justification: excusing oneself or one's actions.
Self-confidence: over feeling of trust in one's abilities, qualities, and judgment.

Jude: Verse 16 says selfish people ***"brag loudly about themselves, and they flatter others to get what they want."*** Verse 19 says, ***"These people are the ones who are creating divisions among you. They follow their natural instincts because they do not have God's Spirit in them."*** Author Bob Goff informs us, "A life focused on yourself and the meeting of your own needs will never be a great life, because it can get no larger than just you. Every great life is focused on meeting other people's needs."[1] Selflessness in leadership is focused on bringing people together. Be the leader that is self-aware enough to know that one of the most beautiful purposes of leadership is to lift the lives of those you serve and lead. Selfish leaders create irrevocable emotional damage when they belittle and put others down with their selfishly motivated words and actions. The selfish leader fails to realize or meet others' needs because they do not care about others' interests.

In the introduction of this book, we identified that every word of God is the Truth. Let's read what the wisest leader ever anointed and appointed by God reveals are the differences between being selfless and selfish. Who better to tell us than King Solomon himself? King Solomon, who would reign as King of Israel for forty years, asked God for Wisdom.

> ***Solomon son of David, took firm control of his kingdom, for the Lord his God was***

with him and made him very powerful. (2 Chronicles 1:1)

That night God appeared to Solomon and said to him, "What do you want? Ask, and I will give it to you." (2 Chronicles 1:7)

Solomon replied to God, ***Give me the wisdom and knowledge to lead them properly, for who could possibly govern this great people of yours?*** (2 Chronicles 1:10)

Solomon asked God, ***"Give me an understanding heart so that I can govern your people well and know the difference between right and wrong. For who by himself is able to govern this great people of yours?"*** (1 Kings 3:9)

God said to Solomon, "Because your greatest desire is to help your people, and you did not ask for wealth, riches, or fame, or even the death of your enemies or a long life but rather you asked for wisdom and knowledge to properly govern my people—I will certainly give you the wisdom and knowledge you requested. But I will also give you wealth, riches and fame such as no king has had before you or will ever have in the future!" (2 Chronicles 1:11–12)

So King Solomon became richer and wiser than any other king on earth. Kings from every nation came to consult him and to hear the wisdom God had given him. (2 Chronicles 9:22–23)

> ***God gave Solomon very great wisdom and understanding, and knowledge as vast as the sands of the seashore. In fact, his wisdom exceeded that of all the wise men of the East and the wise men of Egypt. He was wiser than anyone else.*** (1 Kings 4:29–31)

> King Solomon states, ***I said to myself, "Look, I am wiser than any of the kings who ruled in Jerusalem before me. I have greater wisdom and knowledge than any of them."*** (Ecclesiastes 1:16)

From these verses of Scripture, we learn that God divinely gave King Solomon unparalleled wisdom. Wisdom represents knowledge and insight. Wisdom is God's gift of understanding and provides a person with the truth to a joyful and peaceful life. James 3:17–18 tells us the benefits of listening to wisdom, ***But the wisdom from above is first of all pure. It is also peace loving, gentle at all times, and willing to yield to others. It is full of mercy and good deeds. It shows no favoritism and is always sincere. And those who are peacemakers will plant seeds of peace and reap a harvest of righteousness.*** Wisdom promotes selflessness. Throughout the Book of Proverbs, King Solomon's wisdom reveals the contrast between a wise selfless person and a foolish, selfish person.

From the Book of Proverbs 1–31, King Solomon Reveals

Wise		*Foolish*
Acts of Selfless People	**vs.**	***Acts of Selfish People***
Cry out for insight	vs.	Hate knowledge
Ask for understanding	vs.	Reject advice
Walks with integrity	vs.	Actions are crooked
Seeks wisdom and knowledge	vs.	Turns on wisdom
Shows discernment	vs.	Great foolishness
Detest deception	vs.	Heart that plots evil

Uses good judgment	vs.	Lack good judgment
Speaks the truth	vs.	A lying tongue
Hates pride and arrogance	vs.	Are haughty
Walk safely	vs.	Slip and fall
Use life-giving words	vs.	Words conceal violence
Actions of love	vs.	Actions of hatred
Speaks wise words	vs.	Babbling of a fool
Accepts discipline	vs.	Ignores correction
Pleases others	vs.	Irritates their employer
Gives wise advice	vs.	A tongue that deceives
Humble	vs.	A proud heart
Godly	vs.	Treacherous
Rescues the righteous	vs.	Destroys their friends
Keeps quiet	vs.	Belittles their neighbor
Kindness	vs.	Cruelty
Gives freely	vs.	Stingy
Integrity	vs.	Crooked hearts
Loves discipline	vs.	Hates correction
Listens to others	vs.	Think their ways are right
Speaks truthful words	vs.	Speaks lies
Quiet in their wisdom	vs.	Broadcasts foolishness
Controls their tongue	vs.	Opens their mouth
Hates lies	vs.	Cause shame and disgrace
Thinks before acting	vs.	Fools don't
Walks with the wise	vs.	Associates with fools
Fear the LORD	vs.	Despise the LORD
Does not lie	vs.	Breathes lies
Acknowledges guilt	vs.	Makes fun of guilt
Cautious, avoiding danger	vs.	Plunge ahead recklessly
Controls their anger	vs.	Short-tempered
Uses gentle words	vs.	Uses harsh words
Stops/avoids fights	vs.	Starts/joins in fights
Uses pleasant uplifting words	vs.	Words of destruction
Plans for good	vs.	Plots evil
Keeps silent	vs.	Loves to quarrel
Practices honesty	vs.	Takes secret bribes

Cares for others	vs.	Cares only for themselves
Justice is a joy	vs.	Terrified by justice
Love to give	vs.	Greedy for more
Foresees danger	vs.	Goes blindly
Honesty	vs.	Corruptness
Does not envy	vs.	Envious of others
Does not betray others trust	vs.	Gossips
Content	vs.	Desire is never satisfied
Are bold	vs.	Runs away
Brings stability	vs.	Destroys
Understands justice	vs.	Don't understand justice
Inherits good things	vs.	Fall into their own traps
Confesses their wrongs	vs.	Conceals their wrongs
Lifts others up	vs.	Oppresses others
Hard worker	vs.	Lazy
Trustworthy	vs.	Untrustworthy
Walks in wisdom	vs.	Trust their own insights
Gives to the poor	vs.	Closed eyes to poverty
Despises the unjust	vs.	Despises the godly
Does not reveal secrets	vs.	Goes about telling secrets

King Solomon's Book of Proverbs is filled with advice and counsel on pretty much every ethical dilemma a leader will face during a lifetime. In Proverbs 1:2–5, King Solomon reveals his purpose for his words.

> ***Their purpose is to teach people wisdom and discipline, to help them understand the insights of the wise. Their purpose is to teach people to live disciplined and successful lives, to help them do what is right, just, and fair. These proverbs will give insight to the simple, knowledge and discernment to the young. Let the wise listen to these proverbs and become wiser. Let those with understanding receive guidance.***

The nature of a selfless person is one that draws others to them. A selfless leader keeps an "open-door policy" because they want to be available to others for their issues and needs. A selfless leader gets up from their desk and gets out and about to make themselves available to serve others. A selfless leader asks those they lead, "How are you doing? What can I do for you?" with sincerity. A selfless leader makes sure that the organization's needs and those they serve and lead are met to the standard of those they serve. A selfless leader does not work for a stellar self-promoting evaluation report they can compare to their peers. Instead, they focus on the mission and the needs of others before their advancement.

Reporting to a new organization as a senior leader, I soon sat in the organization's top senior leader's office. I knew this senior leader's reputation as being very intense, very focused, and very Army. On the other hand, I preferred to be more laid back, and while I loved the Army, it was not going to be my everything in life. I was not sure if he and I would see eye to eye on how to run things. Before entering his office for our first formal introduction to each other, I asked God, "Be with me, please."

I sat and listened as the top senior leader discussed his leadership philosophy and vision for the organization (all of which were inspiring). But I was afraid that he would not appreciate my leadership philosophy or even my style of leading. When I was selected over thirty-two of my peers for this promotion in position of responsibility, one of my superior's said to me, "Dawg (he called everyone Dawg… I don't know why), you can't go to that new unit being the laid back, love and take care of everybody guy you are here. That large organization and tough crowd will eat you alive." I prayed that night on what he had said and asked God to show me how to serve the new organization best. I asked God, "Do I need to change?" God eased my anxiety and placed in my heart His words "Be who I made you be, and lead as the one that allowed you to be selected over many others for this organization," in other words, be true to the leader I made you to be.

So when it came to my opportunity to speak to my new boss, I subconsciously thought, "Here we go." I told him that "I will give

110% to the organization and everyone in it. I will lead from the front and lead by example (here it comes, how will he take it?), but if my family calls and they need me for an emergency or help only I can provide, I will immediately depart to care for them. My family is for life, the military is for today." I expected him to say, "Well, you are not the right leader for leading here; there is the door." Instead, his words of humility blew me away. He looked at me intensely and said, "I need you to help me make my family more of a priority as we lead together. Will you do that for me?" He had me; here was a leader, as great a leader as there will ever be, willing to admit to me in our first conversation that he longed to be a better father and husband.

Now, this was powerful, but it gets even better. We then talked about those we were to lead together, and yes, we talked about our higher headquarters and what they expected of us. He said to me, he had not read his last five years of leadership evaluation reports given to him by his superiors, and he had no clue what they said about him as a leader. I asked, why? What mattered to him was if those he served and led were good with his performance. Suppose they were good with his selfless leadership, and the organization always achieved its objectives and completed its mission. In that case, everyone senior to him should have no problem with his performance, "Why read what they write?" he asked.

His selfless mind-set represents a leader willing to hear the truth from those that see the leader for who he is. Too many "leaders" strive to present a picture of themselves to those senior to them as they desire to be seen. If you want to learn a leader's motives, go and talk to those they currently serve and lead or have led in the past. The truth of a leader's motives for leading is revealed to those who hear and see them out of earshot and view of the leader's superiors. Everyone, including a leader's peers, sees a leader's true motives when they attempt to impress other leaders.

After serving in this most recent position of greater responsibility for two years, I was blessed to be selected for promotion to my career field's top leadership rank. Upon selection, the Army notified me that I would be leaving for a new assignment; this meant the organization would select someone to succeed me. Over the previous two years, the organization's people became like family to me, and I loved them as such. I sincerely hoped that the person selected to replace me would care for them the same as I had. I bumped into a peer within our higher headquarters. He said, "Man, I know I should put my name in the hat for consideration to be your successor, everyone that successfully survives that position always gets promoted to the top."

He said nothing about the organization's people or about the great opportunity to serve such a large group of people and make sure they were cared for. He selfishly looked at the position as a chance to get himself promoted. I don't hold back when I feel a leader's motives are misoriented. I bluntly told him, "Don't bother putting your name in the hat for consideration for the position. I will let those making the decision know that I strongly protest your consideration since you only care about what the position will do for your career." What I said to him did not even register with him. He had no idea there was any other reason to take on the job of leading such a large and challenging organization other than it would help his career; he had selfish motives.

The motive of the selfish leader is their gain, their advancement. Selfish leaders dictate over others at whatever the cost (hate, aggravation, chaos, irritations, meanness, disloyalty, abrasiveness, and reckless behaviors) to those they lead to advance their agenda. Consideration of others is nonexistent in their selfish mind-set. A selfish leader is like rotting fruit; they spoil everything and everyone they come in contact with. On the contrary, a selfless leader serves as a fertilizer, enhancing others' growth, which helps them thrive and flourish. ***But the Holy Spirit produces this kind of fruit in our lives: love, joy, peace, patience, kindness, goodness, faithfulness, gentleness, and self-control. There is no law against these things!*** (Galatians 5:22–23)

In the last chapter, we discussed loving those we serve and lead. Just like any meaningful, loving relationship, love requires selfless actions of giving to others. We make self-sacrifices to benefit those we love and serve. Pastor Tony Evans tells us, "When you walk in love, you don't use people to satisfy your impure desires; you don't take from them to satisfy your greed, and you don't abuse or belittle them with your mouth. Distance yourself from these kinds of things and the people who practice them."[2] When leaders are selfless, they make themselves available to others, which is critically essential to building the relationship required in leading. Being selfless leads us to one of the most extraordinary success moves any leader can ever make; they surround themselves with great people—something a selfish leader would never do.

Reflection Time

Do your actions and words meet the needs of others or seek gains for yourself?

How often are your decisions and agendas based on the needs of others and not yourself?

What are you willing to give up so that someone else can rise?

---

1 Bob Goff, Live in Grace, Walk in Love, A 365-Day Journey (Nashville: Nelson Books, 2019), 270.

2 Tony Evans, Time to Get Serious: Daily Devotions to Keep You Close to God (Wheaton: Crossway, 1995), 309.

Surround Yourself with Great People and Let Them Soar

For as in one body we have many members, and the members do not all have the same function, so we, though many, are one body in Christ, and individually members one of another. Having gifts that differ according to the grace given to us, let us use them.

—Romans 12:3–4

There is an old saying about leadership: "It's lonely at the top." This saying represents the lonely endeavor of being the senior person in charge. When at the top, there are no peers to hear your venting of frustrations. There is no one you can express your anxieties to or discuss your challenges with. There is no one you can be brutally honest with, without fear of judgment. This becomes the role of a respected mentor or leadership advisor for encouraging the psyche of the lonely senior leader. Every leader requires someone to express, and when needed, share their burdens with. Loneliness at the top applies to the top person not the organization's need for concerted leadership collaboration.

Organizationally, no leader at the top should be alone if they are applying God's truth in leading. No single leader can do it all, nor does any single leader know all the answers. God's word instructs leaders to surround themselves with others for advice, insights, and varying perspectives.

Seek and Take Advice/Wise Counsel

Two people are better off than one, for they can help each other succeed. If one person falls, the other can reach out and help. But someone who falls alone is in real trouble (Ecclesiastes 4:9–10). (Mother Teresa stated, "You can do what I cannot do. I can do what you cannot do. Together we can do great things." Two people are always better to have when strength is required to overcome challenges. The workplace and the rest of our lives are filled with challenges. Most challenges we face in the home or workplace are emotional, not always physical (unless you work in the furniture moving industry☺.) Each of us requires the emotional strengthening and encouragement others provide when we succumb to life's challenges. God created us to be in relationships; we need each other. And you, as a leader, need others to help you with workplace challenges. No matter how smart, how skilled, or how many degrees you have, you required the teaching and help from others to get you where you are. The same goes in the workplace; you need others alongside you. Challenges will come; they always do.)

It is better to be a poor but wise youth than an old and foolish king who refuses all advice (Ecclesiastes 4:13). (I enjoy the music in the beautiful song written by Paul Anka, "My Way." You know the song; it has the line "I Did It My Way." While these words are great lyrics in a song, they are no way for a leader to lead. Every leader who refuses to receive advice from others only knows what the leader knows. No leader knows everything about everything. The wisest man to ever live, King Solomon, sought insights from counselors and advisors. Don't be the "foolish king who refuses all advice." If you want to be great at leading, you must first be great at listening to others.)

The words of the wise are like cattle prods—painful but helpful (Ecclesiastes 12:11). (Ouch, the truth hurts sometimes! But without the facts, a leader will stumble down a path of unknowns, and unknowns can quickly become a leader's overwhelming adversary. Hearing the wisdom of the truth may not always be what you prefer to hear. The truth sometimes cuts into our agenda, the profit margin of a potentially lucrative contract, or our personal goals and desires. Knowing the truth upfront can save a leader from more significant losses and pain down the road. The wise words are like ripping a band-aid off of a hairy part of the body. Painful but thankfully over with quickly so that the wounded area gets much-needed air to dry and heal.)

Plans succeed through good counsel; don't go to war without wise advice (Proverbs 20:18). (No military analogies here, although I have a bunch to offer. Before a leader makes decisions of any sort, they should receive insights and counsel from any party to provide information to be weighed by the leader. Good counsel allows a leader to see the big picture of the pros and cons of their decisions now and for the future.)

Timely advice is lovely, like golden apples in a silver basket. To one who listens, valid criticism is like a gold earring or other gold jewelry (Proverbs 25:11–12). (As a leader, establishing a routine in your decision-making process of first being informed by advisors before making a final decision is a routine that will equate to greater success.)

So don't go to war without wise guidance; victory depends on having many advisers (Proverbs 24:6). (Automakers now build into automobiles the dreaded "Check Engine" light to illuminate when the automobile has a problem requiring the vehicle operator's attention. The extended operational ability of the vehicle requires the operator to have a professional auto technician to investigate further. The auto technician hooks the vehicle up to an On-Board Diagnostic System reader to reveal what is wrong. Suppose the auto tech tells the operator a repair is needed now before becoming much worse later. In that case, the operator is wise to have the item fixed now, saving them from more significant expenses later. As a leader, the advisor's wise guidance early in the decision-making process equates to using an On-Board Diagnostic System. Identifying potential long-term consequences today by receiving advice establishes a path to tomorrow's organizational victories.)

Get all the advice and instruction you can, so you will be wise the rest of your life (Proverbs 19:20). (I often wish back in my youth I would have read and taken to heart all of King Solomon's wise advice found in the book of Proverbs. Keep learning from and listening to the wise advice those you serve and lead have.)

Without wise leadership, a nation falls; there is safety in having many advisers (Proverbs 11:14). (Every successful person, organization, and society has equipped itself with smart and foresighted advisors. Too much is at stake to risk going at life or business without many advisers.)

Walk with the wise and become wise (Proverbs 13:20). (Never let pride get in the way of admitting you don't know everything about everything. Seek and surround yourself with people that will take your intellect higher, not fools that seek to bring you down.)

Those who take advice are wise (Proverbs 13:10). (The smartest people in society are the ones intelligent enough to learn from others.)

People who despise advice are asking for trouble (Proverbs 13:13). (I have a friend who hates others' advice. To the point that they have said if they fail in their career, they will stand on a corner with a sign begging for other's handouts. Their pride is so severe that they are willing to risk their quality of life before listening to others' advice. Sure enough, they are now experiencing quality of life challenges. I pray for them daily. Never be too proud to seek advice and act on it appropriately. God uses others to speak into our lives for Him. When we fail to heed their advice and counsel, we are saying to God, we know better than those He has provided to help us have His peace and joy in life.)

Fools think their own way is right, but the wise listen to others (Proverbs 12:15). (How true!)

Plans go wrong for lack of advice; many advisers bring success (Proverbs 15:22). (So says the wisest man ever to live!)

> ***Two are better than one, because they have a good reward for their toil. For if they fall, one will lift up his fellow. But woe to him who is alone when he falls and not another to lift him up! Again, if two lie together, they keep warm, but how can one keep warm alone? And though a man might prevail against one who is alone, two will withstand him—a threefold cord is not quickly broken.*** (Ecclesiastes 4:9–12)

(A wise leader strengthens their decision-making process when their decisions represent advice and insights from many.)

Iron sharpens iron, and one man sharpens another (Proverbs 27:17). (A wise leader should question, encourage, coach, and challenge others. And a wise leader will allow others to do the same to them.)

No person or leader is intelligent enough to know everything required to fix issues that need to be addressed. However, when a person or leader is blessed to know they need to surround themselves with great people, they can ride their wave of abilities to an organization's success. When leaders surround themselves with others, they do not surround themselves with people who see all issues the same as the leader. A leader should not surround themselves with "yes" people.

A leader should seek people with varying perspectives, experiences, and new ideas and methods to achieve organizational success. The motives of advisors should be the same; motives for the organization's good and its people, their personalities will and should differ. A leader should surround themselves with positive and forward-thinking people, not naysayers, and people with personal agendas. The right mix of talent and experience may not necessarily be present to select from within the organization. In this case, you may have to look external to the organization and bring in new people with the strengths needed to provide the expert advice and counsel required.

Upon return from a combat deployment, I was called and told that I had been selected to lead a leadership training academy in the Army. I had spent the previous twenty-one years in the Operational (warfighting) side of the Army; I had never served in the Army Training (schoolhouse) side before. I asked if there was a course or class I could take to learn what I did not know and was told, "You will figure it out." I had been selected to change leadership development training from the peacetime curriculum currently being instructed. I was to design, build, and emplace curriculum that prepared leaders to lead soldiers in the combat operations environment's complexity.

I verified with my leader my change parameters. How much could I change, and whose permission did I need to make those changes? I learned I had the authority to change what was needed within the Academy's teaching curriculum regarding leadership. After I was briefed on the current leadership curriculum being instructed, I identified what needed to be removed and added. A problem I incurred in this change was that two thirds of the instructors had not been to combat and did not understand or have the experience required to build or teach the new leadership classes of instruction.

I worked with the Army's Human Resources Command and had the inexperienced instructors reassigned. I then requested recent combat-experienced leaders be assigned to the Leadership Academy. I selected an individual who would serve as the second in command. They were assigned to the Leadership Academy after their return from a recent combat deployment. I surrounded myself with prior combat experts who understood my vision and required changes. Their previous experiences would better prepare leadership students for leading in combat. Without them, I would have failed regardless of how much experience and knowledge I had.

Leaders create a vision for their organization and its people. Still, it is those the leader has around them that make achieving the vision a reality. All the world knowledge cannot physically enable a leader with the energy and stamina required to do it all. ***Even youths will become weak and tired, and young men will fall in exhaus-***

tion (Isaiah 40:30). Surrounding yourself with great people has many benefits. One that is especially beneficial is how the company of others sustain and energize you. Pastor and author Adrian Rogers revealed, "There can be no shining without burning, and when you burn, you are consumed. The pathway of service can deplete your stamina and strength."[1]

Engineers studying Geese's method used to fly great distances with their Flying V formation discovered a flock of geese could fly 72 percent further during one flight then a single goose flying alone. When a goose moves to the front of the Flying V formation, it uses more energy to cut through the air. The other geese in the flying V formation benefit aerodynamically from the lead goose's efforts and can often be heard "honking" (encouraging) the lead goose onward. Whichever goose is leading is encouraged and knows when they grow tired, they can count on another goose to fly up and take the lead. This will make flying easier and sustain the former flight leader's ability to keep flying. Just like a single goose can go much further when surrounded and encouraged by other geese, a leader must surround themselves with great people to go further for the organization and its people.

Essential when surrounding yourself with great people is sitting down and having an honest conversation with yourself. A conversation of identifying what aspects of the organization's mission leaves you feeling uncomfortable with your knowledge or experience level. Once you have identified your weaknesses and challenges, surround yourself with the right person(s) whose strengths in those areas will shore up your knowledge for decision making. ***As each part does its own special work, it helps the other parts grow, so that the whole body is healthy and growing and full of love.***

Allow for frank, honest, and sometimes brutal truth to be provided without fear of retaliation (psychological safe zone environment). Knowing the truth will set you and others free to make the right and best decisions. Closed Ears = Closed Minds. Others will pay the cost.

Empower and Delegate Authority to Others

After surrounding yourself with the right great people, you are ready to take your longest leap of faith in leading, empowering and delegating authority to others. You selected those around you, so you should feel confident about their abilities. Hang on a minute; you don't think Roger is telling you this, do you? I am only telling you what God's Word says; let me show you.

> ***The next day, Moses took his seat to hear the people's disputes against each other. They waited before him from morning till evening. When Moses father-in-law saw all that Moses was doing for the people, he asked, "What are you really accomplishing here? Why are you trying to do all this alone while everyone stands around you from morning till evening?" Moses replied, "Because the people come to me to get a ruling from God. When a dispute arises, they come to me, and I am the one that settles the case between the quarreling parties. I inform the people of God's decrees and give them his instructions." "This is not good!" Moses' father-in-law exclaimed. "You're going to wear yourself out—and the people, too. This job is too heavy a burden for you to handle all by yourself. Now listen to me, and let me give you a word of advice, and may God be with you. You should continue to be the people's representative before God, bringing their disputes to him. Teach them God's decrees and give them his instructions. Show them how to conduct their lives. But select from all the people some capable, honest men who fear God and hate bribes. Appoint them leaders over groups of one thousand, one hundred, fifty, and ten.***

> ***They should always be available to solve the people's common disputes but have them bring the major cases to you. Let the leaders decide the smaller matters themselves. They will help you carry the load, making the task easier for you. If you follow this advice, and if God commands you to do so, then you will be able to endure the pressures, and all these people will go home in peace."*** (Exodus 18:13–24)
>
> ***Then the LORD said to Moses, "Gather before me seventy men who are recognized as elders and leaders of Israel. Bring them to the Tabernacle to stand there with you. I will come down and talk to you there. I will take some of the Spirit that is upon you, and I will put the Spirit upon them also. They will bear the burden of the people along with you, so you will not have to carry it alone."*** (Numbers 11:16–17)

Jesus practiced empowering and delegating His authority; ***Jesus called his twelve disciples together and gave them authority to cast out evil spirits and to heal every kind of disease and illness*** (Matthew 10:1). The Twelve Disciples of Jesus learned the lesson of delegating from their leader. As the Disciples witnessed and led more followers to Christ after his death and resurrection, they delegated to others to help their ministry. **"We *apostles should spend our time teaching the word of God, not running a food program. And so, brothers, select seven men who are well respected and are full of the Spirit and wisdom. We will give them this responsibility"*** (Acts 6:2–3). King Solomon, the wisest man and greatest King, practiced empowerment and delegating of authority in his leadership. ***King Solomon appointed 250 of them to supervise the people*** (2 Chronicles 8:10). ***Solomon also had twelve district governors who were over all of Israel*** (1 Kings 4:7).

Empowering and delegating authority does not imply a leader recklessly abandon their responsibilities or releases their position of authority in leading. When a leader empowers and delegates, the power has parameters and limits. When I called my leader and asked how much authority I had to change the leadership course of instruction for the Leadership Academy, I was not given free rein of authority outside of that work scope. My leader still retained overall authority and responsibility for the work the leader hired me for.

When empowering and delegating authority to others, a leader observes and monitors their actions. I did not say the leader micromanaged those they empower; to the contrary, a leader allows them to run with the ball. Once a leader has clearly stated their intent for the area those empowered are responsible for (in Deuteronomy 1:18, Moses said to the leaders he had empowered and delegated his authority to, **"At that time I gave you instructions about everything you were to do."**) The empowered person has communicated a clear understanding of the leaders' intent and let them go to work. Suppose a leader observes the empowered person sliding off course of their intent. In that case, course corrections (tugging left or right on the orientation reigns of the empowered) are made, and the empowered person is placed back on the right path. I did not say the leader pulls back on the reins; they reorient and steer them back on course as required.

"Inspiring and challenging others, and watching them rise to their full potential, is the complex yet enormously rewarding role of the leader."[2] Empowering and delegating authority to others is an impactful method used to grow tomorrow's leaders today. The Books of 1 Timothy, 2 Timothy, and Titus are empowerment instructions from the Apostle Paul to his former understudies in teaching the Gospel. The real legacy of a leader's effectiveness is revealed in the competencies and selflessness found in the leaders they prepare for tomorrow. Joshua, who after Moses's death, led Israel into the promised land after Moses had prepared him to lead, ***Now Joshua son of Nun was full of the spirit of wisdom, for Moses had laid his hands on him*** (Deuteronomy 34:9).

God's word offers valuable insights into the many other benefits of leaders surrounding themselves with great people.

This makes for harmony among the members, so that all of the members care for each other. If one part suffers, all the parts suffer with it, and if one part is honored, all the parts are glad (1 Corinthians 12:25–26). (Everyone seeks to be acknowledged for their contributions when success is achieved. When a leader trusts others for their advice and counsel, the leader is inviting more people to succeed--what an excellent method for building a team mind-set in the workplace. With the harmony created by surrounding yourself with a great group of people to speak into your decision-making process, you say to everyone they are considered vital to the organization's success. We win together, and we may even lose together, but through it all, we are together.)

We are many parts of one body, and we all belong to each other (Romans 12:5). (If an organization creates a job position for a required skill or talent, then the organization is saying whoever fills that role is necessary for its success. Everyone is essential, and everyone's contributions matter. This is the mind-set needed for an organization to create a sense of belonging; and a vital part of the organization's success. This is the mind-set of those that leader surrounds themselves with. When the leader says, "I need and want to hear your input," they have just stated, "We are in this together, I trust you to help me make the right decisions."

Then make me truly happy by agreeing wholeheartedly with each other, loving one another, and working together with one mind and purpose (Philippians 2:2). (Working with and uniting a workforce requires everyone's voice to be heard. Creating a single mind-set and purpose is never achieved by a leader who says it's all about "my way" of doing things. Unity is only formed when everyone's way is considered and respected equally. An organization is not who the leader wants it to be; an organization is what the workforce makes it. For an organization to achieve and maintain success, the workforce must care about each other, value one another, and listen to one another. The leader establishes this mind-set by the example they set in doing the same.)

A friend is always loyal, and a brother is born to help in time of need (Proverbs 17:17). (A leader who surrounds themselves with others is stating they trust others. Trust creates loyalty, and a person or a leader can never have enough people in their corner when they need help.)

Great leaders see the value of surrounding themselves with exceptional people. Through empowering others and delegating to them, they accomplish extraordinary things. Dr. Billy Graham lead with the leadership style of empowering and delegating. Here is how his leadership style was seen:

> *The leader with a large vision knows the means of accomplishment is to select those with great capacities who can slash their own trail through the thickets and get the job done. Delegation means providing clear, simple 'lines' and freedom, but also generating strong loyalties and a sense that each person's contribution is highly valued.*[3]

Henry Ford, a master at organization and cooperation, stated,

> *Coming together is a beginning.*
> *Keeping together is progress.*
> *Thinking together is unity.*
> *Working together is success.*

How do I know that God's leadership principle of surrounding ourselves with great people and riding their wave of success works as His word declares? I spoke earlier about being selected as the US Army Leadership Academy leader and surrounding myself with great people. Following sixteen months of developing and implementing all of the changes required to prepare leaders for leading in combat operation's complexity, we were visited/inspected by the US Army's senior leader, a Four-Star General, The Chief of Staff of the US Army.

The first question the General asked me was, "What qualifies you to lead this Academy?" Afterward, he asked every instructor/leader he met, "What qualifies you to instruct other leaders on these subjects?" For two hours, the General allowed us to show him what we implemented and were teaching. After his visit/inspection, the General looked at my leader and said, "This is the finest leadership academy I have witnessed in thirty-six years of being a leader." Through empowering and delegating other great people, we together had achieved my leader's intent. Now it is time to Celebrate Their Successes and Bring Along Those Who Are Lost.

Reflection Time

Do you feel comfortable empowering others and letting them shine? If not, why?

Think about all that you have learned from the people in your life. Not teachers, professors, or parents, but from those you have surrounded yourself with in daily living. How have they enriched your life?

Have you ever been micro-managed by a leader? How did that make you feel? Does your leadership style micro-manage or empower and delegate?

---

1 Adrian Rogers, Mastering Your Emotions (Memphis: Love Worth Finding Ministries, 2012), 56.

2 Harold Myra and Marshall Shelley, The Leadership Secrets of Billy Graham (Grand Rapids: Zondervan, 2005), 131.

3 Ibid., 130.

Celebrate Their Successes and Bring Along Those Who Are Lost

> ***Love each other with genuine affection and take delight in honoring each other*** (Romans 12:10).

I don't know about you, but when I am watching others receive recognition for their successes, I always feel happy for them. Receiving public praise for their accomplishments acknowledges that they create value and bring honor not only for themselves but also for the organization. The last line on the award citation of every award medal given by the United States Army (regardless of the level of the award being presented) says: "*This award reflects great credit upon yourself, your organization, and the United States Army.*" Everyone that has pulled up alongside and assisted them during the awardee's career can take a bow in recognition of contributing to their acknowledged success.

> ***This makes for harmony among the members, so that all of the members care for each other. If one part suffers, all the parts suffer with it, and if one part is honored, all the parts are glad*** (1 Corinthians 12:25–26).

God's Word teaches us when it comes to those we serve and lead; we should celebrate their successes and bring along those feeling a little lost. It is vital that people feel appreciated, valued, part of something greater than themselves, and agree with others (harmony). ***How wonderful and pleasant it is when brothers live together in harmony!*** (Psalm 133:1). An organization that celebrates member successes, and brings along those who are lost, invest in retention, commitment, loyalty, unity, hope, and the belief that the organization and its leadership genuinely cares for those in the organization. Let's break it down and see what God says for both.

Celebrating Accomplishments

A time to cry and a time to laugh. A time to grieve and a time to dance (Ecclesiastes 3:4). (Life will get severe enough by itself. When tough times come, stand with those you serve and lead, and if needed, cry with them. With every win of success, regardless of its magnitude, celebrate and rejoice in other's accomplishments. The memories of, and the hope for future celebration helps significantly in getting past the tough times of grieving our losses.)

We must celebrate with a feast (Luke 15:23). (When my son was preparing to head off to the Navy, we prepared a large meal and had family and friends over. We were celebrating his start of a new and exciting adventure. Celebrating over a meal with those you serve and lead for the individual, team, or organizational successes is an excellent method for developing togetherness bonds. Who doesn't love to eat, and what better excuse to do so than to use food as a means to bring others together? How often have you seen an office or an organization have a celebratory farewell meal for an employee leaving the organization? Why is it that the only time we recognize someone's contributions is when they are on the way out the door? Get some food, get everyone together, and identify what they are doing for you and the organization today. Let's celebrate with others while enjoying some good food!)

We had to celebrate this happy day (Luke 15:32). (I would ask you to think back in your life to the times when you accomplished something, and others made a big deal over it with praise and celebration. It may not have been something others consider extraordinary. Still, to you, it was a huge success, and you wanted to celebrate. It's like the person earning their PhD and the person graduating high school. Both are significant accomplishments for where the person is in their educational journey. Does one achievement outweigh the other in deserving of a celebration? No, the success value of each achievement is not how others see the level of accomplishment. The success value is the personal achievement for the individual achieving significant success. Celebrate their happy day, rejoice with them in their triumph: it's all about them!)

He will take delight in you with gladness. He will rejoice over you with joyful songs (Zephaniah 3:17). (One great way of celebrating other's successes is by speaking their praises to others. Share the news of successes on organizational social media accounts, bulletin boards, or whatever method you find to publicize their accomplishments. When a leader lauds over the achievements of those they serve and lead, they reveal how blessed they are to have the person on their team. That has to make people feel good about themselves!)

And people should eat and drink and enjoy the fruits of their labor, for these are gifts from God (Ecclesiastes 3:13). (You have probably heard the saying, "Work, work, work, that's all I do is work." My dad once built a big beautiful house for a Medical Doctor friend of his. Years later, they were talking, and dad asked him if he was enjoying the home? The Doctor said, "George, I get up every morning before the sun rises, get dressed, fix a cup of coffee-to-go, get in my car, drive to the hospital, and work till late that night. When I finally get home, my family is asleep. I heat my dinner left for me in the microwave, and I eat alone. I shower, go to bed, and sleep. Almost every day is the same routine. My family enjoys the home. I just work to pay for it." Enjoy the fruits of your labor. Allow those you serve and lead to do the same. I have never read a Cemetery Headstone with the words, "I wish I could have worked more" on it. Take time to enjoy and celebrate life; everyone deserves to.)

Remember, the Lord will reward each one of us for the good we do, whether we are slaves or free (Ephesians 6:8). (If we are to lead as God's Truth tells us to, then we must also do as He does. Reward the good that those you serve and lead achieve. Never take for granted the good they do. Their good makes your job of leading easier.)

Every time I think of you, I give thanks to God (Philippians 1:3). (Let others know that you thank God for placing them in your life.)

Let the whole world know what he has done. Sing to him; yes, sing his praises. Tell everyone about his wonderful deeds (Psalm 105:1–2). (A leader's public praise and recognition of the successes of those they serve and lead is a leader's best tool for making an organization the place everyone wants to be part of. People want to work in a place where their contributions are valued and recognized. When leaders tell the whole world about their people's accomplishments, they tell the world as a whole, here people matter!)

Do not withhold good from those who deserve it (Proverbs 3:27). (Withholding acknowledgment of successes from those deserving of it is wrong! Any leader that withholds praise is a selfish and ungrateful person. I would also suggest they are a hypocrite. I am sure they would want to receive recognition for their accomplishments. When others are deserving of special mention, be the first one in line to shake their hand and celebrate their achievement.)

The master was full of praise. 'Well done, my good and faithful servant. You have been faithful in handling this small amount, so now I will give you many more responsibilities. Let's celebrate together!' (Mathew 25:21). (I love the example of celebrating other's accomplishments in this Scripture verse. In this Scripture, we find a person (The Master) who has already achieved great success, acknowledging the success of someone subservient to him. Not only does he recognize their accomplishment, but he also wants to go and celebrate it with them. What is not a challenge to the leader may be a challenge to those they lead. When those you serve and lead overcome an individual challenge, celebrate it with them.)

They have been a wonderful encouragement to me, as they have been to you. You must show your appreciation to all who serve so well (1 Corinthians 16:18). (Appreciation is revealed/given by one person and received by another. Gratitude cannot be taken from a leader, regardless if it is well deserved. A leader must provide appreciative words or actions for them to be conveyed appropriately. Never assume that those you serve and lead know they are appreciated; say the words, show them with your actions.)

The godly are showered with blessings (Proverbs 10:6). (Another word for godly is faithful. Blessings represent favor, care, and safety. The faithful people a leader serves and leads should be recognized and taken care of. Don't take their faithful and good work for granted. Show those you serve and lead that you are thankful for their good and faithful service. Make a big deal of it all!)

The godly can look forward to a reward (Proverbs 11:23). (A leader should make rewarding others a normal part of the organization's calendar of events. In the military, the last weekday of the month for every organization was committed on the calendar to reward and recognize deserving individuals' achievements and successes. People should know that part of the organization's culture is rewarding and celebrating people's successes. Rewards are an organization's way of saying, "We do not take your hard work for granted, we appreciate it and we will celebrate and recognize it." The focus or importance of celebrating achievements by the leadership of any organization conveys a strong message to everyone. Make celebrating successes meaningful!)

Wise words bring many benefits, and hard work brings rewards (Proverbs 12:14). (We assume hard work brings rewards, but there is always the exception. Don't be the exception. For some, it is "Work hard, play hard!" For those that you serve and lead, it should be, "Work hard, celebrate bigger!")

Good people receive their reward (Proverbs 14:14). (This should be true in every sector of society. We need good people and good people should be rewarded for all the good they represent. The next time someone does something "good" for you and you did not expect it, realize we cannot take "good" for granted in today's world. Sad, but true.)

Celebrating a person's success in today's modern work environment is represented in many ways. Rewards are represented by financial bonus incentives, position promotions, public ceremonial recognitions, citations, organizational trade paper announcements, and organizational celebratory events and functions. In lesser forms of celebrating an individual's success, the pat on the back or handshake with a sincere thank you from leaders and others is ever so important. The main goal is for people to know they are valued and appreciated for their accomplishments.

Celebrating successes should always be done in public and given in view of others. I once worked in an organization that would bring people into the Director's office and recognizes their accomplishments privately. A manager said they didn't want the awardee's peers who were not being recognized to feel bad about themselves. I disagree with this philosophy. Maybe this is why this organization had such a tremendous turnover rate of employees, also equating to a terrible retention rate? I could not wrap my head around their train of illogical thinking. Why would any leader minimize the significance of a person's accomplishments by rewarding them in private? This organization had the weakest people pretending to serve as leaders; they cared only about their job security. Part of the real reason they recognized people's success in private was they feared others would make claims of impartiality against them and jeopardize their career. Celebrating people's successes publicly is an excellent tool for motivating others to excel and receive recognition when earned. Success is available for everyone to achieve and should be strived for by everyone in the organization. Make success desirable!

When the king smiles there is life; his favor refreshes like a spring rain (Proverbs 16:15).

Leaders who celebrate other's successes are smiling on the career of those they serve and lead. Like a spring rain, they are promoting a season of growth in people's lives. Remember, we are orienting our leadership methods toward building a relationship with those we serve and lead through establishing trust. When people trust that their accomplishments will be recognized, valued, and celebrated, they are endeared to the leader and the organization.

Making Everyone Important, Especially the Lost

In Matthew 18:12–13 Jesus asks,

> ***"If a man has a hundred sheep and one of them wanders away, what will he do? Won't he leave the ninety-nine others on the hills and go out and search for the one that is lost? And if he finds it, I tell you the truth, he will rejoice over it more than over the ninety-nine that didn't wander away!"***

In team sports, a group of individuals has mastered their skill sets to be designated a member of the "starting team." Meanwhile, players good enough to be on the team, but they still require developmental work on their skill sets; these are the substitutes (second or third string) for the starters as needed. The substitute players still need some work on their skill sets but are prepared to relieve a starter if called on. In professional football, they have an additional level of "practice squad" players, who are a little behind in their skill set developmental process. However, they are anticipated to rise to become a substitute player shortly if needed.

In an organization, there are no substitutes (second or third string) people. There are either people that perform as required or those in need of improvement. People that serve as needed seem to succeed at everything they do, while the rest of us need to improve ourselves just to keep up in today's fast-paced workplace. In youth sports activities, we see that participation warrants recognition, whereas in previous generations, winning warranted recognition. If you did not win and you wanted recognition, you practiced and worked harder to win the next time. Everyone wants to be recognized for their achievements, and they should be. But who is responsible for helping those who require more development in their abilities and skill sets? That would be you, their leader. ***He will not crush the weakest reed or put out a flickering candle*** (Isaiah 42:3).

A leader understands what equates to success, and a leader realizes when additional development is required for some. When the Army's Human Resource Command reassigned the Leadership Academy noncombat experienced members, those leaders were reassigned to organizations preparing for and deploying to combat operations in the near future. Reassigning these leaders was not a form of punishment. Their reassignment was critical to their career development. In the future, the reassigned leaders would be competing with peers for hard to achieve promotions. Without combat experience, they would be at a severe competitive disadvantage. Part of my responsibility as their leader was to put them in places that would allow them opportunities for continued success and promotions. A leader is responsible for preparing those they serve and lead for their professional career's future by helping them stay on the right path today.

> ***You who are godly should gently and humbly help that person back onto the right path… Share each other's burdens,… If you think you are too important to help someone, you are only fooling yourself. You are not that important.*** (Galatians 6:1–3)

God's Word reveals, ***God blesses those who are merciful, for they will be shown mercy*** (Matthew 5:7). (When a person is trying their best but coming up a little short, who is anyone to judge or ridicule them? There is not a single person on this earth that did everything right and perfect from their beginning. We are all a work in progress. For some, a few little tweaks here and there may be needed, others may require more substantiative work to get up to the standard required. Either way, as a leader, patience and understanding are virtues required. Remember to treat others as you want to be treated. Honest shortcomings deserve mercy!)

Make allowance for each other's faults (Colossians 3:13). (If you are honest with yourself, you realize people are making allowances for the unattractive or unsatisfactory leadership methods and decisions you have made over time. You didn't get everything right, and you will miss the mark a few times more; we all do in life and leadership. A leader must realize the same goes for those they serve and lead. People are going to fall short, do things wrong, or flat out fail in a task. However, if they fell short trying, did something wrong accidentally, or failed while giving it their all, we cannot fault them. Accept their efforts, identify where they need help, help them, and move forward to future successes. Someone did the same for you and me at one time or another. Don't be a hypocrite!)

Teach and counsel each other with all the wisdom he gives (Colossians 3:16). (A leader wears many hats. A leader serves others as a teacher, coach, counselor, or mentor. Never get so wrapped up with the title "leader" to think you are above teaching, counseling, and mentoring others to succeed. Share your knowledge, impart your wisdom, and be the light in other people's search in the dark for success.)

But everything that is done must strengthen all of you (1 Corinthians 14:26). (All development opportunities must be available to everyone. While a chain is only as strong as its weakest link, an organization can only endure tomorrow's stressors to its weakest workforce members' abilities. There can be no "haves or have nots" in an organization. An organization can only consist of "have's." As a leader, let every decision be made for the greater good of the whole, not parts thereof.)

I will strengthen you and help you (Isaiah 41:10). (This should be the mantra of every leader.)

The LORD your God said, "***Don't be afraid, I am here to help you***" (Isaiah 41:13). (Have you ever approached a small hurt animal with the intent of helping it? You intended to help, not hurt, but the little hurt animal doesn't know this because it doesn't know your heart. When those you serve and lead know your heart, they know you sincerely care about them. When they honestly fall short or need help and see you coming their way, they will know that help is on the way. If they are afraid when they see you coming, then leader, you have some work to do.)

Brothers and sisters, we urge you to warn those who are lazy. Encourage those who are timid. Take care of those who are weak. Be patient with everyone (1 Thessalonians 5:14). (We have discussed honest failures and mistakes, all of which require mercy. However, laziness is a different challenge. Laziness needs a leader to have a frank conversation with the lazy person, "Step up, or we will show you the door." Those who are not lazy but are anxious, nervous, or need some developmental strengthening, give them time and opportunity to find their comfort level with everyone. Find ways to ease them into the mix. Pair them with those that have a natural knack for making others feel welcomed. Laziness is a no-go; everything else, we can get you where you need to be.)

Don't think of them as enemies but warn them as you would a brother or sister (2 Thessalonians 3:15). (Have you ever heard the term "tough love"? There are times in leading that tough love is the necessity for the moment. Enforcing certain constraints or measures to alter substandard work or conduct is a form of tough love in the workplace. A leader warns those they serve and lead as we warn those we love and care for. We warn others to protect them from potential more significant consequences if the substandard work or conduct continues.)

Let everything you say be good and helpful so that your words will be an encouragement to those who hear them (Ephesians 4:29). (Negativity never encourages. Let your comments promote motivation, inspiration, positivity, belief in their abilities, confidence in them, and their potential for greatness. It is easier for those you serve and lead to believe in themselves when they have a leader that believes in them and is encouraging.)

In the workplace, a leader serves many people. There will typically be a person **(Person A)** that stands out as exemplary in their performance, conduct, and resourcefulness. However, not every person comes with "having it all together." There will be individuals **(Person B)** whose performance requires some improvement, and their conduct is questionable at times. They wait to be provided with information and resources before acting. When trying to determine why one person does well, and another person struggles to find success, an investigation is required.

It is time to bring on the scene the Leadership Scene Investigator (LSI) team (leadership's version of Crime Scene Investigators) to discover clues. The LSI team comes in and applies fingerprint dust on the hands, upper back, and shoulders of **Person A** and **Person B**. On **Person A**, the dusting reveals their leader's handprints on their hands from shaking their hands and acknowledging their successes. On **Person A's** shoulder and upper back are many handprints from pats on the back from encouragement and acknowledgment of great work from their leader. However, the dusting of **Person B** leaves the hands, upper back, and shoulders of **Person B** dusty with no visible handprints revealed anywhere.

It is easy for a leader to rely on and acknowledge the individual's success that always performs outstandingly like **Person A**. It appears **Person A** has it all together and is performing as required. However, the initial investment of a leader's time is required by followers who need improvement **(Person B)**. Jesus says in Matthew 9:12, ***"Healthy people don't need a doctor—sick people do."*** **Person B** requires handprints of encouragement, assistance, mentorship, and developmental support on their shoulders and upper back from their leader and the organization's talent development elements. **Person B's** hands should have their leader's handprint on theirs from being given a hand-up. **Person B** should receive the leader's and the organization's developmental focus. ***He feels pity for the weak and the needy, and he will rescue them*** (Psalm 72:13). **Person B** was a little lost, but now they have been found, encouraged, helped, and placed on a path toward individual and organizational success and celebration.

Jesus says, ***"He was lost, but now he is found." So the party began*** (Luke 15:24).

How important is the role of leaders bringing along those who are lost? I considered every loss of a person who failed to meet the organization's standards of discipline and conduct a leadership failure. Everyone is subject to making mistakes, to falling short in life. Everyone deserves help to overcome shortcomings. Couples attend "couples counseling" to identify and understand how to meet their significant other's needs. People use the valuable services of counselors, psychiatrists, and pastors to help them in personal areas needing growth and encouragement. In an organization's workforce, leaders serve to identify, strengthen, and orient a person's professional needs onto the right track. Galatians 6:1 says, ***You who are godly should gently and humbly help that person back onto the right path.***

A method for leaders to inform those they serve and lead to how well or how poorly they perform to standard is "performance counseling." Performance counseling should be performed monthly for new employees until they have settled into the organization's ways and fully understand their work requirements. For others, performance counseling is conducted quarterly. During performance counseling (in writing), the leader identifies what areas of a person's performance are being performed well. The leader would then discuss with the person the areas of their performance requiring improvement. This is where the leader identifies areas of understanding that the leader will assist/help the person grow and improve. The leader will then write out specific methods/actions they will implement to overcome their shortcomings.

> ***"I am the LORD your God, who teaches you what is good for you and leads you along the paths you should follow"*** (Isaiah 48:17).

The counseled employee then acknowledges their understanding of their performance counseling and will write on the performance counseling document their role in becoming stronger in their weaknesses and sign the document. Everyone is now on the same page and knows what is expected.

> ***Don't look out only for your own interests, but take an interests in others, too*** (Philippians 2:4).

Everyone deserves to understand what is required of them. Waiting until the person has gone so far off track that they are hopelessly lost is unacceptable as a leader. As parents, we correct our children because we love them and care about their future. Leaders are required to do the same for those they serve and lead. Correcting others through performance counseling is not the best part of being a leader. Still, it comes with the mantle of leadership. If not taken seriously and without the care those you serve and lead deserve, it is a responsibility that may impact their quality of life. Helping the lost find their way back into the organization's fold through performance counseling is a leader's method for watching over those they serve and lead. ***The LORD says, "I will guide you along the best pathway for your life. I will advise you and watch over you*** (Psalm 32:8).

When a soldier established patterns of misconduct or severe shortcomings not overcame in time, they were released from the Army. I hated those moments because I felt we (their leaders) had failed in grasping their attention or had not helped them overcome their shortcomings. Do you think what we do to help the lost find their way back matters to the lost person? Yes! One terrible day, we had to discharge two soldiers from the Army for their patterns of misconduct. That evening my home phone rang twice. Both calls were from the discharged soldiers. As I heard each former soldier's voice on the other end of the call, I figured they would tell me out of anger that they were going to threaten retaliation for "kicking them out" of the Army. I was wrong and blown away by what both former soldiers said. Both called to say, "Thank you for trying to help me. I am sorry I let you down; I know you tried to help me before it was too late."

I sat in amazement. I told both former soldiers I was sorry it had come to this and that I only wanted the best in life for them. I offered my words of support and belief that God has a more excellent plan in life for them. I extended my hand of help when they sought future employment opportunities if listed as a reference. My actions in their dismissal from the Army were NOT personal; it was my professional responsibility to enforce the standards and discipline only. I believed and told them both, "Sometimes the Army is not for everyone, and sometimes everyone is not for the Army." I sought to encourage them in this challenging situation.

Look for the lost; they desperately want to be found by a leader that cares and wants to help them find success. Do all that you can to prepare them for the organization's needs. Before combat deployments, as we trained and prepared for what lay ahead, I would tell leaders, "Don't let your soldiers ever look at you in the stress and dangers of combat and say to you; you did not prepare me for this." Leaders in every organization owe the same to a person whose quality of life and sense of self-worth rely on leaders who care enough to bring them along when they are lost. As a leader, you must be like Christ. Christ, who is the One that never leaves the one behind, is revealing that we must bring everyone along with us. One lost sheep requires we leave the ninety-nine and find them and bring them safely back into the fold. Let them know you care; let them know you are in this for them. Let them know they can come to you when they feel lost, and you will help them find their way back. Be Approachable!

> ***So it is right that I should feel as I do about all of you, for you have a special place in my heart*** (Philippians 1:7).

Reflection Time

How big of a deal do you make of the accomplishments and successes of those you serve and lead?

Do those you serve and lead know you value, appreciate, and recognize their contributions to the organization's successes? If so, how do they know?

When is the last time you stopped moving forward to pause and bring along someone in need? Remember, it is about their success and growth; help them.

Be Approachable

Give all your worries and cares to God, for He cares for you.

—1 Peter 5:7

Make Yourself Available

Leaders need to know and understand the truth in all factors during their decision-making process. People must know they can safely and welcomingly approach their leaders with the truth, good or bad. I love the words of Jesus in John 8:32, ***"And you will know the truth, and the truth will set you free."*** Of course, Jesus was referring to himself as the "truth," and he certainly is the truth in everything. We all need Jesus's truth for a life of peace and joy. We learn to trust and know God through our time spent in his Word and conversation with him in our prayers. God, our Father, welcomes us anytime and anyplace into conversation with himself. Jesus says, "***For everyone who asks, receives. Everyone who seeks finds. And to everyone who knocks, the door will be opened*** (Luke 11:10). People will learn to trust and know their leaders only if they feel that they can approach their leaders and feel welcomed in doing so.

Then Jesus said, "Come to me, all of you who are weary and carry heavy burdens, and I

> ***will give you rest. Take my yoke upon you. Let me teach you, because I am humble and gentle at heart, and you will find rest for your soul. For my yoke is easy to bear, and the burden I give you is light."*** (Matthew 11:28–30)

Whether you are leading a team of a few individuals or leading a large organization, no one can imagine leading all of humanity as Jesus does. Yet I love what Jesus says at the beginning of Matthew 11:28, ***"Come to me."*** Scripture tells us that the LORD tells us to come to Him, to approach His throne of grace. ***Come. Let anyone who is thirsty come. Let anyone who desires drink freely from the water of life*** (Revelation 22:17). ***"Come now, let's settle this," says the LORD*** (Isaiah 1:18). In Scripture, the LORD tells us to ***"come,"*** in other words, approach me. This makes me wonder if God did not want us to approach Him with our needs, concerns, or thoughts, would we genuinely have a relationship with him? Oh wait, this also means if a leader does not make themselves welcomingly approachable, can they have a genuine connection with those they lead?

The wonderful and remarkable thing about our Heavenly Father is that he is approachable. Imagine having a leader that embraces your presence, that welcomes your problems, that desires to know your concerns and challenges, and that you can always trust to care about you. Throughout Scripture, God's Word tells us who God our leader is, and he wants us to approach His throne of grace, trusting in him.

"***If you look for me wholeheartedly, you will find me. I will be found by you," says the LORD*** (Jeremiah 29:13–14). (Most people hate to "bother" others with their problems and challenges. Pride prevents many from asking for help. Earlier in this book, we discussed "Let Them Know Your Method to the Madness." An essential requirement for telling others how we lead and our motives in leading is to help them understand our working mind-set. I would tell those I served and lead, "Never refrain from telling me if you need my assistance. Never refrain from allowing me to do my job of taking care of your needs. Never apologize as if you are "bothering" me with your problem. Your needs are never a "bother" to me.

On the contrary, your needs allow me to serve and make your life better. I am in this for you." I wanted to emplace a mind-set in those I served and lead that if you seek my help, you will get it; gladly.)

Jesus said, "***However, those the Father has given me will come to me, and I will never reject them***" (John 6:37). (At the beginning of a potentially valuable and long-term relationship, we always display our best behavior. You know what I am talking about. When you started dating that special someone, you went out of your way to look your best and be attentive to their every need. Later on, in the relationship, it becomes easy to take others and their needs for granted.

We don't drop everything to address their need as quickly as we did in our relationship's blossoming. We wear our comfortable sweatpants and favorite old shirt most of the time with them instead of the former fashionable clothes meant to impress. Soon, we look and act more like we are pushing them away, then desiring to lure them in. Serving and leading can be challenging and wearing on a leader. You are potentially spending over a third of your day doing your organization's work and serving the needs of those you lead. It can become easy to discount the people for the organizational aspects of leading. It can become easy to take the needs of those you lead for granted and find yourself rejecting their needs. It can become easy to think "I am too busy and too important" for others' seemingly insignificant problems.

Maintaining a mind-set of "serving and leading" means just that. Serving others and leading them for the organization's mission success. Every day do the part of leading that is so much more important than your climb up the corporate ladder, serve those you lead. Never allow a person to look at you and say, "I came to see you about my need, but you were 'too busy' for me." Make and find time for those you serve and lead first and always!)

And since we have a great High Priest who rules over God's house, let us go right into the presence of God with sincere hearts

fully trusting him (Hebrews 10:21). (Any person we trust, we believe we can count on them to help us when needed. We do not hesitate to approach them for help because we know they sincerely care and want to help. Trust is essential in being approachable as a leader. Those you serve and lead must trust that you care and believe you sincerely want to help them.)

Those who know your name trust in you, for you, O LORD, do not abandon those who search for you (Psalm 9:10). (I enjoy the television series Law and Order Criminal Intent. Whenever the detective's boss (their Captain) wants the detectives to ramp up the pressure on a criminal suspect, he always says, "Step into them." Being approachable is a two-way street. One-way for others to come to you and one-way for you their leader to go to them. Use your way to "step into them." Step in to ask how they are doing. Step in to convey your appreciation. Step in to make yourself available. Step in to say, "Here I am for you." Stepping in is the opposite of abandoning them. Step into them!)

The LORD is righteous in everything he does; he is filled with kindness. The LORD is close to all who call on him, yes, to all who call on him in truth (Psalm 145:17–18). (A demeanor of kindness is one that people are drawn to. As a young boy, I had five Aunts, three from my mom's side of the family and two from my dad's side. All five were lovely and sweet, but one of them was super kind. She would go above and beyond in being considerate, indulgent, and helpful. Any and every opportunity I could find, I wanted to be in her presence. Her kindness made me feel special. Finding people in our lives to make us feel this way is not always easy. However, those you serve and lead should have this kindness in their lives through you, their leader. Kindness is not a weakness; it is your greatest strength in the lives of others. I could not wait to see my kind Aunt; those you serve and lead should look forward to your kind presence in their life.)

In my desperation I prayed, and the LORD listened; he saved me from all my troubles (Psalm 34:6). (Prayer is how we communicate our thanks and needs to God. God has provided prayer as the method we use to approach His throne of grace. What steps have you taken as a leader to make yourself more accessible for those you serve and lead? Look around you; are there any barriers preventing others from approaching you? Even Jesus had to break down barriers to make Himself approachable to those in need.

> ***One day, some parents brought their children to Jesus so he could lay his hands on them and pray for them. But the disciples scolded the parents for bothering him. But Jesus said, "Let the children come to me. Don't stop them! For the Kingdom of Heaven belongs to those who are like these children." And he placed his hands on their heads and blessed them before he left.*** (Matthew 19:13–15)

Making yourself approachable to help others takes effort on your part. Knockdown barriers preventing you from being available to meet the needs of those you serve and lead.)

The LORD hears his people when they call to him for help. He rescues them from all their troubles. The LORD is close to the brokenhearted; he rescues those whose spirits are crushed (Psalm 34:17–18). (Being approachable empowers a leaders' ability to serve others. How will you know your help is needed if others are apprehensive in approaching you?)

But may all who search for you be filled with joy and gladness in you (Psalm 40:16). (By making yourself approachable, you open the door of opportunity to enrich the lives of those you serve and lead. Let your presence in the lives of those you serve and lead be a blessing from God, through you. What an incredible opportunity to have!)

God is our refuge and strength, always ready to help in times of trouble (Psalm 46:1). (A leader with a mentality of "I'm in this for you," is a refuge and strength for those they serve and lead. By being approachable, a leader says, "I am available to help others in their times of trouble.")

The Dangers from Not Being Approachable

A surprise birthday party is something most people enjoy being the recipient of. The moment of surprise is one of celebration and laughter. Everyone present was aware of the pending surprise; the only one in the dark (intentionally) is the birthday person. Surprises of this type are fun. In the workplace, surprises can often be associated with more significant underlying organizational and leadership problems brewing under the surface for some time. No one wanted to say anything, and the organization goes on like everything is fine, but is it?

I am revealing my age here, but from 1965 to 1971 a television show titled *Hogan's Heroes* was filmed. It has run in syndication ever since (still funny too). The show represented the daily exploits of a group of allied prisoners of war (POW's) military personnel in a German POW camp during World War II from a comical perspective. One of the main characters was a German guard, Sergeant Schultz. He was only trying to survive the war away from the front lines of combat, and he did not want to make any waves. Sgt Schultz wanted to keep things as peaceful and harmonistic as possible in the POW camp until the fighting was over. Anytime Sgt Schultz encountered an allied POW doing something that might disrupt the harmony, he would turn his head, close his eyes, cover his ears, and say, "I know nothing, I see nothing, I hear nothing."

Do you think a leader in today's fast-paced and complex global work environment would survive very long with Sgt Schultz's "I know nothing, I see nothing, I hear nothing" mentality? We both know this would never work. Being approachable as a leader enables knowing, seeing, and hearing the truth. However, some "leaders" in today's workplace unknowingly have the same mentality as Sgt Schultz. As long as their paycheck shows up by direct deposit in their bank account, they are happy remaining unaware, blind, and deaf to the truth around them. God's Word warns leaders against this.

Jesus said, ***"They are blind guides leading the blind, and if one blind person guides another, they will both fall into a ditch"*** (Mathew 15:14). (Any leader who makes decisions without knowing all of the facts is making blind decisions. Blindness is seen in the leader without foresight. The foresight of the internal and external organizational challenges that leaders must be aware of. Organizations are responsible for looking outside the organization to identify their customer's needs and their industry competitor's strategies to meet customer needs. This knowledge and insight determine the organization's strategy for future initiatives. Internal to an organization, leaders must know the workforce's strengths and weaknesses to achieve future organizational initiatives successfully. Being approachable allows the truth of strength and weakness to be identified. Those you serve and lead should be able to approach you with more than their issues; they must be able to come to you with issues or problems that may affect the organization's ability to achieve success. Failure to know these pertinent truths will place everyone and the organization off course and in a ditch eventually.)

They will reject the truth and chase after myths (2 Timothy 4). (When a leader is unapproachable, others will not trust their motives whenever they are in the rare situation of conversing with the leader. These situations lead to people telling leaders what they think the leader wants to hear. "Don't tell me what you think I want to hear. Tell me the truth, what I need to hear." However, the unapproachable leader rejects the truth and makes decisions on their false knowledge of what the truth is.)

But this is what you must do: Tell the truth to each other (Zechariah 8:16). (Truth comes with trusting someone. To hear the truth, people must trust you enough to approach you with it.)

They are like silent watchdogs that give no warning when danger comes (Isaiah 56:10). (Unapproachable leaders cannot hear the truth from others. Likewise, they provide no opportunity to share the truth with others. Everyone deserves to be on the same page as the truth. Otherwise, no one knows what dangers lurk ahead. This is how rumors and untruths take nest in an organization. The truth sets everyone free to prepare and overcome together.)

What makes a leader approachable so that they will know the truth from those they lead? (This is your best insight into the truth of reality.)

- A humble demeanor
- Genuine and sincere kindness
- A presence and voice of gentleness
- A welcoming salutation
- A leader with a patient demeanor
- A leader who remains truthful and trustworthy in word and deed
- A leader who evokes inviting facial expressions (a smile, a look of concern, a look and action of attentiveness)
- A leader who presents an extended handshake of greeting
- A leader whose door to their office remains open when they are not privately meeting with others
- A leader who creates easy access to themselves by merely maintaining an open-door policy
- Leaders who let others know they are available as needed (When we see each other, and I ask you how are you? That is an invitation to tell me how I can help you.)
- A leader who is out and about with those they serve, making themselves available as needed by others
- The leader who eats where others eat and take breaks in their break area
- A leader continuously providing hope and encouragement
- A leader always conveying a willingness to serve others and help as needed

All of these approachable qualities in a leader require an intentional effort on the leader's part. The mantle of leadership is one that can be draining and burdensome. Getting caught up in the organization's mission is easy to do. Making ourselves approachable requires a degree of selflessness beyond our natural humanistic character. I admit that as a leader being approachable was something I had to work toward continuously. For me, it began with forcing myself to approach them first. My position and the stigma of a rigid and insensitive nature often associated with the role required me to sell who I was as a person. I wanted them to know the person behind the title. People were going to respect the authority of my leadership position. Still, I cared more about them respecting the person's heart filling that position. This did not compromise my authority; it allowed those I served and lead to know they had someone whose positional power in leadership was present to help them.

Spontaneously stopping for a moment in the presence of those you lead to ask how they are doing may not fit into your schedule, often dictated by competing priorities. Being approachable, however, is a priority. You became a leader because you are competent, diligent, and have the self-discipline to prioritize and schedule the activities that must be accomplished throughout the day. This is why leaders must schedule a block of time within their day where they make themselves approachable and available.

An organization that wants its leaders to be approachable intentionally refrains from packing their leader's schedules with countless meetings. They provide space in leader's daily plans affording leaders time to get out and about with those they lead. They leave time for their leaders to schedule office calls to address the needs, concerns, and challenges of the people they serve and lead. They provide their leaders time to know, see, and hear the truth of what is happening with those they lead and the organization. This is one of the most significant investments in the organization's people the organization can make.

What can stifle the people and an organization's success? Unapproachable leaders. What makes a leader unapproachable?

- Pride
- Selfishness
- Arrogance
- Leaders with a demeanor of being annoyed
- Leaders who speak lies and are deemed untrustworthy
- Leaders inattentive to people speaking to them while they "multitask."

- Leaders whose office door is always closed
- A leader who deters access to themselves by emplacing/maintaining layers of a bureaucratic staff
- Leaders who never get out and about with those they serve
- A leader who never promotes their availability and never invites others to share their needs or concerns
- A leader who never visits/uses the common areas of the organization (breakrooms or the cafeteria)
- A leader who tears others down with discouraging or oppressive comments
- A leader who looks the other way when those they lead are in need.
- A leader who is easily angered and loses their temper. ***Stop being angry! Turn from your rage! Do not lose your temper—it only leads to harm*** (Psalm 37:8).

Organizations often play a big part in creating unapproachable leaders. Organizations that prioritize mission and profit over people dictate a leader's mind-set. Look at an organization that promotes an unapproachable leader mind-set of mission and profit over people. You will see an organization with a high turnover rate of people or low retention rates. You will see a workforce plagued with low morale, high disciplinary rates, a high absence from work rate, lower productivity, and a lack of organizational loyalty.

As a leader, making yourself approachable is like giving others a light source to be turned on when darkness approaches. Everyone needs to know there is a source available and desiring to help as needed. It's kind of like the assurance we have for a response to a 911 call. Emergency Services has provided a means of approaching them when help is required. Emplace pathways for those you serve and lead to come to you when they need your light into their darkness. ***I pray that your hearts will be flooded with light so that you can understand the confident hope he has given to those he called*** (Ephesians 1:18).

When a leader is approachable, they are telling others, "You matter to me." Being approachable tells those you lead, "I'm in this for you." Being approachable as a leader says to others you care. You are saying what others think and have to say is important to you and the organization. Being approachable enables a leader to understand things before they are introduced as an unwelcomed surprise. Being approachable allows a leader to know what they don't know and the information they need. Being approachable creates a bond of trust; without it, we have no relationship with those we lead. Being approachable as a leader says to others that they are more important to us than ourselves. Being approachable makes you available to hear others. If a leader is unapproachable or unavailable, they have just diminished their ability to influence others. Leading is all about influencing, so how are you leading by influencing if they can't get close enough to you to be influenced? Move barriers out of the way so others can get to you; when you are in this for them, you are available. This requires leaders with sincere and authentic Humility! Time to get humble.

Reflection Time

List the ways you make yourself approachable for those you serve and lead.

List the ways you can make yourself more approachable for those you serve and lead.

Who in your inner circle do you trust with letting you know when you need to be more accessible to those your serve and lead? Are you willing to empower them to do this?

Humility

Though he was God, he did not think of equality with God as something to cling to. Instead, he gave up his divine privileges, he took up the humble position of a slave and was born a human being. When he appeared in human form, he humbled himself in obedience to God and died a criminal's death on a cross.

—Philippians 2:6–8

Virtues represent a person's natural tendency to be a good person. Not only is doing right a natural tendency for a virtuous person, but they do the right thing intending to do good. Virtues are learned and developed; they can become a habit of anyone; it is never too late to increase one's virtue at any age. Virtues are good works, which are revealed by a virtuous person in consistently doing the right thing. Ultimately, virtues are the underlying framework of a person's character. A virtue required in a leader's character, according to God's Word is Humility.

Humility is not weakness, quite the contrary. Humility represents your character's inner strength, and reflects your selfless attitude, propelling the person/leader beyond the person in the mirror. A leader's Humility reveals they are strong enough to take on the needs of others. When John the Baptist spoke of Jesus in John 3:30, stating, "***He must become greater and greater, and I must become***

less and less," John spoke of Jesus's significance in God's ministry on earth. Humility for a person or as a leader means we see others as more significant in worth and value than we promote ourselves. It does not imply John was insignificant or weak; to the contrary, it reveals that John the Baptist was a strong enough leader of the gospel to step into the background while Jesus stepped into the limelight of God's ministry on earth. John the Baptist knew his place and was secure enough as a leader to make it about Jesus, not himself. Can we all say this about those we serve and lead? To become great in leading is to move past ourselves and make others' lives more meaningful.

Being humble and filled with Humility is not thinking less of yourself but thinking of yourself less often and focusing on others' needs more often. Every person must humble and submit themselves to God before they can humble themselves before people. As a leader, if we cannot submit in Humility to God, we will never submit to Humility in our lives of serving and leading others. Humility requires commitment and being okay with ourselves. The only person we answer to in life, and the only person that matters, is our Father in Heaven, not some group of people at work. Ultimately, we should respond to God in life, not man. The LORD says, ***I will bless those who have humble and contrite hearts, who tremble at my word"*** (Isaiah 66:2).

Humble leaders don't worry about what others think about them; they don't worry about being thought of less. Humble leaders don't compete with their peers for recognition; they let their talk and walk be oriented outward toward those they serve and lead. Humble leaders do not seek to stand out; they care more about standing up for those they serve and lead. Jesus says, ***Those who speak for themselves want glory only for themselves, but a person who seeks to honor the one who sent him speaks truth, not lies*** (John 7:18). Jesus teaches us in John 8:50 that others may "glorify" (give honor or praise to Him). Still, He does not lead and teach to boast of himself, ***"And though I have no wish to glorify myself, God is going to glorify me. He is the true judge."*** How important is being humble to God? God addresses the importance of being *humble* seventy-one times in the Bible. The word *humility* is spoken twenty-five times in the Bible (King James Version).

How humble was Jesus, the only perfect leader to ever live? Let me see if I can place Jesus's level of humility in perspective for us. First, we must understand the culture of the society in the time which Jesus walked the earth. Certain positions of occupation warranted varying levels of prestige and honor. If we were ranking every occupation in order of Highest in prestige and honor to the Lowest of low, being a shepherd was considered the lowliest occupation.

Jesus, who knew precisely how society viewed shepherds assumed their significance of power in that day. Jesus said, ***"I am the good shepherd"*** (John 10:11). Jesus did not say: "I am the President, I am the King, I am the Prime Minister, I am the Emperor, I am the Chief Executive Officer, or I am the General." Jesus did not compare himself to any person or position of authority that people of His day or people of today claim for representing their power. Jesus knew who He was. He did not have to claim a highly respected title to be the leader of this world. Jesus allowed His humble and caring demeanor to represent His position in this world, not an occupation or position admired by society. God's Word uses the words *exalt* (to elevate by praise or in estimation (used over seventy times in Scripture). The word *haughty* (arrogant and full of pride) is used in more than a dozen verses to warn against being haughty as a contrast between Humility and pride.

God Honors the Humble

True humility and fear of the LORD lead to riches, honor, and long life (Proverbs 22:4). (Thinking more of others than of ourselves and leading as God's Word instructs us to are the essential elements for a life of joy and peace that money alone cannot buy. Humbleness allows joy and peace to enter into our lives because it is a welcoming demeanor, not one that deters and divides like pride.)

Always be humble and gentle (Ephesians 4:2). (Placing the needs of those you serve and lead ahead of your interest states you consider others more significant than yourself. A leader who gently encounters others in need is saying, "I am here for you. What can I do to help you?")

Be humble, thinking of others as better than yourselves (Philippians 2:3). (No person is more important than another person, and no person is more valuable than any other person. We are talking about seeing others as God see's us. The world does enough to try and pit people against one another. The world says we are different because of our skin color, how much money we do or don't have, our work title, our educational degree, the make of our automobile, the brand of clothing we wear, or how socially popular we are. We must see past the world's view of seeing ourselves in comparison to others and see others as a person we would be fortunate to serve as a friend. Nothing human-made makes any person better than another person. We are all God's creation, trying to find happiness, love, and peace in our lives. Be these things for everyone else, and you will have happiness, love, and peace too!)

Serve each other in humility, for God opposes the proud but favors the humble. So humble yourselves under the mighty hand of God, and at the right time, he will lift you up in honor (1 Peter 5:5–6). (Do not worry about man's approval. Do not let the ridicule or judgment of others prevent you from taking the position and heart of humbly serving those you lead. Leading with a heart committed to others' success instead of leading with selfish desires for self-success will be your greatest strength. And with this great strength, God will give you more significant positions of responsibility because He knows your heart is right where He wants it to be, with those you serve and lead.)

Then if my people who are called by my name will humble themselves and pray and seek my face and turn from their wicked ways, I will hear from heaven and will forgive their sins and restore their land (2 Chronicles 7:14). (God wants us to get over and past ourselves. Every person is created for God's purpose in their life. This purpose is to serve others for God's glory. When we humble ourselves before God, then and only then can He use us for His purpose. If you want to maximize your leadership effectiveness, get over yourself and get after serving those, God allows you to lead. Serve God by serving others in your leadership.)

Jesus said, ***The greatest among you must be a servant. But those who exalt themselves will be humbled, and those who humble themselves will be exalted.*** (If the King of Kings, the Son of God, came to serve those he leads, who can say we are to lead in any other way? The greatest leader ever left us with the recipe for success in leading. If you are proud and full of yourself, you will eventually be brought down low. If you consider others more significant than yourself, you will be lifted high. This contradicts this world's ways, but great leaders lead in God's ways.)

Humble yourselves before the Lord, and he will lift you up in honor (James 4:10). (When we get over ourselves and submit all that we are to God, we are taking a servitude position to God. Now, God can use us to do great things for others to bring glory to God. When we go low in the perspective of ourselves, we are now positioned for God to take us higher than we could have ever climbed on our own.)

God blesses those who are humble, for they will inherit the whole earth (Matthew 5:5). (Assuming a humble demeanor positions us to serve others' potential needs, not judging others because of their needs. People seek relationships, and leaders require relationships with those they serve and lead. What better way to start a relationship than approaching others humbly? It is not arrogant, not as if we are superior, and not as if we are better than others, but humbly seeking to help them in their needs. Who would you want leading you? An arrogant, selfish person, or a person whose Humility says they care more for you than themselves? Arrogance and pride lead to inheriting a lonely failure. Humility and service to others lead to inheriting numerous victories for those we serve and lead.)

Since God chose you to be the holy people he loves, you must clothe yourselves with tenderhearted mercy, kindness, humility, gentleness, and patience (Colossians 3:12). (Just as you choose which clothes you will dress yourself with each day, you must also choose to clothe yourself with the virtues God desires for us to lead with. No one can force a person to be tenderhearted, merciful, kind, humble, gentle, or patient. These virtues do not come naturally to a person's character. They must be chosen, pursued, and practiced to become a part of our character. As we seek a closer relationship with God through reading and studying His Word, and through prayer, God's virtues begin to take root in us. What are you feeding your character? Are you providing it the world's view and the world's virtues, or are you feeding it God's Word? Feed your leadership character, God's virtues and watch a harvest of God's peace and joy manifest in your life and your leadership.)

LORD my heart is not proud; my eyes are not haughty. I don't concern myself with matters too great or too awesome for me to grasp (Psalm 131:1). (Be humble and content with where God has you in service to others. Know that if God has more incredible things for you to achieve, He will make it happen for you. In Proverbs 3:5–6, the wisest man to lead, King Solomon teaches us, ***Trust in the LORD with all your heart; do not depend on your own understanding. Seek his will in all you do, and he will show you which path to take.*** God's will for leaders is for them to serve others. Do so humbly and leave everything else to God. ***Your own ears will hear him. Right behind you a voice will say, "This is the way you should go," whether to the right or to the left*** (Isaiah 30:21).

Humility is a choice; we are told in James 4:10, "***Humble yourself.***" People are not born humble but being humble comes by way of learning to be humble. Almost every person is born with some type of God-given natural talent (artist, musician, builder, athlete, physician, etc.), something that they have a passion for doing. Humility is not given at birth but is a choice of where one positions themselves concerning others. When a person or leader is confident in their abilities, they don't need to prove themselves to anyone. A humble person or leader allows their selfless actions to speak to their qualifications, abilities, and motives for serving and leading others. As a leader, we are not interested or focused on self-promotion; we are interested and focused on others' needs and their promotion.

For a moment, sit and think about humble leaders you have witnessed in life. We have all read stories of humble people and humble leaders, but how many have you personally seen? I witnessed many men during my youth, growing up in rural North Carolina, who was very modest. My father and the men he associated himself with were great examples of Humility in their character. But what about leaders in our professional lives? Finding a leader in the military who was consistently humble was sometimes challenging, but they existed.

Every eighteen or twenty-four months in an Army organization, there is a "Change of Command." This is where the organization's current/former senior leader hands the reins of organizational leadership over to an incoming/new leader. Typically, a new leader would spend time receiving overview briefings and going out into subordinate organizations to view their facilities and to meet their people, much like any new leader in any organization will do. One of our subordinate organizations was geographically located over 1,600 miles away in the Arizona desert, which meant we would fly out and visit them. The new senior leader and I had been out in the most southern part of Arizona for a day or two visiting the organization. This allowed time for briefings and orientation to the organization's facilities and to meet their great people. As we left the military base on our way to our hotel one evening, the temperature was well over one hundred degrees, and the sun was still beating down on the desert floor. I was driving our rental vehicle, and ahead on the side of a busy road was an elderly gentleman standing behind his truck looking despondently at a rear flat tire. There was no way I could drive by this elderly gentleman in our air-conditioned rental car and leave him to his predicament in the scorching heat.

I pulled off the road and parked behind him with the emergency flashers blinking. I told the new senior leader that I would be right back and left the rental car running with the air conditioner blasting cool air. As I approached the elderly gentleman, he stated he had a spare tire underneath the vehicle bed. Still, he could not physically remove it or change it. Before I could retrieve the spare tire, the new senior leader had left the rental car and walked around behind me. The next thing I knew, the senior leader grabbed the lug wrench and worked on taking off the flat tire. Together, over the next twenty minutes, we changed the tire for the elderly gentleman. When finished, we were covered in sweat and dirt, leaving our military uniforms filthy. The senior leader never said a word, other than making sure the elderly gentleman was okay and asking him if he needed anything else. Before this moment, the jury was still out in my mind about what kind of man the new leader would be. As we climbed back into the rental vehicle, I knew he was a man of humility. He never let his senior leader status or his position of authority invoke or imply privilege. He viewed himself as no better or higher than any other person but served and lead as a humble servant to all. I had the pleasure of witnessing this senior leader's Humility for the next twenty-four months. He never failed to place others before and above himself. Serving with him was indeed a wonderful and fulfilling experience. This leader's Humility and kindness represented not only that he was a good person, but more importantly for those of us he led, he was a great leader!

How else do we know God wants us to lead with Humility? There are numerous times in Scripture we are told how much God opposes and detests pride.

God Opposes the Proud

Stop acting so proud and haughty! Don't speak with such arrogance! For the LORD is a God who knows what you have done; he will judge your actions (1 Samuel 2:3). (We do not require man or society's approval. Galatians 1:10 reminds us, ***I'm not trying to win the approval of people, but of God.*** God knows our heart. Pride and arrogance are about the person. Humility and service are about others. Which does God see in your heart?)

You rescue the humble, but your eyes watch the proud and humiliate them (2 Samuel 22:28). (Humility invites God's grace and mercy into your life. Pride and arrogance bring God's humiliating consequence of His judgment onto your life.)

Pride leads to disgrace, but with humility comes wisdom (Proverbs 11:2). (Pride says "I know it all," and failure and dishonor eventually follow. Humility says, "Tell me what I don't know," and wisdom is gained.)

The LORD detest the proud; they will surely be punished (Proverbs 16:5). (No one likes the word *punished.* God's Word does not hold back from teaching us the reward of doing good and the consequence of being wrong. Remain humble and in a position for God's bounty. Man's reward is temporary; God's reward is eternal.)

Pride goes before destruction, and haughtiness before a fall (Proverbs 16:18). (The wisest King knows what he is talking about. Look quickly around the world at the proud strutting their "success." I say look quickly, because their mighty fall is up ahead. Ask the arrogant and ruthless Saddam Hussein, who was found humiliated and hiding in a hole in the ground, how his pride and arrogance worked out for him? Oh wait, you can't ask him because he was publicly hung to his death. God's Word warns us, why do some leaders think they are the exception to God's law? Every person and every leader will answer for how they lived and how they led.)

Haughtiness goes before destruction; humility precedes honor (Proverbs 18:12). (Pride leads to destruction; Humility leads to respect. Not respect for a leader's position of authority, but respect for the person leading.)

You rescue the humble, but you humiliate the proud (Proverbs 18:27). (God has your back when you seek to serve others for His glory. God is famous for delivering those who follow His ways (Daniel in the Den of Lions; Shadrach, Meshach, and Abednego in King Nebuchadnezzar's blazing furnace; the Israelites trapped between the Red Sea and the Pharaoh's approaching Army) and God will be present for you when you humbly serve and lead others.

Haughty eyes, a proud heart, and evil actions are all sin (Proverbs 21:4). (A sin is an immoral act considered to be a transgression against God's law. Humility is an act of consenting to God's law. Humbly serve and lead as God's law commands.)

Pride ends in humiliation, while humility brings honor (Proverbs 29:23). (The choice is ours to make. Whenever a wise person invests in a financial venture, they want to know the risks involved. God's Word repeatedly tells us the danger of pride and arrogance. Smart people make the right choice for long-term success; they invest in Humility.)

If you have been a fool by being proud or plotting evil, cover your mouth in shame (Proverbs 30:32). (Shame is one of many consequences of the proud and arrogant person. Guilt is a painful feeling of humiliation or distress caused by the consciousness of wrong or foolish behavior. Also known as the *consequence* of evil and dumb actions.)

Otherwise, you are boasting about your own plans, and all such boasting is evil (James 4:16). (Boasting is a form of excessively proud and self-satisfied talk about one's achievements, possessions, or abilities. Everyone has encountered this type of person. If you want to know how good they are, just ask them. I once witnessed a new leader introducing themselves to the people of the organization they were to lead. Their audience was a group of hourly wage-laborers. Their audience of people worked very hard for not much money. They hoped to hear words of hope and encouragement that their hard work would warrant pay raises and promises of a better tomorrow from their new leader. Instead, the new leader started by telling them how successful he was and how wealthy he was. The second the leader said these things, he lost them. He lost their hope that he could empathize with their needs. He lost their respect as a person because they understood the only person he cared for was himself. He lost their loyalty because they knew he was only loyal to himself. A person or leader boasting is full of themselves and will never go low for others' needs. They care nothing about lifting others; they only want to lift praises for themselves.)

God opposes the proud but favors the humble. So humble yourselves before God (James 4:6–7). (Get on the winning side of life and leading. Let serving others be like the customer service folks at Chick-Fil-A say, "My pleasure." Do not see serving others as demeaning; see serving others as an honorable act of service. When we are humble, we are honoring God's commands, and in this, we find favor from God.)

> ***This is what the LORD says: "Don't let the wise boast in their wisdom, or the powerful boast in their power, or the rich boast in their riches. But for those who wish to boast should boast in this alone: that they truly know***

> ***me and understand that I am the LORD who demonstrates unfailing love and who brings justice and righteousness to the earth, and that I delight in these things. I, the LORD, have spoken!"*** (Jeremiah 9:23–24)

(No matter how far up the leadership chain you go, how much money you make, how educated a piece of paper in a frame says you are, give all honor and praise to God, not yourself. When we write our resume for pursuing a new employment opportunity, we use this time to toot our own horn of our qualifications and credentials. Organizations require this information to determine who they will select to fill personnel vacancies, which is a suitable method for hiring the best-qualified applicant. There are times and circumstances where people must validate their qualifications by talking about themselves and their accomplishments. Being humble does not mean we disavow our capabilities and successes. Being humble means when we are selected or accepted based on our qualifications and successes, we give God the credit and praise for our abilities and successes. Being humble before God says we achieve nothing without His grace and mercy. We should quickly acknowledge to others that we would have no success without God's help. Humility in leading admits we are not worthy of leading other people; however, we are blessed by God to do so.)

In Luke 18:14 Jesus says, "***For those who exalt themselves will be humbled, and those who humble themselves will be exalted."*** (God's way, clear enough!)

Human pride will be brought down, and human arrogance will be humbled (Isaiah 2:11). (Have you caught onto God's theme yet? God detests prideful people!)

Human pride will be humbled, and human arrogance will be brought down (Isaiah 2:17). (When God's Word keeps saying the same things in different ways, we would be wise to hear and obey them all!)

Pride leads to conflict (Proverbs 13:10). (Why does "***pride lead to conflict***?" Because pride can never admit it was wrong. A prideful person cannot acknowledge their defeat when beaten by an opponent. An arrogant or prideful person will go down swinging, insulting, demeaning, and arguing before ever humbly accepting defeat. Prideful people cannot utter the words "I'm sorry," "I was wrong," or "my mistake." Pride fuels a person's vanity to the point they are blind to reality. Pride makes the person, no matter how wrong they are, believe their lies of denial. Here is the sad truth of it all; the only person they are fooling is themselves.)

Don't be impressed with your own wisdom (Proverbs 3:7). (Impressing others is not something humble people strive to do. My father was a humble man, and he had fun teaching me to be humble. As a young country boy, I was often challenged to conform to the rules of how my dad would have me to behave. No one was more surprised (and relieved) when I came home from the military recruiting station and revealed I had signed up for the next four years in the Army. God blessed my military career with promotions and recognitions. Each time I would tell my dad about them, he would say. "I just can't believe you are doing so well."

I did not take Dad's observations personally; I knew he was proud of me. Still, I also knew he knew me as a wayward boy. We always laughed, and he would remind me that God was proving his might in my success. Dad had already gone to be with God in heaven before I finished my post-graduate studies. When the day came and I received an email from my dissertation chair congratulating Dr. Kingston, my sister and I laughed as we knew our dad would say, "I just can't believe it." When I read the congratulatory email, the first thing I did was drop right here beside my desk and thank God. I know this, there is no way this simple country boy could have ever graduated without God's wisdom, help, and grace. I laugh now because, just like my dad, I can't believe it either. I don't even know what I don't know. But I know this, there is so much more to learn in life, especially in learning to lead as God would have you and I lead. Seek His wisdom in leading every day.)

The LORD mocks the mockers but is gracious to the humble (Proverbs 3:34). (God laughs at the pride of those who laugh at others' expense, for he sees through their arrogant foolishness. God sees the mocker's insecurities as they attempt to cover them with their mockery of others. Meanwhile, God sees the humble person's heart for others and pours His kindness into their lives.)

When people commend themselves, it doesn't count for much (2 Corinthians 10:18). (I, I, I no matter how many times a leader says I when commending themselves is just an individual all by themselves. But when a leader says we or you when praising and recognizing others, they are impacting, encouraging, and celebrating those they serve and lead. A humble leader makes others count.)

O people, the LORD has told you what is good, and this is what he requires of you: to do what is right, to love mercy, and to walk humbly with your God (Micah 6:8). (Humbleness is not a world thing. Humbleness is a God thing! All things in leading and life will ultimately be good when we continuously honor God's Word.)

Live in harmony with each other. Don't be too proud to enjoy the company of ordinary people. And don't think you know it all! (Romans 12:16). (I have sat here for the last few minutes thinking about times when I have witnessed a person who the world says is important and successful by its standards enjoying the company of ordinary people. NEWSFLASH, WE ARE ALL ORDINARY PEOPLE! However, there was one person, definitely not ordinary, but absolutely extraordinary, that I do think of. You know Him also. When Jesus walked this earth, he only sought the company of the everyday person. In His splendor, he was humble. In His might, he was meek. In His power, he came to serve others. And unlike you and I, Jesus did know it all. Humility, meekness, and being a servant to others was good enough for the most extraordinary person and greatest leader to ever walk this earth. How can we not follow His lead?)

A person or leader filled with pride is only striving for themselves to make it to the top. They are like a whale in the cold arctic waters where whaling is still legal at times. When they get to the top of the water's surface, and they are ready to blow their air of hubris, that's when they are harpooned. Be humble, or you will stumble. Pride middle letter is "I," only "I" matters to the proud person or leader. Humble and Humility's second letter is "U," as in this is not about me. It is about you. Pride and arrogance results in a division between the person/leader and colleagues, friends, family and most importantly, God.

People and leaders who walk around in pride feel morally superior to others. Who do they think they are? Pride filled leaders strut around comparing themselves to others, claiming their intellectual and competence superiority over everyone else. However, God sees them vastly differently, ***But they are only comparing themselves with each other, using themselves as the standard of measurement. How ignorant!*** (2 Corinthians 10:12). What makes their small, insecure minds believe they are morally superior to any other person? Do they think that they have it all figured out, and the rest of us are lucky to be in their presence? The most powerful and morally superior leader to ever walk the face of this earth walked and served in Humility. In Mark 1, verses 40–44, we find Jesus healing a man with leprosy. Rather than seek honor and praise for his act of healing and service to someone in need, Jesus told the man after recovering him completely, ***"Don't tell anyone about this."***

Being humble before God means we submit to His Will for our lives; we get ourselves out of the way of God's way. Humility is seen in the person whose humble demeanor invites others in instead of repelling them away. We stop trying to make things happen and surrender to God. According to Dr. and Pastor Tony Evans, "God needs you to set down your pride, dignity, and rationale. God needs you to seek Him and His Word concerning your situation so He can tell you what to do. And then He wants you to obey completely."[1] Great leaders understand that it is not themselves which provides strength through Humility, but it is the power of God's grace and mercy exercised through them that is their strength and greatness.

> *I have been driven many times to my knees by the overwhelming conviction that I had nowhere else to go. My wisdom, and that of all about me, seemed insufficient for the day.* (Abraham Lincoln)

Being humble means, others' needs are more critical than a self-serving title or position of authority. Humility harmonizes; arrogance divides. Pride and arrogance are destructive in relationships; Humility builds and reinforces relationships. When a leader is humble, they are happy being behind the scenes serving those they lead. Now, those they lead can be recognized and celebrated for their contributions to the organization. It is not about you, the leader; it is about those that you serve and lead.

As observed by Estelle Smith, "Humility is strong—not bold; quiet—not speechless; sure—not arrogant. Humility is not denying the power you have. It is realizing that the power comes through you, not from you."[2] The humble and great servant leader Dr. Billy Graham himself stated, "*God measures people by the small dimensions of humility and not by the bigness of their achievements or the size of their capabilities.*"[3]

If pride prevents others from wanting to be around us, how can a prideful leader establish relationships with others? Humility mends divisions and welcomes others in. Humility says to others, "You are important to me." Part of feeling close to someone else in a relationship means we feel like they see us as important and valued. Humility invites and establishes trust. Humility places the importance and value of being trustworthy for others at the forefront of a humble leader's motives. Since we believe that leadership is strengthened through relationships and we know trust is vital to relationships, Humility becomes an essential building block in building the relationship leadership requires. Through being humble, we have significantly fortified our foundation of relationships in leading. The nemesis of a firm foundation is a crack. It's time to look at what creates destructive cracks in the foundation of a relationship built on trust. We are talking about the evil and debilitating action of hypocrisy found in untrustworthy leaders. Let's take a look at how God sees hypocritical leaders, onward!

Reflection Time

Do you view a humble person as weak or strong? Do you judge a person's intellectual abilities if they appear humble? How you see Humility will determine your inclination to being humble.

Think of a person you have known that was genuinely humble in their character. What were their strengths, and what were their weaknesses?

Think of a person you have known that was arrogant and very prideful. What were their strengths, and what were their weaknesses?

---

1 Tony Evans, Your Comeback: Your Past Doesn't Have To Determine Your Future (Eugene: Harvest House, 2018), 18-19.

2 Harold Myra and Marshall Shelley, The Leadership Secrets of Billy Graham (Grand Rapids: Zondervan, 2005), 198.

3 Ibid., 203.

Hypocrisy (Say No)

In Matthew 7:15–20 Jesus tells us what a hypocrite looks like:

> ***"Beware of the false prophets who come disguised as harmless sheep but are really vicious wolves. You can identify them by their fruit, that is, by the way they act. Can you pick grapes from thornbushes, or figs from thistles? A good tree produces good fruit, and a bad tree produces bad fruit. A good tree can't produce bad fruit, and a bad tree can't produce good fruit. So every tree that does not produce good fruit is chopped down and thrown into the fire. Yes, just as you can identify a tree by its fruit, so you can identify people by their actions."***

So far, we have focused on the characteristics, attributes, and motives for creating trusting relationships with those we lead. However, some of the best lessons I ever learned in leadership came from observing and being subject to some of the worst leaders I have encountered over the years. These bad leaders taught me everything I never wanted to be associated with in leading others. Some were excessively prideful or selfish, but the worst of the worst were hypocritical leaders. They would talk as if they cared but then turn and reveal their hearts were far from me by their actions. Their only cared for themselves. ***For their tongues shoot lies like poisoned arrows. They speak friendly words to their neighbors while scheming in their heart to kill them*** (Jeremiah 9:8).

Bob Goff informs us of the word *hypocrisy*'s origin and motive,

> *The word hypocrisy is derived from the Greek word for actors on the stage who spoke from behind masks held in front of their faces. Hypocrisy is all about hiding behind a mask. Because you think people will be more impressed with the mask than they are with you—and, most likely, because you are doing something behind the mask that you don't want other people to see.*[1]

God's Describes Hypocrisy as Wicked and Evil Behavior

For they are all wicked hypocrites, and they all speak foolishness (Isaiah 9:17). (Morally bad leaders are only out for themselves and lack good judgment. These are leaders that do not have the intestinal fortitude, integrity, or personal courage they require of others. They talk a big game, but coward in the face of adversity.)

So get rid of all evil behavior. Be done with all deceit, hypocrisy, jealousy, and all unkind speech (1 Peter 2:1). (Look at the company hypocrisy keeps in this Scripture: deceit, jealousy, and unkindness. These are all forms of ***"evil behavior,"*** according to God's Word. Evil is defined as profoundly immoral and wicked. In other words, a hypocritical leader is an immoral and wicked person. These are deep convictions a leader must avoid.)

False weights and unequal measures—the LORD detests double standards of every kind (Proverbs 20:10). (Whatever is good enough for those you serve and lead is good enough for you. Whatever they must do for the organization, so must their leader do. Remember, being a leader does not provide hypocritical privilege; it requires equal standards of conduct and equal adherence to organizational policies and requirements.)

If someone claims, "I know God," but doesn't obey God's commandments, that person is a liar and is not living the truth (1 John 2:4). (Any leader who says they know the organization's rules, standards, and regulations but does not serve in compliance with them is a liar. Only a hypocritical leader would say one thing and then do another. Only a hypocritical leader would require others to obey and conform to rules, standards, and regulations that the leader does not follow. You know that leader, they are the one who says, "Don't worry about what I do, worry about yourself.")

In Matthew chapter 23, we find Jesus criticizing the hypocritical leadership style of the day's Religious Leaders. Throughout Matthew 23, Jesus holds no punches and calls out the Religious Leaders and exposing their failures. Matthew 23:27–28 Jesus condemns hypocritical leaders of the Church, ***"Hypocrites! For you are like whitewashed tombs—beautiful on the outside but filled with dead people's bones and all sorts of impurity. Outwardly you look like righteous people, but inwardly your hearts are filled with hypocrisy and lawlessness."*** When He addressed the Temple's hypocritical leaders, Jesus unleashed a verbal rebuke as witnessed nowhere else in His life of ministry. Jesus called out those who were given great responsibility in leading for their "do as I say, not as I do" hypocritical leadership. Jesus detested hypocrisy, and so do those we lead today. James 3:1 warns ***for we who teach will be judged more strictly.***

In Matthew 23, Jesus uses the following words or terms numerous times to call the religious leaders what they were:

- ***"Hypocrites"***: six times
- ***"Blind"***: five times (***"blind guides," "blind fools," "blind Pharisees," "how blind"***)
- ***"Snakes! Sons of vipers! How will you escape the judgment of hell?"***
- ***"Your hearts are filled with hypocrisy and lawlessness."***

In the King James Version of the Bible, the word *hypocrite* is mentioned thirty-one times. Throughout Jesus's ministry, we hear the compassion in his words and see it in His actions. Jesus forgave people of their sins and did not judge them for sinful lives. In John chapter 8, a woman is caught in adultery and the teachers of religious law sought to stone her. They attempted to persuade Jesus into condemning her actions. ***Jesus answered them, "All right, but let the one who has never sinned throw the first stone!"*** (John 8:7). All of the accusers (teachers of religious law) shrunk back and left the area. ***Then Jesus stood up again and said to the woman, "Where are your accusers? Didn't even one of them condemn you?" "No Lord," she said. And Jesus said, "Neither do I. Go and sin no more"*** (John 8:10–11). However, when it came to hypocritical leaders, Jesus did not hold back from calling them out. Jesus forgives a person's sins and mistakes with compassion, but to be a hypocritical leader, Jesus jarringly rebukes this behavior.

Leaders are in a unique position, they are held to higher standards of expectation by those they lead, and they should be. A leader is in a place that often requires the judgment of others. God's Word warns leaders about judging as a hypocrite.

> ***You may think you can condemn such people, but you are just as bad, and you have no excuse! When you say they are wicked and should be punished, you are condemning yourself, for you who judge others do these very same things.*** (Romans 2:1)

> ***Since you judge others for doing these things, why do you think you can avoid God's judgment when you do the same things?*** (Romans 2:3)

Making judgments is part of everyday life for a leader. At times we are professionally obligated to judge those we lead; this can present hypocritical dilemmas. When you have an accused person that requires judgment, and you know you have performed a similar wrongful action in your past (but were not caught or found out), what do you do without being hypocritical in your judgment? You cannot judge and condemn others for the same infractions you got away with in the past without being a hypocrite.

Our organization was deployed into the California desert to work jointly with other US government organizations in combatting illegal drugs from entering the United States along its southern border. Whenever we were "deployed," there was an order of no alcohol consumption. Within our organization was a group of people whose support role was vital to our operational success. This group of people worked long, hard hours every day of the week. Following two weeks of nonstop operations, our organization's senior leader authorized this group of support personnel to have twenty-four hours of "downtime." Unfortunately, this group of people took this to mean they could go downtown and have a beer or two. They were found in a local bar establishment by a "courtesy patrol" of leaders charged with checking such locations to enforce the no alcohol consumption order.

All of the support personnel were brought to the military facilities medical station and were confirmed through blood screenings to have consumed alcohol. No one was above the legal limits, but they violated the no alcohol consumption order. Our organization's senior leader would now have to judge their infraction and decide on the severity of their pending Uniform Code of Military Justice disciplinary punishment. Their punishment could range from a verbal reprimand (fancy way of saying being chewed out), all the way to punishment that would reduce their rank with a loss of pay, ultimately ending their military careers. Everyone in the organization would be watching to see the severity of their punishment and the senior leader's tolerance for misconduct.

The next evening, the organization's senior leader knocked on my door of the room I was living in. When I opened the door, I was surprised to find him of all people at my door. He asked if he could come in and talk to me? I invited him in; he took off his hat and sat on a chair in my room with his head down. I asked, "Sir, is everything okay?" The senior leader looked at me and said, "I need some advice and counsel. What do I do with these support personnel that was caught drinking downtown last night? If I go severe in punishment, I will have to redeploy them. We will have to cease operations until a new team of support personnel can be deployed out here. If I go to light in their punishment, I will be seen as weak and what will prevent someone else from doing the same as they did." I could tell this decision was tormenting the senior leader. Still, I also suspected he was looking for a way to send a message without jeopardizing these hard-working support person's careers.

Under my breath, while he was talking, I asked God, "What do I tell this man? Help me say the right thing for everyone involved." I said, "Sir, you have every right under your authority to throw the book at all of them. They violated the order of no alcohol consumption. But I want to ask you a question that only you know the answer to. Suppose in your entire military career, and especially in your junior officer years, you never once violated an order or violated any policy of the Army. In that case, you can impose whatever punishment you deem appropriate without being a hypocrite. But if you know that this may not be the case, and the only difference is, you were never caught in your infraction of the rules. How can you punish them severely and not be a hypocrite?

> Jesus says, ***"Do not judge others and you will not be judged. For you will be treated as you treat others. The standard you use in judging is the standard by which you will be judged. And why worry about a speck in your friend's eye when you have a log in your own? How can you think of saying to your friend, 'Let me help you get rid of that speck in your eye,' when you can't see past the log in your own eye? Hypocrite! First get rid of the log in your own eye; then you will see well enough to deal with the speck in your friend's eye."*** (Matthew 7:1–5)

> ***The LORD detests double standards; he is not pleased by dishonest scales.*** (Proverbs 20:23)

Sir, you can make this a painful learning opportunity for those involved and at the same time present a stern warning to everyone else in the organization. Your latitude in the severity of punishment allows you to do both if you know what I am suggesting." The senior leader raised his head and looked at me, and said, "I hear what you are saying. I have some thinking to do." He thanked me for the counsel and departed.

The next afternoon, word went out that everyone in our 450-person organization would meet in a formation that night for the senior leader to talk to everyone. When we met, the senior leader called all of the support personnel caught in violation of the no alcohol consumption order to stand in front of everyone present. Over the next five to ten minutes, the senior leader verbally reprimanded all of the support personnel. He finished by telling them they would all receive Official Letters of Reprimand, which would result in the severe stagnation or end their military careers if filed in their official Army personnel records. Now, here was what was not said to everyone in attendance. The Official Letters of Reprimand do not automatically get filed in the person's official military personnel record. The senior leader has the authority to let those letters sit in his desk drawer while he is in command. Whenever he chooses, they can be destroyed as if they never existed. That was exactly what the senior leader intended to do, but no one besides himself at the time knew this. The support personnel were not sent back home; they stayed with us and worked harder than ever.

Everyone present knew the senior leader meant business and was not looking the other way. I knew this was a senior leader that could not be a hypocrite and punish someone for something he may have done in his junior officer days. As the formation ended and people went back to work, the senior leader walked in my direction. As he was walking by, he winked at me with a smile on his face and said, "We can't have any hypocritical leaders, can we?"

I said, "No, sir, and thank you."

He said, "No, thank you." That night, I thanked God for his words of wisdom He allowed me to speak to the senior leader.

Hypocrisy is a tough thing to be free from if you have lived several or more decades in life. We have all made hypocritical mistakes and have instances in our lives that leave us with feelings of shame and or regret. Things that we judge others for when we are no better than they are, and sometimes our actions are even worse. Some of my most substantial regrets in life were from the same things I warned others against or judged others for doing. I was a hypocrite for selfish reasons, and my hypocrisy fractured several relationships. Submitting my life to God, he forgave me, and I promised never to be that man again. Writing on this subject fills my mind with memories of my hypocritical actions. I regret them still to this day, I always will. ***I turned away from God, but then I was sorry. I kicked myself for my stupidity! I was thoroughly ashamed of all I did in my younger days*** (Jeremiah 31:19). So just like me, we all must move forward into becoming the person and leader God intends us to be. When we seek God's forgiveness and repent from former hypocritical ways, God forgives us and forgets our past. Now we have a chance to do things right. We must realize as a person and leader, we will be judged as we judge others. I don't know about you, but I need all the mercy and grace God and others can give me. While we all fall far short of perfection, we must keep on striving for excellence in leading others without hypocrisy.

> ***But if we confess our sins to him, he is faithful and just to forgive us our sins and to cleanse us from all wickedness.*** (1 John 1:9)

> ***He will wipe every tear from their eyes, and there will be no more death or sorrow or crying or pain. All these things are gone forever.*** (Revelations 21:4)

Hypocrisy is asking someone you lead to do something you have not done or will not do. Hypocrisy is the leader that sets expectations for others that the leader exempts themselves from. Hypocrisy is the leader that says we are to do one thing while they do another. To avoid placing ourselves in positions where our decisions and actions represent hypocritical behavior, a person must be self-disciplined and self-aware. As our character (discussed later) becomes more like the character of Christ in leading, we will naturally walk and talk with integrity, not hypocrisy.

> ***Since he himself has gone through suffering and testing; he is able to help us when we are being tested*** (Hebrews 2:18).

Standards and policies apply to everyone in an organization. If they are good enough for the people, they are good enough for the leader. Leaders are not exempt from the same standards and policies as everyone else. Leaders establish the standards and must remain disciplined to adhere to them. Just as the leader expects others to follow the rules, others expect and deserve leaders who do the same. When we *rationalize* hypocritical behavior as a leader, we tell ourselves *rational lies* instead of speaking the truth to ourselves. Leaders verify their words by their actions! What is the best way to prevent becoming a hypocritical leader? Lead by Example!

Reflection Time

What fruit would a person you serve and lead pick from you if you were a tree of leadership? Remember, the fruit represents the roots and context of what the tree is. Would you provide good fruit produced from truth and honesty, or bad fruit which appears tasty, but under the skin is rotten from dishonesty and selfish motives.

Have you successfully done all the tasks and jobs you ask others to do? In other words, do you expect those you serve and lead to do something you would not do yourself? Have you been hypocritical in this area?

Does your walk reflect your talk?

---

1 Bob Goff, Live in Grace, Walk in Love, A 365-Day Journey (Nashville: Nelson Books, 2019), 203.

Lead by Example

And you yourself must be an example to them by doing good works of every kind. Let everything you do reflect the integrity and seriousness of your teaching. Teach the truth so that your teaching can't be criticized.

—Titus 2:7–8

We now have a clear understanding of God's disdain for hypocrisy in leadership. For the correct way to serve and lead, we must look to God's Word. God's Word instructs leaders to become an example of His Truth in leading. Jesus revealed God's nature in His walk as an example of how we are to serve and lead. Leading by example says, "Do as I do, and follow my ways." Throughout Scripture, this is revealed to us time and time again.

We wanted to give you an example to follow (2 Thessalonians 3:9). (The Psychology of Leadership is understanding how others are influenced to enable the leader to achieve the organization's goals. Perhaps there is no better way to influence others than to lead as an example of how you would have them serve the needs of others and the organization. When a leader is on time, true to their word, committed to doing the job correctly, and treats others with respect and consideration, they set an example they would like those they serve and lead to follow. Be what you would have others be.)

In Matthew 20:26–27 Jesus said, "***But among you it will be different. Whoever wants to be a leader among you must be your servant. For even the Son of Man came not to be served but to serve others and to give his life as a ransom for many."*** (Allowing others to see that your walk of service represents your talk of service to them and the organization amplifies a message of "I am an example for you to follow." Jesus never told people to do things one way, while he did things another way. Instead, Jesus let his walk of being a servant to those he led be an example of what He required from others. A leader's example of selflessness, service for others, and loyalty to those they lead and the organization establishes the norms for how they expect others to be.)

And those who are peacemakers will plant seeds of peace and reap a harvest of righteousness (James 3:18). (Most everyone is familiar with the saying "You reap what you sow." This saying comes from God's Word.

> ***You will always harvest what you plant. Those who live only to satisfy their own sinful nature will harvest decay and death from that sinful nature. But those who live to please the Spirit will harvest everlasting life from the Spirit. So let's not get tired of doing what is good. At just the right time we will reap a harvest of blessing if we don't give up.*** (Galatians 6:7–9)

(Whatever example a leader makes for those they serve and lead represents a leader sowing seeds of what is acceptable. Seeds of kindness, service, respect, care, listening, timeliness, humbleness, and honesty planted by a leader's example produce a harvest of peace and harmony in the organization. Life in this world is chaotic and unpredictable for those you serve and lead. Make the workplace a place where your example of what is good and right by God shines hope into the lives of those you have been anointed to serve and lead. You are God's example of love and hope. It still exists by the example you show others as their leader.)

Remember your leaders who taught you the Word of God. Think of all the good that has come from their lives and follow the example of their faith (Hebrew 13:7). (When people see good things happening from the way you lead, they want to have those same successes for themselves. Talking success is just talk. Let your walk as a leader serve as an example for others to seek for themselves. A leader's example of doing the right thing by others is an investment into those they serve and leads future leadership mindset. My father's faith was on display every day in his humble and kind demeanor. He lived a life surrounded by good friends and was very content with whatever God blessed his life with. My father had real success in life, family, friends, and peace. He served as an example of what I eventually realized was the true meaning of success in life. Real success is not represented by a title, position, or life of luxury, but of real wealth in being a person of great Christian character. My father was a person of faith, and how he served in life became the example I came to want to for my life. ***Yet true godliness with contentment is itself great wealth*** (1 Timothy 6:6). Thank you, Dad, for being a great example of what matters in life.)

Don't lord it over the people assigned to your care but lead them by your own good example (1 Peter 5:3). (We cannot force our ways on others. Human nature is to resist others telling us what to do and how to act. The quickest way to push someone away is to force our beliefs and methods for leading on them. I once inherited seven subordinate senior leaders who were very talented, very driven, Type A personality individuals. I needed them to come together as a team of leaders. Between the seven of them, they led over four thousand people. Each of their organization's had unique missions that individually could achieve some level of success. Still, suppose I could influence them to want to work in unison and combine their organizations abilities with the others, united. In that case, we could achieve so much more. I introduced a slow simmering team building environment oriented toward moving them past themselves as leaders and bonding as people. I began bonding with each of them on their terms and pushing past our leadership positions to our commonalities in life. I was not trying to motivate them toward each other through being pushy; I was slowly speaking into them and moving them toward one another with a humble, loving demeanor. This endeavor required a subtle approach. Any revelation of my motive and they would refuse to be willing to participate in my plan. I would humbly allow their pushback at first and make a point of letting them know I was attempting to get to know each of them more as we gathered in group settings and discussions. Over the next few months, I observed them eating together by their own choice. They started enjoying one another's company and sharing their issues and vulnerabilities as a person and leading their organization. I allowed them to know me as a person and bring them in as a collective group of leaders who all wanted the same ultimate goals for our people and the organization. Soon, they sought advice from one another, and ultimately, they offered each other's organizations assistance from their organization. Even though they ultimately answered to my authority position, I wanted them to want to work together because they cared about each other's personal and organizational success, not just their own. Through an example of caring and valuing each leader's abilities, they eventually felt the same for one another. Together we achieved great success.)

Be an example to all believers in what you say, in the way you live, in your love, your faith, and your purity (1 Timothy 4:12). (Every word you say and every action you make is setting an example for others to follow.)

Promote the kind of living that reflects wholesome teaching (Titus 2:1). (Let your walk represent what you say.)

Let your good deeds shine out for all to see, so that everyone will praise your heavenly Father (Matthew 5:16). (As a Christian leader your talk, and your walk should be a reflection of God's Word. People are searching for hope in this world. As a leader, let your conversations and your walk be one that leaves people thanking God for your leadership in their lives. To God, be all the glory!)

When the godly succeed, everyone is glad. When the wicked take charge, people go into hiding (Proverbs 28:12). (We just came out of a season of electing our political leaders. The closer we came to election day, I started reading more and more quotes from "celebrities" saying that if a particular candidate was re-elected, they were moving to another country. These people so disliked the personality and leadership of a particular candidate that they would live ('go into hiding') in another country to avoid being led by the person if re-elected for another term in office. This is how impactful a leader's style of leading affects people. Lead as God's Word tells us to lead and people will seek you, not hide from you.)

In Matthew 23:2–4 Jesus says,

> ***"The teachers of religious law and the Pharisees are the official interpreters of the law of Moses. So practice and obey whatever they tell you, but don't follow their example. For they don't practice what they teach. They crush people with unbearable religious demands and never lift a finger to ease the burden."***

(Jesus tells us, do not follow the example of hypocritical leaders. Do not follow the example of people who say one thing but do another thing. Lead as an example of what to say and do for those you serve and lead.)

And you yourself must be an example to them by doing good works of every kind. Let everything you do reflect the integrity and seriousness of your teaching. Teach the truth so that your teaching can't be criticized (Titus 2:7–8). (The way you prefer others talk and walk in life and the workplace begins with the example you make. What example are you making for those you serve and lead?)

We are careful to be honorable before the Lord, but we also want everyone else to see that we are honorable (2 Corinthians 8:21). Jesus tells us in Matthew 6:1–4,

> ***"Watch out! Don't do your good deeds publicly, to be admired by others, for you will lose the reward from your Father in heaven.***

> ***When you give to someone in need, don't do as the hypocrites do—blowing trumpets in the synagogues and streets to call attention to their acts of charity! I tell you the truth, they have received all the reward they will ever get. But when you give to someone in need, don't let your left hand know what your right hand is doing. Give your gifts in private, and your Father, who sees everything, will reward you."***

These are not contradictory Words of Truth from God. Jesus is talking about being charitable to those in need without seeking acknowledgment from man. Being honorable means we are respectful. And just like we are to be respectful to God, we are respectful toward other people. As examples of respecting others, we are saying that respect is a two-way street in treating other people. To be respected, one must give respect. Set the example of respect for others to follow.)

Every leader is always "on display." Every word, action, behavior, and characteristic of a leader is broadcasting a message to others. The leader is continuously setting an example for others to follow. What example are you setting for those you lead? Is it okay for them to do and say things the way you do? These are hard questions for all of us. We may not like some of the examples we have been setting for those we lead, at home and in the workplace.

How does a leader's example multiply with those they lead and their organization as a whole? A leader is like one grain of corn planted in the ground: One kernel of corn produces a corn stalk with two to three ears of corn, resulting in up to one thousand grains of corn. The leader's example plants in the minds and actions of the few they lead an example of what right looks like in leading. Those they lead will grow to lead multitudes of people over future generations eventually. What example are you planting? Your example today has the potential of impacting societies of tomorrow.

A leader is most beneficial to an organization and its people when their example aligns with and epitomizes God's Truth in leading. Let's look at a variety of challenges every leader encounters in leading. We will review what God's Word tells us is His guidance for each challenge, followed by practical applicational thoughts and some experiences for your consideration.

Being on Time

For everything there is a season, a time for every activity under heaven (Ecclesiastes 3:1). (It appears the higher some leaders move up in position, the more relaxed they become at being on time. Late for work, late for meetings, and late with timely decisions. When a person is working their way up the corporate ladder, most go above and beyond to be on time for work and complete their assigned work on time. Why is it that once they make it to the top, they feel as if they can "do as they please" when it comes to being on time with everything? If it is okay for the boss to be a little late, it becomes okay for others to be late. If others are late, the boss will not know because the boss is late also. Being late for meetings throws others' schedules off; this is disrespectful of their time. Making decisions late reduces productivity as people sit and wait for your decision. You were on time during the years you were working to become a leader. Stay that way as a leader.)

Being Honest in Word and Deed

Honesty guides good people; dishonesty destroys treacherous people (Proverbs 11:3). (Leaders must lead with the absolute truth in word and deed, always. The people you serve and lead must be unconditionally sure that whatever you tell them is the truth. Tell a lie, and doubt creeps in their minds. Your integrity comes into question, and people become suspicious of everything you say. The truth may hurt at times, but the truth ensures the trust you require from those you lead remains strong.)

Adhering to All Standards

> ***They should be obedient, always ready to do what is good*** (Titus 3:1).

(In the Army, we had a saying, "standards + discipline = safety." In other words, if a standard of operation was approved as a requirement of how we do things (even in dangerous training operations) + everyone was disciplined to adhere to the standards of operation, this should = a safe operation. While leading day to day may not present any "dangerous operations," every day leading provides the challenge of adhering to all the organization's standards. Leaders most often establish the standards, and just like everyone else, leaders are responsible for adhering to those standards. Leading does not bring the privilege of being exempt from the standards; leading brings the responsibility of being the standard!)

Do Not Take Shortcuts

Good planning and hard work lead to prosperity, but hasty shortcuts led to poverty (Proverbs 21:5). (Take a shortcut, and a precedent has been set for others to follow. Remember, once a leader is known to take shortcuts in organizational operations, they compromise their authority to be judgmental of anyone else that takes a shortcut, especially when things go wrong. How can you punish someone for doing what they have seen you doing? Adhere to the prescribed and proven methodologies of the organization. If you or someone you lead develops a more efficient way of completing a task, have it approved by the appropriate authority. Allow them to incorporate the more efficient method into the standards of operations. This is the right example to set for others to follow.)

Do Not Bad-Mouth Others

> ***They must not slander anyone and must avoid quarreling*** (Titus 3:2).

Throw out the mockers and fighting goes too. Quarrels and insults will disappear (Proverbs 22:10). (One of the most unprofessional acts a leader can make is talking bad about others, in private or public. When this occurs, the leader has stepped out of their professional perspective and allowed their personal perspective to enter the situation. Suppose a leader in their professional capacity has a problem with someone. In that case, the leader addresses the issue, in private, with the person they have the problem with. Deal with it, talk it out, and move on in harmony.)

Do Things Properly and Keep Things in Order

But be sure that everything is done properly and in order (1 Corinthians 14:40). (One thing that drives some people crazy (and sometimes me) is my obsession with doing things right and in order. It must be the Army's fault because the country boy in me sure wasn't that way before entering the Army. But any profession requires things to be done correctly and in order. Would you want your surgeon to be disorderly and misplace a sponge or instrument during your surgical operation? Well, those you lead will follow your lead in "how we do things around here." When you do things the right way and maintain an orderly environment, others will fall in line with the same attention to detail and the workplace's environmental construct.)

Loyalty to Others

A friend is loyal, and a brother is born to help in time of need (Proverbs 17:17). (When others know you can be counted on to be there for them in both the good and bad times, they know they have a loyal leader. When things are going wrong for others, and they turn and look, there you are for them. When they are struggling in life or work, you are there to encourage them, strengthen them, and help them navigate to the other side of their struggles. The easy thing to do is leave everyone to fight their own battles, but a leader stands with them in their fight. A leader is allegiant and supportive to those they lead every day, in every way.)

Being Selfless

Don't be selfish; don't try to impress others. Be humble, thinking of others as better than yourselves (Philippians 2:3). (Placing the needs of others before your own needs is a situation every parent encounters. You want those new golf clubs, but your kids need new school clothes. You want that sporty two-door car, but your family needs a vehicle big enough for everyone and their "stuff" on trips. Selflessness is just this simple; we prioritize other's needs before our wants. Based on the severity of other's needs, they should become a priority over our own needs. We sacrifice to see others be safe, successful, or feeling valued and cared for. We place others in positions to be successful and receive praise instead of seeking it for ourselves. Selfless leader's actions speak louder than anything else they can do when boosting their worth in the organization. And a selfless leader's actions, most importantly, let those they lead know they matter, and they come first.)

Be Kind to Everyone

> ***Instead, be kind to each other, tenderhearted, forgiving one another, just as God through Christ has forgiven you*** (Ephesians 4:32).

(Kindness does not equate to being weak. The most potent and most powerful leader to walk this earth (Jesus Christ) was kind and loving to everyone he encountered in need. Kindness is revealed when we give the fallen person another chance to stand back up. Kindness means we are easily able to be compassionate and sincere with others, regardless of the circumstance. Kindness means we value the person, and we care about them. When a leader is kind to everyone, they say, we are in this together, and I empathize with you. Kindness in word or deed is endearing acts that build trust and strengthen relationships beyond measure.)

Always Have Time for Others Needs

Don't look out for your own interests, but take an interest in others, too (Philippians 2:4). (Taking a moment of your valuable time as a leader and giving that time to others' needs is the best use of your time. A few moments of a leader's time given to others' interests or needs may require the leader to sacrifice other things that require the leader's attention. The difference the leader has made in the lives of those they make time for is worth so much more. Giving your time to others is one of the most significant investments a leader can make in relationship building. Taking an interest in the interests of others says, "I'm here for you, and I care about what you care about. You matter to me." Go an inch for them, and they will go miles for you.)

Have Faithful Integrity

People with integrity walk safely, but those who follow crooked paths will slip and fall (Proverbs 10:9). (Doing the right thing when no one sees what you are doing indicates that everyone can count on you to always do things right by them and the organization. Integrity represents doing the right thing, telling the truth, being the same person regardless of the situational dilemma. Integrity reveals what a leader believes in and fortifies their pattern of conduct as one above reproach. Integrity reveals honorable motives in leading others. Integrity is an essential ingredient in the formula of creating and sustaining trust in every relationship in our lives.)

Work Intently Without Grumbling

Do everything without complaining and arguing, so that no one can criticize you (Philippians 2:14–15). (Never, never, never, never complain about the organization or others in the organization, especially in the presence of those you lead. You may disagree with a decision made by your leaders, but when you talk to others, you keep your disagreement to yourself. As far as everyone else knows, you fully support the decision and do so in your words and actions.

Leaders do not have the privilege of saying how they feel when they disagree with those serving above them in positions of responsibility. Do you want those you lead to complain or argue with your decisions openly? No, you want them to adhere to your decision and trust that you see the bigger picture of where your decision is taking them and the organization. Grumbling is a method of muted disloyal and second-guessing complaints against decisions and policies made by leadership. Disagreeing is indicative of human nature; complaining is indicative of character flaws that require adjusting.)

Use Good and Proper Language

> ***Don't use foul or abusive language. Let everything you say be good and helpful, so that your words will be an encouragement to those who hear them*** (Ephesians 4:29).

Whoever loves a pure heart and gracious speech will have the king as a friend (Proverbs 22:11). (One of the quickest ways to lose the respect of those you lead is turning lose your tongue and letting ignorance in language flow from it. As a leader, your language should speak for one purpose, positive encouragement directed toward others. Foul and abusive language negates everything right a leader has done before; it reveals their real character. A leader's speech reveals their heart. How do you want your heart to be seen by those you serve and lead? Guard your tongue!)

Respectful of Everyone

Love each other with genuine affection and take delight in honoring each other (Romans 12:10). (The quickest way to detect a leader's humility is to observe how respectful they are to others. Respecting others is not based on others' titles, work positions, wealth, social status, race, ethnicity, physical appearance, physical abilities, or the educational degree they have on the wall. Respect is a human being thing. The differences individuals have in cultural practices and even political party affiliation will never change the fact that we respect one another as our fellow human being. It is acknowledging that we are all created and loved by the same God in Heaven. God has not made one human being, regardless of race or ethnicity, superior to any other person (other than his Son, Jesus). Just like we are to lead as God would have us to lead founded on His Word, we are to respect and love each other as His Word tells us. No person is exempt from deserving of our respectful consideration.)

Nonjudgmental of Others' Personalities

In Matthew 7:1–2 Jesus says, ***"Do not judge others, and you will not be judged. For you will be treated as you treat others. The standard you use in judging is the standard by which you will be judged."*** (A leader is no different than any other person when it comes to falling short of consistently doing and saying the right things in life. At any given moment, everyone is subject to making mistakes, some as intentional acts of wrong and some accidental acts of wrong. Regardless, who is anyone to judge another person in life? Everyone is trying their best to find happiness and joy in life. Some choose the wrong paths, so have you, and so have I. Hope for the best for others and leave their judgment to the only one authorized to judge. God is Holy, and we are not!)

Refrain from Gossiping

A troublemaker plants seeds of strife; gossip separates the best of friends (Proverbs 16:28). (A leader does not have time for the immaturity of gossiping. Gossiping is the babbling of insecure fools talking about and passing hypocritical judgment on others' lives. Stay away from the "water cooler" gossip mill and let your words always be based on facts oriented toward lifting others. James 4:11–12 warns that gossiping is a form of judging for God to do, not man.

> ***Don't speak evil against each other, dear brothers and sisters. If you criticize and judge***

> ***each other, then you are criticizing and judging God's law. But your job is to obey the law, not to judge whether it applies to you. God alone, who gave the law, is the Judge. He alone has the power to save or destroy. So what right do you have to judge your neighbor?***

One last thing on the people that gossip. If they gossip to you about someone else, you can be sure that they gossip about you to others. Squelch gossip in the workplace and our lives. Life is hard enough without a bunch of hypocrites talking about your challenges behind your back. A real leader and friend come to you face-to-face, and instead of gossiping, ask how can I help you, I am here for you, or my favorite, "I'm in this for you.")

Manage Time Well

> ***We must quickly carry out the tasks assigned us by the one who sent us. The night is coming, and then no one can work*** (John 9:4).

(Leaders are required to get things done and make sure others are getting things done on time. Leaders prioritize the priorities of others so that tasks are completed on time. In the business world, time represents costs, and any leader not managing time well, costs their organization forecasted revenues. Leaders establish a schedule for tasks to be completed and allot a proportional amount of time. Once time management rhythms are established, the leader establishes mechanisms within the organization to monitor the timeliness of things being completed. Time management is an area where leaders are required to inspect what they expect. When the leader manages their time effectively and holds others accountable for meeting their timeline requirements, they embed a culture of time management accountability within the organization.)

Accountable for Our Actions

In Luke 17:3, Jesus says, "***So watch yourselves!***" (Every leader is accountable to someone else. If you are an elected political leader, you are accountable to your constituents. If you are the corporation leader, you are accountable to the organization's investors and external stakeholders. Every leader, no matter what level they are leading at, is accountable to others. Most importantly, every person is accountable to God for the life they choose to live. Never think you have arrived at a position or level in leadership that relieves you of accountability. The higher up the success ladder you climb, the more accountable you become. To whom much is given, much is required. Especially as a leader, you will always remain accountable for your words and actions. Be prepared to answer for every decision and action you make!)

Always Faithful in Word and Deed

> Jesus says, ***"If you are faithful in little things, you will be faithful in large ones. But if you are dishonest in little things, you won't be honest with greater responsibilities"*** (Luke 16:10).
>
> In Matthew 25:21 Jesus says, "***The master was full of praise. 'Well done, my good and faithful servant. You have been faithful in handling this small amount, so now I will give you many more responsibilities.'***"

(There is a reason why a person is placed in a position of leadership. They have established a pattern of consistently achieving success in their responsibilities. Promotions in leadership are based on a person's potential to manage greater responsibilities successfully. Similarly, suppose a leader displays honesty and trustworthiness in small tasks. In that case, they show a propensity for honesty and trustworthiness as inherent to their character. These are the leaders we can trust with greater responsibilities. If you desire to get promoted tomorrow, complete today's tasks with excellence. Today is in your control, and others will decide your tomorrow based on how well you controlled what is yours today.)

Always Present and Participating in the Hard Work

> ***Then make me truly happy by agreeing wholeheartedly with each other, loving one another, and working together with one mind and purpose*** (Philippians 2:2).

We are many parts of one body, and we all belong to each other (Romans 12:2). (Ever worked a job that when the work became challenging, grueling, and strenuous, the people that were supposed to be alongside you mystically disappeared? You noticed, and so did everyone else that stayed and worked. Everyone especially sees when the leader suddenly has to leave others to the hard work for an "important" meeting or other "obligation." Realistically, sometimes leaders have to be somewhere else for obligations out of their scheduling control. However, when time permits and schedules can be manipulated accordingly, the best investment of the leader's time is right beside and with those doing the hard work. Leading by example means the leader is right there in the middle of it all, working as hard as everyone else. If a leader wants to amplify their commitment to the team, they show up and stay until the hard work is completed. If the work is good enough for them, then it is good enough for the leader also. We are in this together, for both the good times and the challenging times!)

Meet Work Requirements with Joy

Work willingly at whatever you do, as though you were working for the LORD rather than for people (Colossians 3:23). (Establishing an attitude of gratitude is one of the best mind-sets a leader can channel to those they lead. Leaders must convey that challenges are opportunities to learn, grow, and overcome as individuals and organizations. Leaders who welcome work as opportunities to succeed are inspiring those they lead to embrace work and see it as one reason they come to work each day. Leaders motivate others when they are seen as eager to lean into the challenges work presents. When it comes to challenging work, leaders attack with enthusiasm; leaders never retreat!)

Always Encouraging Others

So encourage each other and build each other up, just as you are already doing (1 Thessalonians 5:11). (Every leader should be so encouraging to those they lead that their people know without a doubt, their leader believes in them. Encouragement creates the difference between self-belief, or doubt in one's abilities to overcome challenges. One of the greatest honors of leading is the opportunity to speak encouragement into the lives of others. Leadership itself gives a person a voice; leaders use their voice to build others up, not tear them down. A leader's word of encouragement can make a bad situation more bearable, sparking hope and belief that things will be better. Let your words create expectations of positivity. Our world has enough negativity in it all by itself.)

Contribute Generously to Others in Need

> ***Remember this—a farmer who plants only a few seeds will get a small crop. But the one who plants generously will get a generous crop. You must each decide in your heart how much to give. And don't give reluctantly or in response to pressure. "For God loves a person who gives cheerfully"*** (2 Corinthians 9:6–7).

Blessed are those who are generous, because they feed the poor (Proverbs 22:9). (Almost every organization supports some local, national, or global cause that solicits charitable donations to support them. Leaders establish a culture of giving to help others by their willingness and zest for giving when it is needed. This leads back to being selfless. Selfless with our time and with our money when others are in need. If the leader's wallet is so tight it can't be pried open with a crowbar, how fast do you think those they serve and lead will be willing to open their wallets? The real test of a leader's worth and heart is not what they keep for themselves, but what they gladly give away to others.)

Take Care of Your Family

But those who won't care for their relatives, especially those in their own household, have denied the true faith. Such people are worse than unbelievers (1 Timothy 5:8). (Show me a leader that does not take care of their family or relatives, and I will show you a leader that will never genuinely and selflessly love those they lead. A leader's care for their family is indicative of how they will care for their professional family. It all stems from the character of the leader. This is more than just providing a home and furnishings. It is moments of affection, emotions, respect, and faithfulness to those God has blessed your life with as a family. Great husbands, wives, dads, and moms are the starting point for becoming great leaders. It all starts at home!)

Show Compassion and Concern for Others

You must clothe yourselves with tenderhearted mercy, kindness, humility, gentleness, and patience. Make allowance for each other's faults and forgive anyone who offends you. (There is nothing else needed here. God has told us exactly how to lead with compassion in his Scripture. His Word says we must do it!)

Walk Your Leadership, Don't Talk It

> ***Talk is cheap, like daydreams and other useless activities.*** (Ecclesiastes 5:7).
>
> ***You can identify fools just by the way they walk down the street!*** (Ecclesiastes 10:3)
>
> ***Let's not merely say that we love each other; let us show the truth by our actions. Our actions will show that we belong to the truth.*** (1 John 3:18–19)

(A leader's walk speaks louder than any words they will ever say. I love the saying by poet Ralph Waldo Emerson: "*What you do speaks so loudly that I cannot hear what you say.*" Walking your leadership visualizes the correct values, ethics, and motivations for emulating to those you lead. It matters less what a leader says and more what leaders do. Talking is important, but walking the talk speaks exponentially louder. If someone asked a person, you lead, "What is their leader's greatest contribution to the organization or themselves?" Would they say it was something you said or something you did? A leader's actions inspire, their words intrigue us to wonder. Tell me something, and you leave me suspect of you; show me something by your walk, and I now know who you are!)

Be a Good Listener

You must be quick to listen, slow to speak, and slow to get angry (James 1:19). (This one can be tough to do in today's fast-paced work environment. It is even hard to do in our homes now with technology vying for our time and attention. A leader must be disciplined to practice good listening. Without listening, we fail to learn what others are trying to say to us. Stopping what we are doing and removing any distractions from our environment to listen requires effort. Still, this effort is an investment in our relationships with those we lead. As a leader, this investment will provide huge returns in the depth of the trust those we lead will have in us. Listening says you care about what others have to say. Listening says that what others have to say is important to you. Listening says your opinion, thoughts, and suggestions are valued and vital to the organization. Others see listening as "You are in this for them!"

Always Self-Improving

> ***All Scripture is inspired by God and is useful to teach us what is true and to make us realize what is wrong in our lives. It corrects us when we are wrong and teaches us to do what is right. God uses it to prepare and equip his people to do every good work.*** (2 Timothy 3:16–17)

> ***Keep putting into practice all you learned and received from me—everything you heard from me and saw me doing.*** (Philippians 4:9)

> ***The shepherds of my people have lost their senses. They no longer seek wisdom from the LORD. Therefore, they fail completely, and their flocks are scattered.*** (Jeremiah 10:21)

The LORD preserves those with knowledge, but he ruins the plans of the treacherous (Proverbs 22:12). (When a plant stops receiving water, it eventually dies. When a leader stops self-improving, their leadership influential effectiveness diminishes greatly. With today's technological advancements in the workplace, generational workforce variances, cultural variances, and a competing globalized economy, leaders must always seek to self-improve their understanding of how to influence a diverse workforce under challenging conditions. When a leader is reluctant to self-improve, they will not remain relevant in today's fast transforming workplace for long. Always be striving to grow in knowledge. Time to hit the books, complete another workshop, embrace another webinar, and evolve into a leader equipped for today's ever-mutating workplace environment.)

Always Prepared for Both the Knowns and the Unknowns of Tomorrow

> ***Be on guard. Stand firm in the faith. Be courageous. Be strong. And do everything with love.*** (1 Corinthians 16:13)

> ***Stay alert! Watch out for your great enemy, the devil. He prowls around like a roaring lion, looking for someone to devour.*** (1 Peter 5:8)

> ***We can make our plans, but the LORD determines our steps.*** (Proverbs 16:9)

(Leaders are responsible for preparing organizations for the future; they plan for the future through their process of strategic planning. Leaders use strategic foresight as a tool in analyzing external trends within their market industry to determine tomorrow's societal needs and applications of their products and services. Leaders also prepare organizations for potential catastrophic events. By emplacing mitigating countermeasures today to survive tomorrow's catastrophes within their market industry, leaders promote resiliency. Preparation today readies an organization for tomorrow's challenges. Be prepared!)

Adhere to Clothing/Equipment Standards

Jesus instructs the disciples, ***"Take nothing for your journey," he instructed them. "Don't take a walking stick, a traveler's bag, food, money, or even a change of clothes*** (Luke 9:3). (Jesus's instructions for His disciples required them to go out equipped in the same way he went about His work of ministry, totally trusting in God to provide for their needs. Today, organizations provide their workforce with uniforms, protective gear, and equipment to perform their work safely and efficiently. These items provided, especially safety equipment, are nonnegotiable in wear and use. With societies current Covid-19 pandemic, personal face masks to cover the mouth and nose are mandated as a safety precaution in preventing the spread of the disease for everyone. This provides an excellent example for leading by example. Leaders are as susceptible as everyone else in contracting Covid-19. However, leaders are still seen on television and in the workplace not wearing their masks. These leaders are only concerned with their outward appearance, not the message of a double standard they project to those they lead. Suppose it is an organizational or societal requirement to wear a protective item. In that case, leaders have the responsibility of leading by example. Wear what you require others to wear (properly), they are being led by your example!)

The higher your position of leadership, the greater impact your leading by example sets for others. Throughout my military career, the mantra "lead by example" is drilled into every leader's mind-set. Perhaps the most outstanding example I observed was witnessed during my eleven years of leading in the 82nd Airborne Division at Fort Bragg, North Carolina. The Division standard for physical training required every Paratrooper to conduct organizationally led physical training five days a week from 0600 to 0730. Regardless of the weather, everyone had to do physical exercise during this period, Monday through Friday.

On Fort Bragg, the main street for our organization to conduct physical training on and adjacent to was Ardennes Street. Alongside and on Ardennes Street every weekday morning were fourteen thousand paratroopers doing all kinds of grueling physical activity and running countless miles. Ardennes Street and several coinciding roads were blocked off from all vehicle traffic during this time, providing miles of pavement for organizations to safely run and call cadence.

Here is where I witnessed a "leading by example" that emphasized to me more than anything else I had seen how leaders "lead by example." The 82nd Airborne Division Commander is a Two-Star General Officer (Major General). His standard for every Paratrooper to conduct physical training five days a week from 0600 to 0730 applied to himself also.

Every weekday morning, regardless of the weather, you would always see the Division Commander doing physical training while running up and down Ardennes Street. He had a big office. He had the phone on his desk that was a direct line to the Pentagon. He commanded an organization that could be anywhere in the world in eighteen hours. He had an entourage of staff and an aide to get him whatever he needed. But the same thing he required of every Paratrooper in the organization, he also did. This was when it hit me more than ever; positions of leadership don't bring privilege. Positions of leadership bring the nonnegotiable responsibility of leading by example. What message is your leading by example projecting to those you lead?

I want to ask you a question to emphasize how much God wants you and me to lead by example. If you were told by a medical professional that you had less than twenty-four hours to live based on every indicator for life expectancy. What would you do? I don't even know what I would do with only twenty-four hours left to live. Still, I am pretty sure it would embody some act driven by my natural human behaviors to be selfish with my last hours of life. But with less than twenty-four hours to live, on his last evening physically alive, Jesus chose to lead by example, yet once again.

John 13:4–5 tells us that Jesus ***got up from the table, took off his robe, wrapped a towel around his waist, and poured water into a basin. Then he began to wash the disciples' feet, drying them with the towel he had around him.***

> ***After washing their feet, he put on his robe again and sat down and asked, "Do you understand what I was doing? You call me 'Teacher' and 'Lord,' and you are right, because that's what I am. And since I, your Lord and Teacher, have washed your feet, you ought to wash each other's feet. I have given you an example to follow. Do as I have done to you."*** (John 13:12–15)

We need to place "washing their feet" in its comparative context. There were no paved or improved walking surfaces in the days of Jesus's ministry here on earth. People wore leather sandals. Every step was taken in the dusty and dirty soils and sands of the middle eastern topography. After a day's travel by walking everywhere they went, a person's feet would be covered in sweat and dirt, filthy. The wealthy people of the day would have servants take care of them. The lowliest of their servants washed the master's feet.

When Jesus, the Son of God, washed his disciple's feet and stated in John 13:15, ***"I have given you an example to follow. Do as I have done to you."*** He was leading by example one last time. Jesus's actions of washing the disciple's feet symbolized that no matter how "high" and "mighty" a person's position in leadership and authority, they are to serve others humbly. Regardless of his majestic power, Jesus assumed the role of being the lowliest servant of their time to those he led. In doing so, Jesus led by example, caring more for others than himself, even when he knew he would be crucified on a Cross within the next twenty-four hours.

> ***Keep putting into practice all you have learned and received from me—everything you heard from me and saw me doing*** (Philippians 4:9).

Reflection Time

What kind of example does your talk set for others to emulate?

What kind of example does your walk set for others to copy?

What kind of example does your heart make for others to come to when they are in need?

PART 6

Who You Are as a Person Is Who You Are as a Leader!

Fix your thoughts on what is true, and honorable, and right, and pure, and lovely, and admirable. Think about things that are excellent and worthy of praise. (Philippians 4:8)

Being Ethical

Understanding Ethics

Before delving into identifying the attributes of ethical leadership, we must understand what ethics are and what forms the foundation for one's ethics. A person or a leader's ethics consist of the moral principles of right and wrong, which govern an individual or a society's behaviors. Ethics are philosophical. They reside within every individual's viewpoint relative to such variables as their cultural background, religious beliefs, societal norms, and other influencers.

Ethics comes from the Greek word *ethos,* which represents a person's customs or character. Ethos focuses on construing and assigning moral essentials and personal conduct, proposing proper and improper ways of acting in behavior. The pursuit of understanding ethics began being recorded by Socrates (469–399 BC). Socrates introduced the micro (person) study of ethics and believed that knowing the difference between right or wrong required an individual to act correctly. Following Socrates, Aristotle (384–322 BC) explored ethics at the macro (societal) level and believed an individual's actions impact others. Excluding where someone is from, their religious views, or whatever they think is their unique perspective on things. Ethics focuses on what is considered morally right for every person.

> ***He will rule with mercy and truth. He will always do what is just and be eager to do what is right*** (Isaiah 16:5).

Ethics reveal themselves due to the mixture of a person's values, beliefs, morals, and virtue. As Ethics are philosophical and subject to varied definitions, people present differing opinions of what ethics are. Perhaps it would be simpler to state what Ethics is **not**:

- Ethics are **not** how someone feels.
- Ethics are **not** norms from cultures or societies.
- Ethics is **not** science. There is no systematically organized body of knowledge on Ethics.
- Ethics are **not** based on following a particular religion or faith.
- Ethics are **not** merely obeying the laws of man.

Ethics represent the humanly accepted standards of behavior that inform us how people should act within different roles in life (parent, father, mother, friend, leader, co-worker.) The study of Ethics entails more than whether a person chooses right or wrong; it involves understanding why individuals' decisions are thought to be right or wrong. When we ask ourselves, "Why are ethics important?" Ethics attempt to establish a qualitative standard of acceptable behaviors for individuals and societies. Society's insistence on ethical conduct between individuals, private and public organizations, and nation-states in today's globalized community attempts to influence all parties toward choosing right over wrong actions in behavior. Ethics prevent societal chaos and try to keep human behaviors within acceptable and anticipated tolerances of proper conduct. Ultimately, ethical behavior is "good and right behavior."

> ***For we are each responsible for our own conduct*** (Galatians 6:5).

However, how does a person or leader form in their minds and present in their actions, "good behavior"? We need to identify the elements required in developing the foundation of ethics. When building a structure to be used as a home, office building, entertainment facility, or any facility expected to shelter and protect individuals or personal property, the first and most important requirement is a solid foundation. Underneath the "seen" exterior and interior is the foundation, the part that solidifies the facility's ability to stand firm. The foundation's strength is a significant factor in a facility's durability, strength, and longevity. An individual or society's ethical foundation is its values, beliefs, morals, and virtues, which determine their ethical durability, moral strength, and ethical longevity. This proper foundation's strength in character will eventually reveal the individuals or society's morality.

Ethical Foundation (Values, Beliefs, Morals, Virtue)

> ***I will be careful to live a blameless life—when will you come to help me? I will lead a life of integrity in my own home. I will refuse to look at anything vile and vulgar. I hate all who deal crookedly; I will have nothing to do with them. I will reject perverse ideas and stay away from evil. I will not tolerate people who slander their neighbors. I will not endure conceit and pride. I will search for faithful people to be my companions. Only those who are above reproach will be allowed to serve me. I will not***

allow deceivers to serve in my house, and liars will not stay in my presence. (Psalm 101:2–7)

- *Values*

Values are what we deem to be essential and meaningful attributes for conducting our lives. Values determine the choices and actions we will take in different situations. Based on an individual's values, their take on what is good or bad or what is right or wrong will guide their actions and choices. Individuals are not born with their values; they are cultivated along a person's life journey. Values are formed and influenced by the physical and social environments surrounding an individual.

Values play a central and significant role in an individual's decision making. Ask a person the simple question, "What is important to you, what do you value in life?" A person may say they value things such as happiness, good health, honesty, salvation, courage, family, success at work, love, marriage, relationships, being a good person, integrity, and a multitude of others. These values represent an individual's values, what is essential in their life and most likely in the lives of those they seek to associate themselves with. Throughout life, a person, an experience, family, religious affiliation, schools attended, cultural beliefs, or traditions have influenced what these values are to each person.

Personal values will lend toward a person's decision making when confronted with a right or wrong ethical dilemma. A person who values their health will make right choices for their health (deciding **no** to illicit drugs). A person who values family or marriage will choose to refrain from conduct that would hurt their family or marriage (deciding **no** to inappropriate personal relationships). A person who values honesty will answer questions with a genuine honesty first thought process (deciding there is only one answer, the honest one). Good values establish ethically repetitive practices for people when confronted with personal or professional dilemmas.

Values are those things a person believes are essential to the way they live and work. Values help determine one's priorities and help a person surmise if their life is turning out the way they want it to be. Somebody cannot physically see values, but a person can surely see the results of a value-based decision. Value-based behaviors represent what is seen as the consistent behaviors of an individual. For example, the US Army receives civilian recruits with their preformed individual values. However, new Army recruits are immersed in the Army's Values required of soldiers from day one. Values represent all soldiers' desired consistent behaviors (loyalty, duty, respect, selfless service, honor, integrity, and personal courage). Army Bases place placards throughout their massive installations with signs on streetlights, store entrances, in gymnasiums, in dining facilities, and even on a tag to wear around a soldier's neck along with their identification tags for constantly ingraining in soldiers the Army Values (Figure 1).

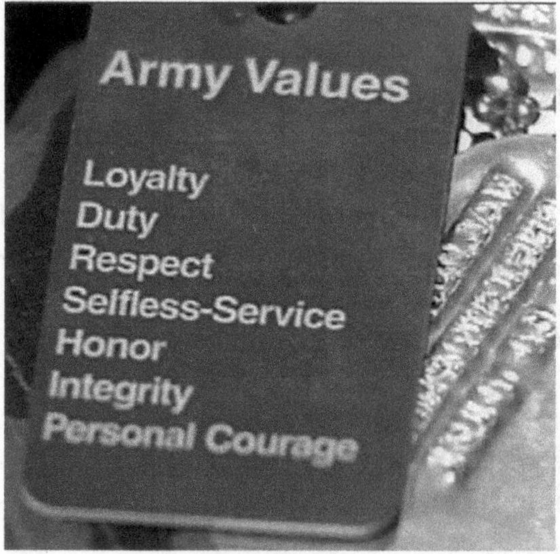

Figure 1: Army Values Tag

A person's Values, once formed, are not set in stone. A person's Values may change along life's twist and turns produced by relationships ups and downs, changing geographical living locations, changing religious orientation, employment opportunities, and societal influencers. Regardless if they change, it is essential to know that a person's Values are reflected by their decisions and actions, right or wrong. Values, which represent the priorities and things necessary to attain a person's happiness, may change with life's circumstances (children, health concerns, family crisis, career status, financial situation). Regardless of what a person's Values are, they will be central to an individual's choice between right or wrong. Values guide a person's behavior, instilling, and acting on the right Values promotes ethical (right) behaviors.

- *Beliefs*

> ***Supplement your faith with a generous provision of moral excellence, and moral excellence with knowledge, and knowledge with self-control, and self-control with patient endurance, and patient endurance with godliness, and godliness with brotherly affection, and brotherly affection with love for everyone. The more you grow like this, the more productive and useful you will be in your knowledge of our Lord Jesus Christ.*** (2 Peter 1:5–8)

Our Beliefs are what we as an individual, consider to be the truth. As Christian's, we believe that the Holy Bible's Words are God's Truth. In politics, a person that identifies with a particular political party believes what that party stands for to be the correct way to govern a society. Like a person's Values, Beliefs are personal, in that not everyone else shares the same ones. A person may believe that a judicial death penalty is an acceptable form of punishment for convicted murderers.

In contrast, another person may not believe in killing any person, regardless of their crimes. (Some beliefs of people are so firmly and intensely in opposition to others' that people have waged war against one another in opposition (Civil War, WWII Nazis)). People have deep beliefs that they have sacrificed themselves in support of their views, as was revealed on September 11, 2001. On this date, one group of individuals with their particular radical beliefs waged war against different beliefs, political beliefs, and religious beliefs. Their beliefs are so strong that their war still wages on today in the Middle East.

Beliefs impact every area of an individual's personal and societal life. Once a person forms a Belief in something, it becomes ingrained in their psychological makeup. Beliefs are strong influencers revealed in our words and behaviors. Beliefs influence a person's Values, or their Beliefs cultivate a person's Values. Either way, it is stated, what a person believes in, will be revealed in their Values, which will significantly influence a person's behavior. Beliefs become a filter for how a person interprets and experiences things occurring around them and in the world at large. These beliefs will influence the behaviors of action and reaction. Beliefs can be so strong that they blind a person's mind from contemplating the potential consequences of wrong choices and actions. Choosing the right or improper behavioral action or reaction based on a person's Beliefs will be judged by others as ethical or unethical.

- *Morals*

> ***Oh the joys of those who do not follow the advice of the wicked, or stand around with sinners, or join in with mockers. But they delight in the law of the LORD, meditating on it day and night. They are like trees planted along the riverbank, bearing fruit each season. Their leaves never wither, and they prosper in all they do.*** (Psalm 1:1–3)

> ***Supplement your faith with a generous provision of moral excellence, and moral excellence with knowledge, and knowledge with self-control, and self-control with patient endurance, and patient endurance with godliness, and godliness with brotherly affection, and brotherly affection with love for everyone. The more you grow like this, the more productive and useful you will be in your knowledge of our Lord Jesus Christ.*** (2 Peter 1:5–8)

A person's behavior, which reflects their acceptable standard of conduct, reveals a person's morals. These are the manifestation of actions extracted from individual Values and Beliefs. When discussing morals, we speak of a person's standards of behavior or beliefs concerning what is and is not acceptable for them to do. Morals are more profound than the physical action of doing what is right. Morals represent an individual's internal wiring that willingly and instinctively selects what their behavior will be. Os Guinness eloquently states, "To be 'moral' does not mean to be 'good' but to exercise one's freedom and responsibility in choosing between good and evil."[1] A moral person is expected to embrace honesty, respect others and their property, display courage, be reliable, and be trustworthy.

Morals implore a person to react appropriately regardless of the situation. Morals reflect what a person truly desires to do when confronted with life's circumstances and decisions. Faced with a bad situation, they may say or think, "This goes against everything I believe in." In other words, this dire situation is morally wrong with them. This would imply that a person's morals manifest their subconscious Values and Beliefs, which propels their physical actions and reactions to circumstances encountered.

A leader's awareness of their morals serves in their ethical decision-making process, specifically when weighing the alternatives for the correct and proper course of action to be applied to a given predicament. A leader's strong moral awareness indicates the leader is conscious of leading and serving ethically for the individuals, organizations, and societies they lead. Doing the right thing is vital to the leader with ethical understanding. A leader with moral awareness is selflessly aware of morality's ever-increasing impact on society as a whole.

> *The foundations of our national policy will be laid in the pure and immutable principles of private morality. (US President* George Washington)

- *Virtue*

> ***Do things in such a way that everyone can see you are honorable. Do all that you can to live in peace with everyone*** (Romans 12:17–18).

Virtues represent a person's natural tendency to be a good person. Not only is doing right a natural tendency for a virtuous person, but they also intend to do good. Virtue is derived from the Greek word *arete*, meaning the aggregate of a person's quality. Throughout Scripture in the Holy Bible, specifically in books found in the New Testament, the Virtuous attributes every person should embody are revealed: Humility/Meekness, Forgiveness, Patience, Hope, Courage/Faith, Generosity, Sympathy/Compassion, Love, Honesty, Gentleness, Kindness, Self-control, and Joy.

Virtues are learned and developed. They can become a habit of anyone; it is never too late to increase one's virtue at any age. Virtues are learned, then developed by practicing and making them a habit of second nature. Transforming the mind from one of impulsive decisions or reactions that result in decisions later deemed as contradictory to one's former character can be achieved, but it must become a habit to become second nature. Deciding to live a life based on God's Word or lead according to God's Word requires transforming our Virtues from a secular world's importance to God's prerogative. ***Don't copy the behavior and customs of this world, but let God transform you into a new person by changing the way you think. Then you will learn to know God's will for you, which is good and pleasing and perfect*** (Romans 12:2).

Virtue is revealed by consistent ethical behavior once a virtuous habit is formed, even under duress or stressful circumstances. Virtue becomes a person's backbone when life's challenging circumstances arise. Their virtues source a person's actions, and their actions reveal their virtues. Virtues are good works, which is revealed in their consistently doing the right thing for the virtuous person. Ultimately, virtues are the underlying framework of a person's character.

Virtues are centric to a person's character. When practicing virtues, the person's virtues become characteristics they are known for, thereby revealing their real character. How vital are virtues to having good character? Virtues are an absolute imperative for the development and sustainment of good character. Place a person or a leader under stress in their decision-making, and their Virtues will be revealed in the decision made.

Leading Ethically

> ***Now listen! Today I am giving you a choice between life and death, between prosperity and disaster For I command you this day to love the LORD your God and to keep his commands, decrees, and regulations by walking in his ways. If you do this, you will live and multiply, and the LORD your God will bless you and the land you are about to enter and occupy.*** (Deuteronomy 30:15–16)

Ask one hundred people their definition of leadership. You will more than likely receive one hundred similar, while different descriptions of their interpretation and expectations of leadership. We will forego any attempts at defining leadership at this time. Instead, we will discuss what has become leadership's increasingly significant and most publicized challenge, ethical leadership. The mantle of leadership comes with its most significant never-ending challenge, moral responsibility. For the leader, ethical leadership is one of the most immense and considerable leadership challenges they will encounter every single day they lead. Ultimately, ethical leadership requires selfless leadership. Leadership is a special relationship, one created by authoritatively empowering an individual responsible for training, equipping, and caring for other people. Ethical leadership creates the all-important relationship bond of trust between the leader and those they serve and lead.

What Ethical Leadership Is

> ***Live clean, innocent lives as children of God, shining like bright lights in a world full of crooked and perverse people*** (Philippians 2:15).

Ethical leadership is the appropriate behavior or the right behavior by leaders for and toward followers and the organization they serve. The ethical leader embodies an ethical demeanor; it is woven into who the leader is as a person. The good virtues, values, and morals of an ethical leader are revealed in their ethical behavior. The decisions leaders make, and their reactions to dilemmas are established within their ethics. The social system's needs in which a leader operates plays a strong role in determining the leaders' moral actions. What is ethically tolerable to society must reside in the ethical mind-set when incurring the moral dilemmas faced in leadership.

To better understand what ethical leadership is, we must identify the characteristics and principles of ethical leadership, revealing a clearer picture. Ethical leaders embody and display humility, selflessness, integrity, reliability, fairness, respectfulness, competence, personal courage, and a natural inclination for encouraging others. Each of these characteristics represents an outwardly focused leader who is selfless and acts in ways that build relationships based on trust and mutual respect. Ethical leadership is characterized by leaders who contemplate and understand that today's decisions, actions, and behaviors represent long-term benefits or potentially devastating ramifications. Ethical leaders do the right thing for others. Ethical leadership builds the all too important trust bond by listening, caring about others' interests, being fair, being honest, and being attentive to others' needs. The characteristics and principles of ethical leadership are exposed through the consistent selflessness exhibited by the ethical leader.

Ethical leadership refuses to focus on the leader in the mirror. The follower's needs and doing the right thing by the organization become the ethical leader's focus. If being ethical is doing the right thing, then ethical leadership implies leaders must do the right thing by and for those they serve and lead. Ethical leadership is a selfless example for emulating and breeds strength in its followers, and the organization through the strong relationship and trust created.

The Actions of Ethical Leadership

> ***If someone aspires to be an elder, he desires an honorable position. So an elder must be a man who is above reproach. He must be faithful to his wife. He must exercise self-control, live wisely, and have a good reputation. He must be able to teach. He must not be a heavy drinker or be violent. He must be gentle, not quarrelsome, and not love money*** (1 Timothy 3:1–5).

The modern-day application of 1 Timothy 3:1–5 in ethical leadership can be interpreted as: If a person aspires to be a leader, they desire a position of honor. A leader must be a person who is above reproach. They must be faithful to others. They must exercise self-control, live wisely, and have a good reputation. They must be able to teach. They must be disciplined and able to refrain from self-destructive or violent behaviors. They must be gentle, not argumentative, and love serving people over serving money.

Aspiring to be an ethical person can be challenging in itself, but what about the leader presented with the moral dilemmas encountered while attempting to meet the needs and demands of followers and the organization? The challenge to remain ethical as a leader is mitigated by the leader's moral inclinations. Ethical leadership requires a leader to listen to what their morals tell them is the right thing to do in a given dilemma. The ethical leader possesses and displays Altruistic behaviors. Ethical leader's actions represent a concern for others' interests, over and before concern for their self-interest.

An ethical leader's activities are intended as ones of service to those they serve and lead and their organization. Ethical activities include a leader's ethical conduct even when outside of their professional leadership role. Every action can ultimately impact their professional lives. The ethical leader conducts themselves in alignment with their espoused values (they walk the talk). Ethical leaders place personal risk last, while mission accomplishment and success of their followers and the organization comes first. Ethical leaders mentor and coach those they serve and lead toward more significant individual achievements. They want to see their follower's goals met.

Ethical leaders provide others with information on problems and issues as they present themselves, keeping everyone on the same page. Ethical leaders create a fair and balanced system for addressing the needs of all stakeholders. Ethical leaders expect and enforce ethical behavior from those they serve. Ethical leaders' standard operating actions pursue honesty, trustworthiness, integrity, remaining credible and proficient, and courageously strong when faced with moral and ethical challenges.

Ethical leaders practice self-control. They are methodical in assessing the ethical implications their words and actions will convey. While the ethical leader's focus is outward toward others, their only time of seeing the person in the mirror comes when they are self-assessing their needs for becoming more of what those they serve and lead require from them. No leader has ever "arrived," the ethical leader seeks daily to improve morally as a person and as a leader.

The Importance of Ethical Leadership

> ***Those who are honest and fair, who refuse to profit by fraud, who stay far away from bribes, who refuse to listen to those who plot murder, who shut their eyes to all enticement to do wrong—these are the ones who will dwell on high.*** (Isaiah 33:15–16)

> ***God blesses those who patiently endure testing and temptation.*** (James 1:12)

Ethical leadership sets the tone, establishes the moral norm, and reflects a society's ethical behavior acceptable tolerances. Ethical leadership subliminally empowers people to do the right thing. Leadership sits at the top. A leader's actions are on full display for those they serve and lead to view, judge, and emulate. A leader's ethical behavior provides followers with reassurances. Corporate mergers, the economy's globalization, and fluctuating job markets create enough stressful concerns for people. Believing in their leadership's genuine concern resulting from ethical leadership allows the follower to focus on doing the best job possible for the organization.

Ethical leadership behavior evokes trust from those they lead and their superiors, empowering them to accomplish objectives within time and resource constraints. Ethical leadership behavior permeates throughout those being led and the organization, instilling a sense of knowing there is competent and empathetic leadership at the helm. Ethical leadership empowers followers to feel comfortable in their jobs, garnering loyalty and psychological safety.

> ***So let's not get tired of doing what is good. At just the right time we will reap a harvest of blessing if we don't give up*** (Galatians 6:9).

Ethical leadership establishes the acceptable behavioral norms within the workforce and which behaviors are valued for career advancement within the organization. Perhaps the most crucial result produced by ethical leadership is the bond of trust followers have with their leadership and the organization. Trust enhances the quality of life for those they serve and lead, their families, and society outside of the organization. It all adds up to the revelation of a leader's Character!

> ***Look straight ahead and fix your eyes on what lies before you. Mark out a straight path for your feet; stay on the safe path. Don't get sidetracked; keep your feet from following evil*** (Proverbs 4:25–27).

In leading, every day will present dilemmas and distractions. These dilemmas and distractions can cause a leader to lose their ethical focus. Every leader should have their sights on the bigger picture toward leading and, most importantly, life success. When you are taking your eyes off the objective, you place yourself in danger of becoming sidetracked and off course. The evil one knows our weaknesses and ethical frailty as a person and leader. Any distraction that can be used to take you off the path God has you on in leading can not only take you on a detour route; it can eventually make you miss your objective of success. Keep your eyes straight ahead. Know your moral weaknesses and avoid their pitfalls. God has a beautiful plan for your leadership. Fix your eyes on leading His way, and stay on the path He has provided for your success.

Reflection Time

Are you okay with bending the rules a bit to get things done?

How about those you serve and lead. Is it okay for them to bend the rules to get things done?

Would you describe yourself as Ethical or Unethical? You are either one or the other. Which would those you serve and lead say when asked this question about you? You are either one or the other. There are no part-time ethical leaders.

---

[1] Os Guinness, The Call: Finding and Fulfilling the Central Purpose of Your Life (Nashville: W Publishing Group, 2003), 85.

Character Matters

> ***The LORD said, "The LORD doesn't see things the way you see them. People judge by outward appearance, but the LORD looks at the heart"*** (1 Samuel 16:7).

The revelation of personal values, beliefs, virtues, and morals is in a person's Character, and a person's Character reveals their heart. When we want to know the true essence of a person, watch for their Character's revelation. What a person values, what a person believes, what a person's chronic human nature is, and their moral fortitude reveals their Character. Character itself is not defined as "good or bad." It merely reveals who the individual is on the inside. Every person characteristically has either a "good or bad" heart.

Fear God and obey his commands, for this is everyone's duty. God will judge us for everything we do, including every secret thing, whether good or bad (Ecclesiastes 12:13–14). Secrets are like a person's Character. There are good secrets like the surprise birthday party or the intelligence secrets that help protect those being protected. Then there are the bad secrets. These are the actions or words of a convicted heart. Sinister secrets are used to hide selfish, illegal, or inappropriate behaviors that a person tries to prevent others from knowing. Ultimately, we have no secrets from God; He knows and sees all. Our thoughts and motives may be kept secret from others, but God knows them. Bad secrets represent the fear of being exposed. Good secrets represent joy when they are revealed. Good Character is revealed in a person who only keeps good secrets. Bad Character creates a life filled with sinister secrets. God knows both, and sooner or later, those you serve and lead will know which kind of secrets you are filled with also.

Character is not what we see of ourselves; Character is what is seen by others when they observe our actions. Os Guinness's wonderful book, *The Call*, contends a person's Character "is the essential 'stuff' he or she is made of, the inner reality in which thoughts, speech, decisions, behavior, and relations are rooted."[1] Character is revealed by a person's walk throughout their life, depicting the 'big picture' of who a person is. A person's character is who a person is at their core. A person's Character will determine their actions, and by their actions, their Character is revealed.

A person's prevalent tendencies determine Character. Not based on remote instances of uncharacteristic behavior, which everyone is potentially susceptible to displaying. No matter how composed we present ourselves, circumstances can "push our buttons" for uncharacteristic emotions and actions. I don't particularly appreciate it, but competition used to bring out a side of me I did not like. I still cannot watch my favorite professional football team play without uncharacteristic comments oriented toward the coaches and players spewing from my mouth. I am not too fond of this side of myself. If only they would win every game, I might get better (I WISH!). From youth throughout adulthood, a person learns, practices, and embodies their ethical principles. Those ethics are expressed in their Character. The great thing about Character is it can evolve toward a better Character. I am hoping when I finally grow up, I will grow out of the immaturity of my uncharacteristic displays toward my favorite football team (it is a challenge!!).

A person's Character conveys to others their level of trustworthiness, honesty, sincerity, reliability, self-discipline, and whether or not they should be associated with. Simply because a person is good at their occupation does not necessarily imply they have a good character. We see people in society celebrated as celebrities or brilliant and wealthy entrepreneurs, but this in no way signifies they have the Character or heart of good morals in life. Have you met a celebrated person you were excited to meet and their real character ruined all of your anticipated expectations of the persons portrayed reputation upon meeting them? ***A good reputation is more valuable than costly perfume*** (Ecclesiastes 7:1). ***Choose a good reputation over great riches; being held in high esteem is better than silver or gold*** (Proverbs 22:1).

Character building is one that must be cultivated and developed throughout one's life. No person is born with a prescribed and established Character. Each person constructs their own unique and individual Character; their Character development begins from their youth. ***Even children are known by the way they act, whether their conduct is pure, and whether it is right*** (Proverbs 20:11). Without contemplating what we want our Character to be, our initial behaviors play a crucial role in our Character as a young person. Character development is influenced by our choices and actions powered by our values, morals, beliefs, and virtues.

As a person grows and matures into becoming an adult, their values often change and evolve. The person has developed through education, experiencing different societal and cultural influencers, and grounding their beliefs in particular religious' faith. A person's initial Character may have aligned initially with their former values, beliefs, and morals. Still, they are no longer the person they were before. As a person matures and as social environments change, a person's motives evolve with newly encountered circumstances around them. How does a person shape their Character to their new values, beliefs, and morals? People require intestinal fortitude and strength of personal courage, and sincere willingness to fortify and embody their developing Character. ***We can rejoice, too, when we run into problems and trials, for we know that they help us develop endurance. And endurance develops strength of character, and character strengthens our confident hope of salvation*** (Romans 5:3–4).

Character begins with an individual thought. Good thoughts promote good intentions toward right actions. Bad thoughts promote bad choices carried out in wrong actions. A person's thoughts, when acted on, ultimately reveals their Character. Jesus describes what bad character entails and who is the promoter of bad character in John 8:44, ***"For you are the children of your father the devil, and you love to do the evil things he does. He was a murderer from the beginning. He has always hated the truth, because there is no truth in him. When he lies, it is consistent with his character; for he is a liar and the father of lies."*** The measures derived from the nature of a person's Character determine where they will eventually find themselves and their destiny. Character is the reflection of a person's chronic personality and will determine a person's future to come.

> Sew a thought, reap a deed.
> Sew a deed, reap a habit.
> Sew a habit, reap a Character.
> Sew a character, reap a destiny.

Everyone needs to understand. Character is not a permanent branding. Over time, people can grow and enhance their Character to who they strive to be, someone they can respect and look at in the mirror without regret and shame. ***My old self has been crucified with Christ. It is no longer I who live, but Christ lives in me*** (Galatians 2:20). Character represents the equation's total: Values + Beliefs + Virtue's = Morals, which are revealed in a person's Character. Character shows who a person is on the inside. Their actions reflect their inside truth, ultimately determining a person's destiny in life. Os Guinness ponders,

> *In what sense is character destiny? Have we faced up to the consequences of our own personality and character? To what extent are we determined by heredity, environment, body, chemistry, instincts, social pressures, and the forces of the universe?*[2]

When a leader must make a high-pressure decision, that moment will reveal the ethical nature of the leader and the real essence of their Character. A leader's ethics are the foundation, the bedrock of what will be revealed in their Character. At a leader's most stressful moment, the real person presents itself, showing the leader's real Character.

> *Character cannot be developed in ease and quiet. Only through experience of trial and suffering can the soul be strengthened, vision cleared, ambition inspired, and success achieved.* (Helen Keller)

When a person dies, people don't eulogize them by their accomplishments or titles and positions of high esteem held in life. They don't list degrees earned, financial wealth achieved, intellect, or list all the things a person would list on their resume as capabilities and qualifications. A person is eulogized for the Character of their heart revealed over their lifetime. Graveyard headstones never say, "Here lays a person that worked hard and made a lot of money." They say things like "Beloved Father and Grandfather," "Beloved Mother and Grandmother," "In Loving Memory," or "A Beloved Friend." Headstones present snapshots of how a person's Character impacted the lives of the people closest to them.

A few months before my retirement from the military, my father passed away. As I eulogized him at his funeral, I spoke of the things which stood out about him in life. I spoke of his good heart; that he always believed in the best in other people; his compassion for others in need; his honesty; his selflessness; his unmovable integrity; how great a father, husband, son, brother, grandfather, uncle, and friend he was in life; his humble demeanor; his loyalty; his gentleness; his patience; and his generosity to those in need.

As I sat back down for others to speak, I realized who my father was in his Character, was not me. Tears came flowing out of my eyes as my heart endured God's conviction on me. Everything in my life changed at that moment. I knew from that moment forward my Character had to change. I was not the man my father was, and I realized that all that he was, was everything I wanted to be. At that moment, I reestablished my faith and committed to transforming my Character. I had lived a life for what this world told me was "success." Still, I realized that my father genuinely knew what success is, being a person of impeccable Character. ***Don't copy the behavior and customs of his world, but let God transform you into a new person by changing the way you think. Then you will learn to know God's will for you, which is good and pleasing and perfect*** (Romans 12:2).

In Matthew 5:48 Jesus says, "***But you are to be perfect, even as your Father in heaven is perfect.***" Perfection is a quest for many, attained by only one. Jesus's Character was filled with what we know as the Fruit of the Spirit. ***But the Holy Spirit produces this kind of fruit in our lives: love, joy, peace, patience, kindness, goodness, faithfulness, gentleness, and self-control. There is no law against these things!*** (Galatians 5:22–23). When our Character is revealed as loving, joyful in attitude, patient with others, we are kind, good, faithful, gentle, and self-controlled. We are displaying Jesus's Character through ourselves. No matter how a leader tries to portray themselves to those they serve and lead, their Character reveals their heart's agenda. Let the Fruit of the Spirit become your Character, and you will have found what perfection consists of in living life and leading others.

Developing or refining our Character away from this world's version of what equates to "success" is a tough and challenging endeavor. Today's media platforms are saturated with images of what the world says represent success. We ingest through our eye's images designed to provoke greed, lust, and otherworldly desires. ***For the world offers only a craving for physical pleasure, a craving for everything we see, and pride in our achievements and possessions. These are not from the Father but are from this world*** (1 John 2:16). Character transformation is a daily endeavor. Through reading and meditating on God's Word, placing our eye's on God's Truth and not this world's lies, our Character evolves. ***Fix your thoughts on what is true, and honorable, and right, and pure, and lovely, and***

admirable. Think about things that are excellent and worthy of praise (Philippians 4:8).

> *When wealth is lost, nothing is lost. When health is lost, something is lost. When Character is lost, everything is lost.* (Dr. Billy Graham)

Serving and leading others will present challenges to every leader's Character. The mantle of leadership exposes a leader to the ethical dilemmas more extraordinary in consequence than any other walk of life. This is why being a leader requires people of proven good Character. Leaders with good Character refrain from impulsive, approval-seeking decisions. Instead, a leader of good Character, contemplates and vets their decision-making through their ethical principles and makes decisions that result in remaining true to their Character. Being true to your Character, and leading with your heart engaged in decision-making, carries you through the dilemma minefield of leadership safely. They are empowering you to fight and win for another day when serving and leading others.

> *Nearly all men can stand adversity, but if you want to test a man's Character, give him power.* (Abraham Lincoln)

Reflection Time

At what point in life did you decide to be of good Character, or one of bad Character? Or have you ever considered which Character you have?

What thing, person, or incident in life's journey do you attribute to being the most significant influencer in your Character today?

Would you trust someone of questionable Character? Should those you serve and lead trust you based on your Character?

---

1 Os Guinness, The Call: Finding and Fulfilling the Central purpose of Your Life (Nashville: W Publishing Group, 2003), 15-16.

2 Ibid., 82.

Integrity in Leadership is Vital to Trust

The LORD detests people with crooked hearts, but he delights in those with integrity.

—Proverbs 11:20

Who wants to be associated with or follow a leader that is known to be dishonest in word and deed or displays a lack of Integrity? How can this kind of leader ever establish trust when they are known to be dishonest? Integrity is about being firm in our moral principles and being an upright person, regardless of the circumstance. God's Word tells us that He highly values Integrity.

He is a shield to those who walk with integrity (Proverbs 2:7). (Every person deserves justice in life. When we see a person suffering injustices for doing the right thing, we naturally want to defend them and help them. As a leader, there may come a time that doing the right thing is not necessarily the most popular thing to do. These are the circumstances when a leader's Integrity is put to the test. Integrity is like an investment in long-term life success. Do we sacrifice Integrity to win the circumstance battle of today, or do we maintain our Integrity and ultimately win the entire war tomorrow? God sees the injustices brought against those who remain faithful to His Word. God sees the leader who walks in Integrity. Keep your trust in God and continue walking in Integrity in each day's battles. He will make you the victor of the war of life.)

As they approached, Jesus said, "Now here is a genuine son of Israel—a man of complete integrity" (John 1:47). (Being recognized as a person of complete Integrity is the highest compliment a person can receive. It means more than any job title and financial success, or any other form of notoriety in life. As a leader, we may not be the smartest person, the best speechmaker, or have a physically impressive stature. Still, if we are leaders with complete Integrity, we are well on our way to great leadership.)

The godly walk with integrity; blessed are their children who follow them (Proverbs 20:7). (Leaders of Integrity provide a substantial measure of peace in the workplace for those they serve and lead. Tranquility is provided by the leader's unquestionable motive of always doing the right thing for the organization's right reason and those they serve and lead. When people are blessed with leaders of Integrity, a selfless and honest leader is leading them. They are blessed to have a person leading them that sincerely cares about them and doing right by them in every situation and dilemma. They are blessed to be led by a leader they can trust.)

May integrity and honesty protect me, for I put my hope in you (Psalm 25:21). (Leaders with great Integrity promote Integrity as a valued attribute of everyone in the organization. When an organization supports Integrity as a welcomed and expected value of personal conduct, they say honest mistakes are okay here. People want to know that they will be afforded more opportunities to find future successes when they try and fail. When Integrity and Honesty become the norm of operational values of those you serve and lead, they know these values protect them from being subject to suspicion of their functional motives. People feel free and encouraged to learn from their mistakes and, in doing so, will push beyond the operational norms when the opportunity presents itself to find more remarkable successes. A leader's Integrity creates a culture of hope for others to thrive in, for there is no fear where the light of hope shines.)

Let God weigh me on the scales of justice, for he knows my integrity (Job 31:6). (Integrity emboldens leaders and those they serve and lead to move out and take challenges head-on. When every endeavor is founded on Integrity, we do not fear those around us, eyes and ears. It does not matter if we are alone or in the presence of others; we will always do the right thing. Leaders and organizations permeated with Integrity can hold their heads up high when storm winds of judgment blow against them. Their core foundation of Integrity protects them from the perils of other's opinions and hypocritical views.)

I know, my God, that you examine our hearts and rejoice when you find integrity there (1 Chronicles 29:17). (When Integrity is the central or innermost part of a person's character, everything they say and do will always be the right moral thing. Whether they are the only one around or in a group of people, whether they are in the darkest of dark or under the brightest of lights, they are the same person consistently.)

To the faithful you show yourself faithful; to those with integrity you show integrity (2 Samuel 22:26). (If we want our home, workplace, or the people we surround ourselves with to be represented by honesty and moral uprightness, we must first be these things to them.)

He cared for them with a true heart and led them with skillful hands (Psalms 78:72). (Nothing can make a person feel more secure and confident than having a leader with a heart of Integrity and hands of service. This is why it is so beautiful to see the look in a small child's eyes when they are in the arms of their parent. They know they are protected, loved, and will be taken care of by a person that will always do the right thing by and for them. I don't know about you, but I never grow tired of feeling loved by the people I am closest to in life. Why does being in the workplace have to be any different? I always wanted people to look forward to coming to work just like they would look forward to going home after work. Either way or either place, I wanted them to feel important, valued, appreciated, needed, and yes, loved for who they were and what they brought into other's lives. A leader's Integrity removes any doubts of a leader's motives; they are in it for those they serve and lead.)

People with integrity walk safely, but those who follow crooked paths will slip and fall (Proverbs 10:9). (Integrity implies the right thing, the right way. Integrity is a path without the need for guardrails to prevent falling into a canyon of unethical disasters. Integrity is a bright light on a safe passage for all to follow.)

And you yourself must be an example to them by doing good works of every kind. Let everything you do reflect the integrity and seriousness of your teaching (Titus 2:7). (As a leader, you are ALWAYS being watched. The higher up in leadership you go, the more people who are watching you. Observing you, judging you, and even imitating you. What message are you sending them? What actions of yours are they imitating? What have they learned from you and your way of leading? As a leader, when you are on full display for all to see and hear, are you encouraging and inspiring, or are you disappointing and defeating others' hopes? Lead them with your complete Integrity. Lead them with your words of encouragement and inspiration. Lead them with your acts of service and support of their needs. Lead them as you would have others lead yourself, with Integrity!)

Integrity's Role in Ethical Leadership

Integrity and ethical leadership go hand in hand. Five-Star General and US President Dwight Eisenhower once stated, "The supreme quality for leadership is unquestionable Integrity. Without it, no real success is possible." Integrity is crucial for success, not a measurable success as in dollar figures, but success in a person's strength or leader's moral character. Integrity is exemplified by a person or leader's honesty and the display of their strong ethical principles, conveyed by their moral uprightness.

Integrity is uncompromising; no test can be too great, and no event can withdraw or challenge an ethical leader's Integrity. Where does a leader find Integrity? Integrity is located in a leader doing what they say they will do, consistently. Integrity in leadership is a personal faithfulness to doing the honorable and right thing, things that are true to a person's morals, and being ethical in words and actions. Integrity is a primary and nonnegotiable attribute required in ethical leadership. Integrity is the essential attribute of a leader who has moral aspirations to be an ethical leader. Integrity is not contingent on the challenge or the circumstance; Integrity depends on a leader's embodied and espoused values.

A person or leader with unwavering Integrity is the exact opposite of what we discussed earlier within the topic of hypocrisy. One of the most respected and ethical leaders known worldwide was the former Reverend Dr. Billy Graham. When asked to define Integrity, Dr. Graham answered,

> *We speak of Integrity as a moral value. Integrity has to do with soundness, completeness, unity, and consistency. It means that a person is the same on the inside as he claims to be on the outside. There is no discrepancy in what he says and what he does. Between his walk and his talk. It means everything about a person is moving in the same direction. Trying to live without Integrity is like trying to drive a car with the wheels moving in different directions. Integrity permeates the fabric of a person, rather than just decorating the surface.*[1]

As one of its highest regarded ethical values, the United States Army leadership promotion study guide simplifies things and defines Integrity as "doing the right thing, even when no one is looking."

An ethical leader demonstrates Integrity by saying what they mean and meaning what they say. An ethical leader does not say one thing to a person or group of people and then turn and say something different to another person or group of people regarding the same subject. Followers can count on an ethical leader's Integrity to remain consistent, regardless of the circumstance or their audience.

A moral leader's words and actions are identical and unvaried with everyone, all the time.

The Results of Integrity in Leadership

An ethical leader's Integrity assures followers that their words will always be commensurate with their actions and behavior. Regardless of the cost, a leader with Integrity keeps their word and does what they believe and value to be the right thing. Leaders of great Integrity inspire, they influence, they establish norms of acceptance for those they lead. An ethical leader's Integrity breeds good character into an organization's DNA.

Integrity prevents and wipes out conflict's destructive agenda. An ethical leader's Integrity practice mitigates the chances of misinformation being used to incubate disputes within the organization. People and organizations know their leaders and can see through any misinformation campaigns as they stand in contrast to an ethical leader's morals and Integrity. Ethical leaderships reliance on Integrity is required as much as society requires ethical leadership; one cannot exist without the other. Too much is at stake; the Integrity found in ethical leaders assures the survival and ultimate harmony for individuals, organizations, and society. Leaders and people with integrity bring dignity and goodness into the lives of individuals they serve and come in contact with. ***Pray this way for kings and all who are in authority so that we can live peaceful and quiet lives marked by godliness and dignity*** (1 Timothy 2:2).

King David was not a perfect man, but he was a leader that sought to live, lead, and rule his Kingdom with a high degree of Integrity. King David determined to live of Integrity, states in Psalm 101:2–8:

> ***I will be careful to live a blameless life—when will you come to help me? I will lead a life of Integrity in my own home. I will refuse to look at anything vile and vulgar. I hate all who deal crookedly; I will have nothing to do***

> ***with them. I will reject perverse ideas and stay away from every evil. I will not tolerate people who slander their neighbors. I will not endure conceit and pride. I will search for faithful people to be my companions. Only those who are above reproach will be allowed to serve me. I will not allow deceivers to serve in my house, and liars will not stay in my presence. My daily task will be to ferret out the wicked.***

We see people's actions with and without Integrity on Television News Networks, in Social Media posts, and all around us in daily life as we are out and about in society. Integrity can be seen in someone who finds someone's wallet and returns it to them with all of the person's contents. We see Integrity in the customer given too much money from the cashier when giving them their change. The customer provides the money back to the cashier. We see it in the person that accidentally damages an unoccupied vehicle in the parking lot. They wait for the owner to return or leave their contact information to make restitution for the damages. We see Integrity in the student that refuses to plagiarize or cheat on a paper or exam, even when the internet provides all types of unethical sources for doing so just a click away. We even see Integrity on display when a professional golfer called a penalty on themselves when no one else witnessed the penalty. This action of Integrity can result in the loss of hundreds of thousands of dollars in potential earnings for the golfer.

Why do these actions of Integrity seem to surprise us so much in today's society? Is it because society has taken to the practice of doing whatever it takes, at any cost, to be successful, to win in life? Some people and some leaders have decided the only thing that matters to them is what they can get for themselves. They seek to achieve what this world tells them is "success." It's almost easy to define and describe actions of Integrity witnessed, because unfortunately, actions of Integrity are not the norm for many. Seeing someone doing the right thing is often reported just because doing the right thing is so uncommon in the world today; how sad.

When looking throughout society for an example of leaders and an organization that places Integrity as paramount to their culture and strategy, one only needs to look at the Billy Graham Evangelistic Association. "Striving for full Integrity had become a part of the organization's DNA."[2] To do so as an organization, they report that the organization took the following approach,

> *When we minimize secrecy and openly admit temptations are there, we can build in safeguards against poor judgment, unconscious motivations, and self-deception. Says Bill Hybels, (Pastor and Author), "Leadership requires moral authority. Followers will only trust leaders who exhibit the highest levels of integrity."*[3]

At the beginning of his ministry, Billy Graham and his founding associate colleagues of the Billy Graham Evangelistic Association sat in a hotel room in Modesto, California. They established an organizational manifesto targeting Integrity as the culture of the organization and every leader in it. The *Modesto Manifesto* stated:

- We will never criticize, condemn, or speak negatively about others.
- We will be accountable, particularly in handling finances, with Integrity according to the highest business standards.
- We will tell the truth and be thoroughly honest, especially in reporting statistics.
- We will be exemplary in morals—clear, clean, and careful to avoid the very appearance of any impropriety.[4]

The *Modesto Manifesto* insisted, "You have to be in the dark what you are in the light!"[5]

The purpose of their manifesto was to build their service to God of one founded and grounded in Integrity. Every leader and every organization must establish and operate their leadership and organizational culture and strategy with Integrity regardless of their industry. For leaders and organizations, their existence and success depend on the trust others have in them. Perhaps the most significant initial investment an organization can make in its future is not requiring investors and their monetary assistance, but initiatives taken by the founders and their leaders in establishing a culture and strategic plan grounded in integrity.

Organizations and their people become a reflection of their leadership. Show me an organization where the leadership looks the other way when infractions occur, and you will eventually see an organization going down. Leaders who promote a culture of *anything goes* as long as *no one knows*, are only assisting others to the edge of a dangerous fall. One that eventually all will suffer. ***If you assist a thief, you only hurt yourself. You are sworn to tell the truth*** (Proverbs 29:24). Let's look at a comparable case analogy of what happens to an organization when leaders don't cultivate a particular culture or focus, which is intrinsically valuable to operational success. For this case analogy we will use the simplistic physical fitness subject in the military to compare a leader's focus.

Case A: The military organization leaders are not physically in shape because they have become lazy and believe they have "arrived" at such a place in leadership that physical training is only for "junior" soldiers. The physical training, the physical stamina, and the organization's physical toughness are no longer an attribute of focus and priority for the leaders. Physical fitness and stamina end up significantly declining as a whole. When deployed into combat operations, the organization suffers massive casualties. It cannot physically stand up to the austere environment and physical toll of combat. The organization is deemed to be combat ineffective.

Case B: The leaders of the military organization are in exceptional physical condition. Leaders are easily able to exceed the fitness requirements of the military. The leaders require everyone to participate in all physical training events and push them to greater physical fitness levels. The leaders push their people's physical limits in training to prepare for the physical rigors of combat. When deployed into combat operations, the organization excels and swiftly defeats all enemy forces. The austere environment and physical toll have been mitigated by physically fit and prepared people and are not a factor in combat operations. The organization suffers minimal casualties and is deemed significantly combat effective.

Look at the leader, and you will see what the organization looks like in one snapshot picture! Watch the leader's actions, and you will have a snapshot of how the organization's people will act. What is vital to the leader becomes important to those they serve and lead. Leaders make what is important to them become essential to all. What does your leadership say is crucial to you?

Leaders must establish and maintain Integrity if they want to see Integrity become their organization's culture. Every organization's mission within their industry requires people with particular aptitudes, skills, and competencies. Still, suppose people are not operating in a culture of Integrity. In that case, the organization will be challenged to achieve its legitimate success potential. Regardless of external challenges, leaders and organizations must establish a mindset of ALWAYS doing the right thing. To be viewed as a leader or an organization with Integrity is to be considered someone everyone else can trust. Integrity is the essential and foundational building block for trust to emerge and produce tomorrow's successes in any personal or professional relationship. Still, leading ethically is no easy quest; it is vital to be aware of The Challenges to Leading Ethically. Let's take a look!

Reflection Time

Is Integrity a word those you serve and lead would use to describe your morals as a leader?

Only two people know if you are in the dark who you are in the light, you and God. What would God say about who you are in the dark? Are you okay with His Truth?

Does speaking the truth come naturally to you?

---

1 Billy Graham, "A Return to Integrity in the Boardroom and Beyond," San Diego Business Journal 24, no. 19 (2003): A2.

2 Harold Myra and Marshall Shelley, The Leadership Secrets of Billy Graham (Grand Rapids: Zondervan, 2005), 57.

3 Ibid., 60.

4 Ibid., 61.

5 Ibid., 61.

Challenges to Leading Ethically

Temptation comes from our own desires which entice us and drag us away. These desires give birth to sinful actions. And when sin is allowed to grow, it gives birth to death.

—James 1:14

People "fudge" (societies softer word for lie/cheat) on their taxes. People damage others' property and leave the scene. Professional athletes use performance-enhancing drugs to win a race or make the team. We see business people doing and saying anything to defraud investors and others out of their money. We see "self-proclaimed people of God" on television pleading "plant a seed (give me your money)" for God to give you a big return on your investment into "my" ministry. All of these actions are from the dishonest hearts of people challenged to live ethical lives.

Dear friends, I warn you as "temporary residents and foreigners" to keep away from worldly desires that wage war against your very souls (1 Peter 2:11).

God's word describes those that are challenged to live ethically:

In Jeremiah 4:22, the LORD said, "***They are clever enough at doing wrong, but they have no idea how to do right!***" (Greed rears its ugly head and devours many. If people who spend all of their time and energy trying to figure out ways to get more money would instead invest their time building and sustaining meaningful relationships, they would find real wealth much easier. I had a friend that worked for a major commercial airline as a pilot. He told me he had to fly so many days a month. He would sit for hours looking over the flight schedule, trying to find a flight for his first day that did not take-off until after 10:00 PM. He would simultaneously try to find an early AM flight to end his trip for his last flight day. He could start flying at 11:30 PM on Monday, fly Tuesday, Wednesday, and a one-hour flight at 6:00 AM on Thursday, and receive credit for flying four days. He said everyone does the same. I said, if you guys worked as hard for the airline as you try not to work, your airline would be number one in the industry.

Why want people do the best thing by others instead of always being wrapped up in looking out for themselves? It is called selfishness, me first. Ethical leaders are selfless leaders who do good and right things. Unethical leaders do selfish and wrong things. Wrong motives represent wrong things. Pride, selfishness, greed, the appearance of success, and coveting what others have all represent ethical leadership challenges. These leaders cannot do right because their motives remain wrong.)

Your fingers are filthy with sin. Your lips are full of lies, and your mouth spews corruption. No one cares about being fair and honest. They conceive evil deeds (Isaiah 59:3–4). (Let's face it, you and I will either be hot or cold in our ethical practices, there is no lukewarm moral person. Either you are honorable in all things, or you are unethical as a person. We cannot have it both ways. What we get involved in at work and in life challenges us ethically. What we say and who and what we allow in our lives challenges us ethically. How we treat other people regardless of the circumstance challenges us ethically. What we are willing to do to achieve our version of success in life challenges us ethically. A person may not be a full-blown, horrifically unethical person as the people described in Isaiah 59:3–4. Still, when a person is challenged to be ethical, they cannot be a little dishonest. Don't give the enemy a chance. Don't think, well, I will do this just once; no one will know. When given in to, unethical challenges start as a snowball that will quickly turn into an avalanche of destructive behaviors. One corrupt failure fuels the fire of unethical behavior, and soon you are in over your head, buried under evil consequences.)

Like a partridge that hatches eggs she has not laid, so are those who get their wealth by unjust means (Jeremiah 17:11). (When I was a young boy playing on a playground, I found a wallet lying on the ground close to the swings. I opened the wallet and saw a picture ID of the owner of the wallet with his address. He lived within walking distance of the playground, so I walked to his home and knocked on the door. The man answered the door and looked puzzled as his eyes fell upon his wallet in my hands. He had not realized he had lost his wallet, and he reached for his back pocket to see if his wallet was present. Before he could say anything, I handed his wallet to him simultaneously, saying, "Sir, I found your wallet on the ground by the swings at the park." He said he was at the park earlier with his kids and pushed his daughter on the swing-set when his wallet must have fallen out of his pants pocket. He quickly opened his wallet and looked inside. All contents were still there, including the cash from his recently cashed employment check. He was very thankful for his wallet and my honesty but was intrigued by it also. He asked me, weren't you tempted to take the money and throw the wallet in the trash? I told him I never looked to see if there was money in the wallet. I just wanted to know who it belonged to, to return it. My focus was on doing the right thing by the man who owned the wallet, not taking money someone else had earned. I did not see the situation as an ethical challenge because I never contemplated doing the wrong thing. Unfortunately, not everyone has this mind-set.

My wife, beautiful Jenny, has a saying about people who gain their wealth by unfair means. She says "their wealth is like a person grabbing a handful of water or sand. It will surely slip between their fingers, and they will lose it as quickly as they grabbed it." Ecclesiastes 5:10–11 reaffirms Jenny's saying, ***Those who love money will never have enough. How meaningless to think that wealth brings true happiness! The more you have, the more people come to help you spend it. So what good is wealth—except perhaps to watch it slip through your fingers!*** Do you remember Bernie Madoff, the one-time market maker, financial advisor, now convicted fraudster? He made hundreds of millions of dollars; no, he stole hundreds of millions of dollars from honest, hard-working citizens. Unjust means equals short term gains. Before Bernie Madoff could spend life basking in the luxuries he sought, he moved into a small jail cell to spend the rest of his life in prison. Unethical challenges want leaders to do the wrong thing the wrong way until it devours their good name and reputation. Do the right thing the right way.)

"Turn from the evil road you are traveling and from the evil things you are doing" (Jeremiah 25:5). (When my father passed away, I realized my character was far from where I wanted it to be in goodness. I decided and was determined to pivot from my old self to who I wanted to be. This required turning away from old habits, attitudes, demeanor, and seriously getting to know God. The first step to overcoming ethical challenges in life is to recognize what they are. Ask God for forgiveness for moral and sinful failures and turn from participating in old unethical and immoral practices (repent). Seek God's Word and wisdom in doing things the right way, for the right reason. God loves us so much He gave His Son's life for our sins and unethical failures. God will help you turn from evil ways and evil things if you sincerely seek Him and ask for His help. Challenges to leading and living ethically will always exist, but so does God's grace and mercy to help us overcome unethical challenges. You don't have to try and be perfect. God already sent someone perfect to pay for our failures. Just do your best and when unethical temptations come, ask God for His strength and fortitude. Don't get on the crooked evil road. It does not lead to success or happiness; it leads to failure and sorrow.)

Don't make your living by extortion or put your hope in stealing. And if your wealth increases, don't make it the center of your life (Psalm 62:10). (There is only one source for all that is good in life, God. Overcoming ethical challenges becomes more manageable when our focus in life is our source of life. The *What Would Jesus Do?* (WWJD) movement of the 1990s sought to have people ask themselves the question, *What Would Jesus Do?* when faced with an ethical dilemma. When we look at ethical challenges in the context of what

God would have us to do, we stop placing our hope in money and put it in God. Be honest, work hard, and keep God first in your heart and life. Now you have wealth money can't provide!)

Luke 16:13 Jesus says, ***"No one can serve two masters. For you will hate one and love the other; you will be devoted to one and despise the other. You cannot serve God and money."*** (Let's get real for a minute. Money is nice to have and necessary for purchasing life's needs (shelter, food, medicine). Money buys things, but it is not everything. We see the news of famous, wealthy people that commit suicide. All of their fame and wealth were not enough to bring enjoyment in living. Only God brings real meaning, real joy, and His peace to our lives; money cannot do this. When former Iraqi dictator Saddam Hussein was found hiding in a hole in the ground like a burrowing rodent, he had hundreds of millions of US dollars stashed in caches throughout Iraq. Saddam had spent decades unethically leading a nation. His greed, pride, and selfishness sought wealth and prestige over the needs of those he led. Still, all of his wealth could not protect him from the consequences of an unethical life. Seeking to lead and live according to God's Truth instead of seeking wealth does not mean you will be poor. It means you will be rich in life.)

> ***Teach those who are rich in this world not to be proud and not to trust in their money, which is so unreliable. Their trust should be in God, who richly gives us all we need for our enjoyment. Tell them to use their money to do good. They should be rich in good works and generous to those in need, always being ready to share with others.*** (1 Timothy 6:17–18)

(Have you noticed a trend in these Scriptures? It certainly appears that God is telling us that money is the root of most of man's ethical challenges. While some leader's ethical challenge is founded on pride, ego, or stature, most ethical challenges originate from a desire to make more money. In the secular world, people believe lots of money makes a person wealthy.

> ***But people who long to be rich fall into temptation and are trapped by many foolish and harmful desires that plunge them into ruin and destruction. For the love of money is the root of all kinds of evil. And some people, craving money, have wandered from the true faith and pierced themselves with many sorrows.*** (1 Timothy 6:9–10)

In God's Kingdom, it is what we give away that makes us wealthy. Wealth is temporary; God is forever. One can cost you your soul, and one can give you life abundantly. Don't allow unethical quick monetary wealth to cost you a life of abundant joy and peace. ***Don't love money; be satisfied with what you have*** (Hebrews 13:5). Trust God first for happiness, not money!)

Movies, documentaries, and literature tell the stories of what society has deemed as great and successful leaders. Military Generals Patton and Eisenhower, US Presidents Lincoln and Roosevelt, President of South Africa, President Nelson Mandela, and Prime Minister Winston Churchill were all depicted in movies portraying their extraordinary leadership successes. These leaders' movies reveal behind the scene glimpses of each leader's challenges and turmoil with the critical and high-risk decisions they were charged with. However, leading at any level faces its challenges, the greatest of which is overcoming the challenge of leading ethically.

A challenge to leading ethically can occur when leaders begin to compare themselves with other leaders and their recognized "successes." Leaders start to want the same successes and the adulations, which often accompany success. A comparison of oneself to another leader will always be using unequal comparative analysis. Comparing two leaders is like comparing apples and oranges. But you say, "Comparing two leaders is comparing two people who lead, so they are the same for comparison's sake." It was stated earlier that there are over 160 varying definitions of "leadership" in publication. If you asked another one hundred people on the street to define leadership, you would get another one hundred different definitions of leadership. Suppose the definition of leadership cannot be agreed upon in society. How is society or any individual capable of comparing success in leaders?

Can we compare one leader's motives or character traits to another leader? Of course, we can, but when it comes to comparing successes, every leader defines success as to what being successful means for them. Some leaders define success based on their professional title, promotions, financial earnings, notoriety, and accolades within their career field. Honors, awards, and the "perks/privileges" they receive define their version of success. Here we find leaders so busy trying to find "their success" they miss out on the very best part of being a leader. They never experience a relationship with those they lead. ***Better to have one handful with quietness than two handfuls with hard work and chasing the wind*** (Ecclesiastes 4:6). These are the leaders that are at greater risk to the challenges of leading ethically. Comparison breeds envy, envy breeds desire, and desire can lead a leader toward unethical pursuits to achieve their version of what success equates to. Os Guinness warns us against envy, "The envious person is moved, first and last, by his lack of self-esteem, which is all the more tormenting because it springs from an inordinate self-love."[1]

> ***Do not love this world nor the things it offers you, for when you love the world, you do not have the love of the Father in you. For the world offers only a craving for physical pleasure, a craving for everything we see, and pride in our achievements and possessions. These are not from the Father but are from this world.*** (1 John 2:15–16)

(Leading by God's Truth represents ethical leadership. Anything else is chasing this world's distorted view of what it calls success.

When we chase success, we take shortcuts to get to success quicker. Shortcuts represent hurdles of moral challenges we must negotiate, or we will surely stumble and fall. Challenges to leading ethically act as a sheer, thin veil over a bottomless pit of ruin and catastrophe. Unethical leaders will always plunge through the veil and end up in this bottomless pit.)

Another leader may gauge what success is by what they have achieved for those they lead. They care about how many of their people have stayed on the team; they care about how many of their people have been successful within the organization. They care about their organization's successes in its industry. These leaders care about the morale of those they lead. They care about their people's eagerness to serve the organization. They care about meeting the needs of those they lead. These are leaders who don't compare themselves to other leaders but are content doing what is right by those they serve and lead. ***Yet true godliness with contentment is itself great wealth*** (1 Timothy 6:6).

One leader looks at how others see them, and one leader looks at how they can serve others. One leader cares about self, and one leader cares about others. One leader desire more for their career and one leader wants more for those they lead. A selfish (me, myself, and I) leader's version of success will be a minefield of ethical leadership challenges. Why? Because ethical leadership is outward focused and concerned with doing the right thing for others. Unethical (selfish) leadership is inward-focused and all about doing whatever it takes (right or wrong) to take care of themself.

"Success" that leaders aspire to achieve depends on what the individual leader defines as "success." Some leaders believe success is represented by how high up the corporate ladder they climb in title or position. For others, success is represented by the legacy they leave behind. However, success is represented by successfully navigating through leadership's ethical challenges without compromising their values and morals for the great leader. Leadership's greatest challenge is not an opposing enemy or the economic environment; ethical challenges represent leadership's greatest challenge. Leaders are not alone in determining their level of "success" achieved; leaders are subject to society's judgment, the people they serve, and ultimately, God.

Unethical leadership, whether as actions of intended or unintended leadership behavior, harms and endangers organizations, the people being led, and ultimately, society.

> ***Their feet run to evil. Misery and destruction always follow them. They don't know where to find peace or what it means to be just and good. They have mapped out crooked roads, and no one who follows them knows a moment's peace.*** (Isaiah 59:7–8)

> ***Everything is falling apart; threats and cheating are rampant in the streets.*** (Psalm 55:11)

Unethical leader's actions are contrary to what their society has deemed as an ethical code of conduct for everyone to adhere to. When leaders fail to achieve success in their climb up the corporate ladder or fail to attain their lofty financial goals, it may be a disappointment to the individual. Still, it does not necessarily negatively affect those they lead and society. However, when leaders fail ethically, those they lead, organizations, and society pay for their unethical leadership. Society needs examples of what right looks like. An unscrupulous leader's emotional toll on society kills hope and belief in other leaders who are successfully doing the right thing. Unethical behavior is nothing new; it has become so rampant in society that the role of leadership has become stained and tainted to the point that society doubts a leader's ability to be ethical. The fact that unethical leadership is a severe and devastating issue to society has been repeatedly reported and surveyed. Dr. and Reverend Billy Graham declared, "Integrity among leaders, or the lack of it, has been front-page news for nearly two decades, and it continues to be today."[2] Unethical leadership gradually erodes the trust of followers. Followers see leaders for who they are, not what the leader attempts to make others see.

To properly evaluate a leader's "success," one must determine their level of trustworthiness.

Historically, unethical leadership took time to be exposed. Before today's twenty-four-hour news channels and social media platforms, unethical leaders could evade being tagged as unethical by changing jobs or moving to a different geographic region. However, today, information outlets saturate society with every tidbit of scandal, and the corrupt leader can hide no more. In the past, a leader could gain a false sense of their ability to hide or minimize their unethical actions avoiding scandals and ridicule. Now, dishonest leaders are only one social media post away from being exposed for who they are. Those being led have always had a voice but were limited in ways to be heard; that is no longer the case. Society is empowering those once silenced to speak up. The truth is setting society free from corrupt leadership's devious and selfish agenda. Unethical leadership has a face with which many are familiar; just watch the news.

The Look of Unethical Leadership

> ***Sin whispers to the wicked, deep within their hearts. They have no fear of God at all. In their blind conceit, they cannot see how wicked they really are. Everything they say is crooked and deceitful. They refuse to act wisely or do good. They lie awake at night, hatching sinful plots. Their actions are never good. They make no attempt to turn from evil.*** (Psalm 36:1–4)

The selfish acts of unethical leadership are revealed in many illicit behaviors such as corruption, inappropriate personal relationships, and power abuse. These unethical behaviors primarily derive from an individual's greed, arrogance, pride, or ego. Many unethical leaders encounter the problem because they have lost sight of what is right and wrong. Dishonest leaders rationalize their unethical behavior to the point they stop contemplating their action's potential consequences. Corrupt leaders only act in their self-interest for themselves, not others. "The leader who rationalizes finds himself or herself reeling in a disaster. One indiscretion can bury a leader's life work."[3]

An unethical leader's selfish desire for personal fulfillment and quick gains increases. In contrast, the needs of others and the quest for long-term success erode from their conscience. Unethical leaders live for their moment, never weighing the long-term consequences unethical behavior always imparts on others. What does the unethical leader look like, what are their actions? They are full of pride and arrogance. They are deceivers, disproportionate in how they deal with others, selfish, untrustworthy, and neglectful of others. They blame others for failures, they are unaccountable for their actions, and they lack personal courage. In addition to the negative attributes of unethical leadership, the primary focus and pursuits of unscrupulous leaders are ones that

- *satisfies personal needs and career objectives,*
- *favors coalitions who offers the most benefits,*
- *attempts to sell a personal vision as the only way for success,*
- *does what is expedient to attain personal objectives,*
- *avoids necessary decisions or actions that involve personal risk to the leader,*
- *uses deception and distortion to bias follower's perceptions about problems and progress,*
- *discourages and suppresses criticism or dissent,*
- *deemphasizes development to keep followers weak and dependent on the leader.*[4]

For the unethical leader, the only thing that matters is their success, recognition, and the pursuance of their plan. The unethical leader's primary focus is on their needs, no one else's. Suppose the unethical leader appears to have concern for others. In that case, it means others concerns benefit the unethical leader in some way.

> *When a man has cast his longing eye on offices, a rottenness begins in his conduct.* (Thomas Jefferson)

What do these unethical behaviors look like in society? A former Hewlett-Packard CEO had to resign for submitting false expense reports. A US Senator was forced to resign for covering up an inappropriate extramarital affair with financial payoffs. A former Chairman of a primary mortgage lender was found guilty and sentenced to prison for numerous bank fraud schemes. A sitting Governor was forced to resign from office following an extramarital affair and attempting to blackmail the co-adulterer into silence. Check out today's or any day's news headlines from around the world, and it is almost a certainty that some high-positioned leader, somewhere, failed ethically. These are just the ones that make the news. Still, that nameless Team Leader or Office Manager practicing the same unethical behaviors will be caught and exposed.

Unethical leadership involves insider trading in the stock market, embezzlement, using organizational assets for personal use, instigating distrust between alliances, providing favoritism for financial gain, selling organizational trade secrets to competitors, or falsifying information. An unethical leader's wants will always win out over others' needs, and selfish, unethical acts occur. As technological advancements continue, other forms and modes of unethical conduct will evolve. Technology is not unethical, but unethical leaders using it have exposed their true nature and who they are when they believe no one is watching. The future will have one thing in common with the past; the selfish leader will continue pursuing unethical behaviors.

What Leads to Unethical Leadership Behaviors?

Leadership can be high stress and a challenging position of authority; everything good, bad, right, or wrong ultimately is the leader's responsibility. Achieving organizational success while caring for others' concerns and needs can be more than some leaders can balance successfully. Technology and the globalization of the world's economy create shorter periods for leaders to achieve demanded successes. For instance, according to the Global Risks Report 2018, the "length of time companies spent in the S&P 500 of the NASDAQ in the 1950s was sixty years. Today, the length of time a company spends in the S&P 500 is twelve years. It will continue to shorten."[5] This results in more pressure for leaders to keep their organizations on top.

Economic competition has moved from the regional and national market to the globalized market. Global players in the financial game increase the stressors on leadership to achieve success. Meanwhile, global leaders are required to negotiate a cultural landscape represented by different ethical tolerances simultaneously. Leaders find themselves in a moral dilemma; compromise their moral standards, or risk losing in the competitive global marketplace.

Feed the family, pay the mortgage, save for the kid's college education, all while standing by personal ethical convictions. These competing life demands place more tremendous moral pressures on leaders as a global society emerges. Unfortunately, some leaders abandon their ethics when faced with increased stress, justifying and rationalizing their unethical behaviors as serving the "greater good" of others. ***Don't let evil conquer you but conquer evil by doing good*** (Romans 12:21). Wrong is wrong, regardless of the leader's motive. In other words, leaders begin to justify their unethical behavior. Once done, it becomes easier to do the next time. Unfortunately, this has the potential to start a downward moral spiral for leaders. Ethical desensitization evolves, and leaders become blind to their evil motives and actions.

When a leader walks in the door of an organization, they walk into a mass of potential ethical challenges. The pressures for the organization to be successful rest on the shoulders of the leaders within the organization. How far is the leader willing to go to achieve organizational success? What does the organization require leaders to be? Team players doing whatever the organization needs to succeed, or leaders staunch in their ethical principles and unwilling to bend? Organizational ethics, established and enforced by founders and senior leadership, will become the organization's moral inclination.

The challenges to ethical leadership come from societal conditions every leader will encounter. We hear people say, "If the temptation were not present, I would not have succumbed to it." In the

Garden of Eden, humankind's character revealed its ethical frailty. As leaders, we must anchor ourselves from swaying in the breezes of ethical dilemmas. Our anchor is our commitment and resolve to always being righteous in life. Conditions around us may change, but our character of being ethical must never change.

> *Be thoroughly acquainted with your temptations and the things that may corrupt you, especially those temptations that either your company or your business will lay before you.* (From the 1600s, English Theologian Richard Baxter)

The ethical influencers within an organization begin with leaders at the top and their tolerances of what practices are allowable. Unethical organizational practices (ways of doing business) can indeed challenge a leader invested in ethical behavior. Corrupt corporate practices can also catalyze unethical actions from a leader who may already be morally deficient. The ethically flawed (corrupt) leader is a leader that has tendencies to place selfish ambitions before the needs of those they lead. When faced with moral dilemmas, the unethical leader will select an ethical egoism (what's best for me) approach when deciding what to do. An unethical leader acts with primary concern for self-interest while simultaneously presenting an image of concern for others' interests. Ethical egoism minded leaders predestine their dishonest acts by their selfish character and bad traits.

What could predestine an individual to be an unethical leader? A leader who lacks integrity and whose self-ambition blinds them from the dangers and consequences of corrupt practices. These are leaders who denounce criticism and tend to keep the company of other unscrupulous leaders. Unethical leaders desire the accolades, financial bonuses, perks, and benefits that come with leadership success. They are willing to do anything to receive them. Fundamentally, unethical leadership stems from individuals with a lack of character, no integrity, low morals, and little to no value for anyone other than themselves; they are anything but a leader. What comes next for the unethical leader? The Damages from Unethical Leadership change the lives of the unethical leader and everyone's lives.

> ***God created people to be virtuous, but they have each turned to follow their own downward path*** (Ecclesiastes 7:29).

Oh, one last thing. So we are CLEAR: Leadership success is achieving good things for others by our service for them, not for the person in the mirror!

Reflection Time

What do you consider to be the greatest ethical challenge in your personal life? Your professional life?

What mechanism or people do you have in place to strengthen your morals and resolve from succumbing to ethical challenges?

What area of your life, both personally and professionally, do you need to strengthen against the challenges of being ethical?

---

1. Os Guinness, The Call: Finding and Fulfilling the Central Purpose of Your Life (Nashville: W Publishing Group, 2003), 14.
2. Billy Graham, "A Return to Integrity in the Boardroom and Beyond," San Diego Business Journal 24, no. 19 (2003): A2.
3. Harold Myra and Marshall Shelley, The Leadership Secrets of Billy Graham (Grand Rapids: Zondervan, 2005), 62.
4. Gary Yukl, Leadership in Organizations: Sixth Edition (Upper Saddle River: Prentice Hall, 2006), 422.
5. Marsh & McLennan Companies. "The Global Risks Report 2018," 16 June 2018, https://www.marsh.com/nz/Insights/research/the-global-risks-report.html.

Damages from Unethical Leadership

For my life is full of troubles, and death draws near. I am as good as dead, like a strong man with no strength left. They have left me among the dead, and I lie like a corpse in a grave. I am forgotten, cut off from your care. You have thrown me into the lowest pit, into the darkest depths. Your anger weighs me down; with wave after wave you have engulfed me. You have driven my friends away by making me repulsive to them. I am in a trap with no way to escape.

—Psalm 88:3–8

Unethical behavior never leads to a long-term positive outcome. The "win" achieved by a corrupt act is only temporary and eventually evaporates once exposed to the light of truth. Ultimately, unethical leadership founded in selfishness impacts exponentially more people than an unethical leader ever considers. Unfortunately, the unethical leader's selfish nature never considers how their illicit behavior will impact anyone but themselves. A leader's unethical behavior ignites consequentially and substantially destructive repercussions for those around them.

> ***They stumble because they do not obey God's word, and so they meet the fate that was planned for them*** (1 Peter 2:8).

(God's Word does not hold back in warning the unethical person and leader of the devastating consequences they will incur.)

But if your heart turns away and you refuse to listen, and if you are drawn away to serve and worship other gods, then I warn you now that you will certainly be destroyed (Deuteronomy 30:17:18). (We find the pursuits of idols (money, fame, inappropriate personal relationships, titles) to be the "gods" we worship and pursue. God warns against pursuing anything but His ways and commands for our lives. Unethical leadership always finds its conclusion in destruction, just as God's Word warns us.)

But people who long to be rich fall into temptation and are trapped by many foolish and harmful desires that plunge them into ruin and destruction. For the love of money is the root of all kinds of evil. And some people, craving money, have wandered from the true faith and pierced themselves with many sorrows (1 Timothy 6:9–10). (When it comes to money, what amount is required for real happiness in life, how much is enough? This question has an answer only you can answer for yourself. Are we trying to keep up with the neighbors next door or down the street? Why are people so concerned with impressing other people who they don't know, with what they can't afford, and what they don't need? People go to unethical extremes to feed their greed and desires for wealth. I wonder how many fraudsters, embezzlers, and greedy criminals sitting in prison would give up the money for their freedom and once again having a good reputation? Having money is a blessing; earning money is necessary, but loving money makes it an idol. God's Word warns us in Hebrews 13:5, ***Don't love money; be satisfied with what you have.***)

Extortion turns wise people into fools, and bribes corrupt the heart (Ecclesiastes 7:7). (Using information that could be harmful if exposed to blackmail a person into paying for silence takes greed to an all-time low. In today's internet-driven society, we are experiencing cyber-crimes. One of which entails an organization's computer systems being hacked into and all of their data being stolen and held hostage until large amounts of ransom funds are paid. In the previous chapter, I mentioned that new unethical practices will occur as people discover more ways to manipulate technology. People sit and think of ways to take what someone else has legally earned through extortive measures. These people don't look for employment; they look for other's vulnerabilities to pray on. When a person or leader violates society's legal norms, they open themselves to being prayed on by extortionists. When a person or a leader accepts a bribe to gain funds for favors or allowing special consideration for other people's interests, they have just become vulnerable to personal and professional disaster. If you want to meet some of these types of individuals, just visit your state or federal prison; that's where they hang out in retirement.)

Fools think their own way is right (Proverbs 12:15). (Fools are people that never contemplate the consequences of their actions, even when convicted of them. A fool lacks a conscience of right or wrong. A fool has only one motive, "What's in it for me?" A fool can be shown the truth and provided examples of the truth, but they will refuse to accept it. A fool is a person blind to how other people feel or what they think.)

A wise person chooses the right road; a fool takes the wrong one (Ecclesiastes 10:2). (In life, there is a hard and correct way to find success and happiness. There is also an easy and wrong road, which leads to failure and consequence. Doing the right thing consistently in life promotes a much greater chance of happiness and success. Doing the wrong something always in life guarantees loss every time. Only a fool keeps doing the wrong something over and over, believing that eventually, life will get better.)

You must never twist justice or show partiality. Never accept a bribe, for bribes blind the eyes of the wise and corrupt the decisions of the godly (Deuteronomy 16:19). (The globalized economy has opened markets worldwide for almost every industry. The problem this presents is some regions of the world see the unethical practice of bribery as "just a way of doing business here." I had a friend that represented an international satellite television provider. He was challenged ethically when working with the newly formed Afghanistan government to introduce their satellite television capabilities throughout the rugged frontier. The lead member of Afghanistan's Ministry of Communication and Information

Technology told my friend before he could present his organization's proposal, they would require $50,000 from him. These funds bought him their consideration. My friend refused to pay their requested bribe money and lost his job as a result. His international organization was okay with paying bribes as a way of doing business. Still, the ethical dilemma was a no brainer for my friend. He would not be corrupted or feed an already corrupt bureaucracy. Meanwhile, a corrupt government leaves its people in impoverished conditions while leaders motivated by greed look for ways to line their pockets through immoral bribes.)

People ruin their lives by their own foolishness and then are angry at the LORD (Proverbs 19:3). (When things go wrong from unethical exploits (and they will eventually), look in the mirror for the responsible party. Since fools lack consciousness, they could never contemplate that their failures are their fault. It's the systems fault, law enforcement's fault, the government's fault, your fault, my fault, God's fault, and everyone else's fault. We have all placed ourselves in a self-imposed pit at some point in life. It may have been in a relationship where we said or did the wrong thing in the eyes of the other person. It may have been at work or in school when we waited until the last minute, and our effort was less than acceptable. Our performance review or grade point average suffered. Regardless of what went wrong, we did wrong, and we endure self-imposed consequences; that's life. I cannot stress this enough in leadership. If you are willing to risk losing everything you have sacrificed for, endured through, and worked for by crossing the moral line for momentary pleasure or financial gain, you will!)

For we are each responsible for our own conduct (Galatians 6:5). (Who caused the destruction, the pain, the consequence? Who achieved success, wealth, and prestige? That would be the person in the mirror. If you want to know who is responsible for how you live your life, look in the mirror. Do the right thing by God first and the person in your mirror second. You want it, do the right thing to get it. If not, it's on you and no one else. God judges each of us for our conduct, not other people's behavior.)

The person who sins is the one who will die...and wicked people will be punished for their own wickedness (Ezekiel 18:20). (When a junior soldier would receive punishment under the Uniform Code of Justice (UCMJ) in the Army, there was the moment when they stood on the other side of my desk. I would inform them of their legal rights and read to them the charges against them. Most of the time, the incident that brought the person to this point in their military life was committed in their military buddy's presence. As I would discuss their pending legal issue, I would always ask them to look around the office and tell me the names of their buddy's present to support them in their dire circumstance. There was never any buddy's present. I wanted them to see that everyone is their friend when the fun and mischievousness is taking place. But when consequences were taking place, no one would stand with them.

This is how it always goes when unethical or wicked actions are exposed. When a convicted criminal in the court of law is being sentenced, everyone remains seated. The Judge orders the condemned to stand and face their punishment. The person stands alone in discipline, and no one wants to go with them to jail. I cannot paint a bad enough scenario to get across to leaders that they will pay severely for unethical exploits. PLEASE BE AND REMAIN ETHICAL AT ALL TIMES IN LEADING!!! The cost and damages from unethical leading go beyond the moment of exposure and the person in the mirror. So much more!)

When a superstar athlete is suspended from participating with their team in competition because they violated a rule of conduct (a sports version of an unethical act), many others and the athlete suffer the consequences. Not only does the team suffer the consequences of being handicapped by the absence of the athlete's abilities, but the fan base suffers due to a team unable to excel. Sporting complexes suffer economically from the loss of ticket sales, merchandise sales, and concession sales once boosted by the star athlete's anticipated performance. An unethical leader's failure resonates much the same; organizations, families, and societies suffer losses and endure consequences. At one time, a person who was expected to enhance others' lives has selfishly brought turmoil into their lives. The effects of unethical behavior incubate and manifest at every level of the dishonest person's life; some are more obvious than others.

Unethical Consequences: The Seen Effects

But no one gave him anything (Luke 15:16). (Jesus tells a parable in Luke about the prodigal son who lived a selfish life of pleasure-seeking. Eventually, the prodigal son found himself in a pit of desperate consequences, one of which was that no one would help him out of his self-imposed messed-up life. People had seen the prodigal son living foolishly and selfishly and were none too eager to lend a helping hand to help him out of the pit his unethical lifestyle had placed him in. Everyone saw his ruin, everyone observed his need, but no one had mercy or compassion. They left him to his self-imposed consequence.)

Television news networks, social media, tabloids, newspapers, and other news journalism forms capture the ethical failure as a headline and a selling point. Each is quick to point out the fallen leader's infractions and show images of the disgraced leader attempting to avoid the media's relentless pursuit. "The press loves to expose the juicy details of leaders who fall, and once the genie is out of the bottle, it can't be stuffed back in."[1] Wait a week, and a newly fallen leader will bump the former fallen leader out of the spotlight and out of the media's piranha-like attacks. Through mass media's saturation of unethical behavior stories, society has become desensitized to the real and vast devastating impact of corrupt leadership. Instead of a societal revolt against unethical leadership, it has become a modern way of life. Throughout our global society, unethical leadership behavior runs rampant and part of everyday life. Dependent on what a particular society deems as corrupt, you can be sure someone is doing something evil.

Media outlets show snapshots of what they believe sells news; they focus on the surface of a story. The media rarely looks beneath the surface at the struggles, turmoil, and chaos affecting the fallen leader and those close to them. Society hears what the fallen leader did. Society hears what punishment they received, and everyone goes back to their routines of life. Everyone except the unethical leader's organization, the people they lead, the family they betrayed, and the society that counted on them to lead ethically. Each of these parties is left with the reality that life just changed from what they once believed it to be.

The deep and lasting impacts of unethical behavior batter the fallen leader, their families, and many others. To reveal the rampant and damaging effects of unethical leadership in modern society, we must see it as it is. Without stating the name of an individual leader that has fallen ethically, the nature of actually reported unethical behavior and its effects warrant being reviewed for understanding. God's Word explicitly warned these leaders, yet they foolishly thought they knew better and would not be found out.

> ***But if you do what is wrong, you will be paid back for the wrong you have done. For God has no favorites.*** (Colossians 3:25)

> ***Don't be misled—you cannot mock the justice of God. You will always harvest what you plant. Those who live only to satisfy their own sinful nature will harvest decay and death from that sinful nature.*** (Galatians 6:7–8)

- A Televangelist Church leader with a spouse and two children was indicted for mail and wire fraud and defrauding the public. The Church leader fleeced followers out of $158 million for building a Church-owned vacation resort and used $3.7 million for the leader's lifestyle. The Church leader also had an extramarital affair with a Church secretary and paid the secretary over $350,000 to remain silent about the illicit affair. The former Televangelist Church leader was sentenced to forty-five years in prison, which later was reduced to eight years. The Church leader lost all material possessions, and their marriage ended in divorce.

- A nationally known News Channel Network Series Host with a spouse and two children paid $13 million to five individuals to squelch talk of inappropriate conduct. They lost a $20 million job contract with the Network.
- A State-level politician with a spouse and a newborn child lost their political job, losing a $175,000 annual salary. Their marriage ended in divorce. The former politician was sentenced to twenty-one months in prison for inappropriate actions with a minor on social media.
- A State Governor with a spouse and two children was impeached for multiple corruption charges and sentenced to fourteen years in federal prison. The fallen leader lost a $177,000 annual salary, family home, and the respect of those who had elected the leader to Office.
- A Head of State with a spouse and one child had an extramarital affair with a subordinate in their Office. When questioned in their impeachment hearing as to why they did it, the leader answered, "Because I could." The leader's character was destroyed, marriage devastated, millions of dollars in legal fees were incurred, and the disappointment of millions who had elected the leader to Office was endured.
- A television entertainer with a spouse and five children, known for promoting family values, was convicted of forcible sexual misconduct with multiple victims. The former entertainer was sentenced to three to ten years in state prison.
- The US Congress maintains records of all instances of misconduct and alleged misconduct by its members. Since the record-keeping began in 1789, elected members of the US Congress have recorded 391 instances of misconduct. These actions of misconduct consist of campaign fraud, corruption, sexual harassment, and discrimination. According to The Office of Compliance since its inception in the 1990s it "has paid over $17 million to victims of U.S. Congressional members."[2]

- A former CEO of WorldCom with a spouse and three children was convicted of fraud. "Losses for WorldCom ultimately exceeded $11 billion and led to the biggest bankruptcy filing in the United States. Approximately seventeen thousand employees lost their jobs due to the CEO's scheme to hide expenses and grossly exaggerate company revenues. The former CEO was sentenced to twenty-five years in federal prison."[3] The spouse divorced the convicted leader.

Who will hear these lessons from the past and see the ruin that awaits you in the future? (Isaiah 42:23). (Time does not change the consequences for unethical conduct. NO ONE IS EXEMPT FROM UNETHICAL CONSEQUENCES, NO ONE!)

Disgrace comes to those who try to deceive others (Psalm 25:3). (NEWSFLASH: God knows everything! Hiding unethical actions in the dark does the dishonest leader NO GOOD. ***I could ask the darkness to hide me and the light around me to become night—but even in darkness I cannot hide from you. To you the night shines as bright as day. Darkness and light are the same to you*** (Psalm 139:11–12). We discussed at the beginning of this book that God appoints and anoints people to lead. As a leader, when we are unethical in our behavior, we will answer to God. God will use man to convict and punish the corrupt leader. But just like God is our source of life and everything good in it, God will be the source of the damages suffered by unscrupulous leaders.)

Unfortunately, it would be of little challenge to continue narrating story after story of countless publicized ethical failures of modern society leaders. Rehashing the unethical failures of leaders of the past is something the fallen leader has plenty of time to do themselves.

Instead, moving forward, we should address the less publicized and detrimental damages levied by unethical leadership.

Unethical Consequences: The Unseen Effects

The actual depth of unethical leadership's toll is revealed by the financial losses incurred, relationships destroyed, careers destroyed, and legal ramifications endured. Displayed in the previous listing of leader's unethical behaviors, each involved a family. Each involved significant financial losses, each affected others in their organization or society, and many incurred legal convictions and punishment. The consequences endured when unethical leaders selfishly pursue more and more money, inappropriate relationships, and professional stature at any cost unfairly encompasses a swath of innocent bystanders. The corrupt leader never considers the price, the damages, or the pain they are ultimately manifesting by their behaviors. Devastation lies in the wake of unethical leaders in many forms.

Crimes committed by leaders in the form of corruption (fraud and bribery), Ponzi schemes, insider trading, racketeering, and embezzlement impose a more significant financial toll on society than common personal property crimes. ***Corrupt people walk a thorny, treacherous road; whoever values life will avoid it*** (Proverbs 22:5). In the United States alone, "According to the FBI, the annual cost of white-collar crimes is over $500 billion, which far exceeds the estimated cost of $15 billion from personal property crime."[4] Today's global society endures even a more significant devastating impact from the unethical behavior of corrupt leaders and systems in the global economy.

There is no escaping from corruptions financial damaging effects on society. Regardless of geographical proximity or distance from corrupt societies, all societies pay for corrupt leadership. The cost of doing business increases as industries are forced to raise prices to recover from losses to corruptive actions. Where society seeks equality and fairness, unethical leadership handicaps societies' efforts to provide for less fortunate societies. "The World Bank estimates that globally more than $1 trillion is handed over annually to corrupt government officials."[5] ***A person who gets ahead by oppressing the poor or by showering gifts on the rich will end in poverty*** (Proverbs 22:16). The unethical leader selfishly seeks to gain more and more for themselves, creating impoverished societies withering and toiling for life's barest necessities.

Unethical behaviors in a leader's professional life threaten to impact their personal life considerably.

> ***There are six things the LORD hates—no, seven things he detests: haughty eyes, a lying tongue, hands that kill the innocent, a heart that plots evil, feet that race to do wrong, a false witness who pours out lies, a person who sows discord in a family.*** (Proverbs 6:16–19)

> ***Greed brings grief to the whole family.*** (Proverbs 15:27)

Families suffer in the ridicule hurled at the corrupt leader when exposed in public. The dishonest leader's children go to school and are potentially subject to the cruelty often conveyed by classmates' crude and damaging self-esteem comments about their corrupt parent. Spouses are often treated as though they are as guilty as the dishonest leader due to their relationship with the fallen leader.

Many spouses cannot forgive the unethical leader's actions and the pain imposed on their lives by them. This is especially the case when inappropriate personal relationships are exposed. Divorces resulting from unethical, inappropriate relationships between leaders and those they lead destroy families and place children's lives in turmoil. The families suffer financially from the loss of employment and careers. Potential legal fees eat away at funds required to support a lifestyle once afforded. Savings for children's college funds cease and are subject to pilferage for daily living needs as income diminishes. Preventing home foreclosures, preventing repossession of vehicles, and affording life's necessities become a challenge. Unethical leadership's devastating consequences are anything but selfish; they eventually impact everyone associated with the fallen leader. Many families are naïve to a leader's unethical behaviors. They are blindsided by the devastating avalanche of relational and financial ruin created by corrupt leadership's exposure.

Unethical behaviors, when discovered, most likely result in jobs lost by leaders. Many leaders are fired from their profession for unethical actions in their personal lives, which often bleed over into their professional responsibilities of ethical conduct. Corrupt leadership stains a leader's reputation within their profession's industry. Finding future employment within the same career field is immensely jeopardized once their unethical behavior is revealed. Industry communities spread the word, and the unethical leader cannot escape ridicule and negative judgment.

Unethical leadership damages the work environment, impacting the workforce and the organization in detrimental ways. People feel betrayed, disappointed, frustrated, and fooled into trusting someone who turns out to be untrustworthy. People become skeptical of trusting other leaders. People's work performance may drop off as they feel a disassociation with the organization after losing their trust in leadership. Organizations are placed in a vulnerable financial position by unethical leadership actions. As in, especially when inappropriate personal acts are involved in unethical behavior. Organizations are subject to expensive legal actions taken on behalf of those betrayed by a leader's unethical conduct.

Unethical Leadership's Self-Imposed Torment

Hiding unethical behavior by a leader is much more challenging and more expensive than the cost of exposing them for who they are. Exposed, a word that strikes fear in the unethical leader's mind and leaves them with nowhere to turn. When the corrupt leader is exposed, there is no place left to hide, no person to call, nothing or no one to save them from the hand they have dealt themselves. "Those who transgress boundaries in their all-consuming life search for knowledge, riches, power, and sexual prowess will overreach themselves until their pact with the devil destroys them."[6]

You will say, "How I hated discipline! If only I had not ignored all the warnings!" (Proverbs 5:12).

Everywhere the fallen leader turns, they are reminded of their falling. Their bank account reminds them. Their family or the loss of it will remind them. Former friends that no longer return calls or seek their company for socializing will remind them. The looks of disappointment by former associates encountered in the community reminds them. The loss of their legacy, both professionally and personally, will remind them. Moreover, perhaps the most devastating reminder for the fallen leader with a conscience is the image they see, staring back at them in their mirror.

> ***And the LORD will cause your heart to tremble, your eyesight to fail, and your soul to despair. Your life will constantly hang in the balance. You will live night and day in fear, unsure if you will survive. In the morning you will say, 'If only it were night!' And in the evening you will say, 'If only it were morning!' For you will be terrified by the awful horrors you see around you.*** (Deuteronomy 28:65–67)

(The curses for disobeying God written by Moses in the Book of Deuteronomy should wake up any person or leader contemplating unethical behavior in their life. Moses knew that disobeying God would bring severe consequences on the people and warned them against it. As a leader, you should know the curses for unethical leadership. God has no favorites, and we are all subject to His wrath when we violate His Truth in leading. God wants to do great things in your life. Do the right thing and allow Him to do great things in your life.)

This time of crisis in a former leader's life is an all-consuming and potentially devastating period that many have endured. They once thought themselves invincible and immune to their consequential reality of unethical behaviors. Way back in time before Jesus Christ walked the earth, the severe damaging effects of unethical behavior have been expressed. Perhaps no more poignantly than we read in Lamentations 3:1–20,

> ***I am the one who has seen the afflictions that come from the rod of the LORD's anger. He has led me into darkness, shutting out all light. He has turned his hand against me again and again, all day long. He has made my skin and flesh grow old. He has broken my bones. He has besieged and surrounded me with anguish and distress. He has buried me in a dark place, like those long dead. He has walled me in, and I cannot escape. He has bound me in heavy chains. And though I cry and shout, he has shut out my prayers. He has blocked my way with a high stone wall; he has made my road crooked. He has hidden like a bear or a lion, waiting to attack me. He has dragged me off the path and torn me to pieces, leaving me helpless and devastated. He has drawn his bow and made me the target for his arrows. He shot his arrows deep into my heart. My own people laugh at me. All day long they sing their mocking songs. He has filled me with bitterness and given me a bitter cup of sorrow to drink. He has made me chew on gravel. He has rolled me in the dust. Peace has been stripped away, and I have forgotten what prosperity is. I cry out, "My splendor is gone! Everything I had hoped for from the LORD is lost!" The thought of my suffering and homelessness is bitter beyond words. I will never forget this awful time, as I grieve over my loss.***

For the fallen leader with a conscience, shame, guilt, and remorse consume them. Feelings of anxiety and depression become adversaries. Loneliness becomes an enemy the fallen leader cannot escape. All of their old places are no longer accessible because everyone knows of the leader's failure and disgrace. Moving to a new location may provide some relief. Still, the fallen leader's unethical reputation will pop its head up the second the fallen leader seeks new employment... another reminder. "True identity is always socially bestowed more than self-constructed."[7] Door after door will close in the fallen leader's life.

For the fallen leader without a conscious, still arrogant, full of pride, full of themselves, and unwilling to humble themselves and admit their failings, they live in denial. They believe they will prove everyone else wrong. However, they will not recover. They will not climb back up; they will not be able to outrun their past. ***Look! Those who do evil have fallen! They are thrown down, never to rise again*** (Psalm 36:12). No one will save them. For them, this warning from Proverbs 15:29: **The LORD is far from the wicked.** The LORD warns the fallen leader who believes they can bounce back using prior arrogant and selfish motives in leading.

> ***"Like those in the pit who have entered the world of the dead. You will have no place of respect here in the land of the living. I will bring you to a terrible end, and you will exist no more. You will be looked for, but you will never again be found. I, the Sovereign LORD, have spoken!"*** (Ezekiel 26:20–21)

For the proud and unrepentant fallen leader, devastation and hopelessness will follow throughout their remaining lifetime.

However, there is hope for the fallen leader with a conscience, beside themselves in regret, shame, and guilt, and sincerely sorry for their unethical behavior. There is a way to stand back up. It starts with God's Truth in living life.

> ***"Today I have given you the choice between life and death, between blessings and***

> ***curses. Now I call on heaven and earth to witness the choice you make. Oh, that you would choose life, so that you and your descendants might live! You can make this choice by loving the LORD your God, obeying him, and committing yourself firmly to him. This is the key to your life."*** (Deuteronomy 30:19–20)

> ***Jesus said, "And you will know the truth, and the truth will set you free."*** (John 8:32)

Pay attention to the responsibility of leading and stop seeking privileges from leading. The right motive of "Leading Is Assuming Responsibility, Not Receiving Privileges" establishes behaviors and attributes found in ethical leadership. Let's keep our focus on leadership's responsibility of honestly serving and leading others. Serving others, now that is a privilege! Onward!

Reflection Time

What devastation have you seen a person endure as a result of unethical choices and actions in life? This is the reality of unethical actions, look at them and fear them.

If you did something unethical that hurt your personal or professional life, contemplate for a moment the number of lives that would be impacted by the damages of your unethical actions.

Are your relationships, career, mental health, finances, life's legacy, or reputation worth risking over unethical decisions? Unethical damages are like a hurricane. They rip apart and destroy everything that once appeared structurally sound.

---

[1] Harold Myra and Marshall Shelley, The Leadership Secrets of Billy Graham (Grand Rapids: Zondervan, 2005), 61.

[2] United States Congress, Office of Compliance. Compliance.gov, https:www.compliance.gov/2017-annual-report.

[3] Carrie Johnson, "Ebber's Gets 25 Year Sentence for Role in WorldCom Fraud," Washington Post. July 14, 2005, B2.

[4] Roomy Khan, "White-Collar Crime—Motivation and Triggers," Forbes.com. 22 February 2018, https://www.forbes.com/sites/roomykhan/ 2018/02/22/white-collar-crimes-motivations-and-triggers/#1cd656bd1219.

[5] Shellie Karabell, "Corruption 101: The Dark Side of Leadership," Forbes.com. 19 June 2015, https://www.forbes.com/sites/shelliekarabell/ 2015/06/19/corruption-101-the-dark-side-of-leadership/#3989a4a039a8.

[6] Os Guinness, The Call: Finding and Fulfilling the Central Purpose of Your Life (Nashville: W Publishing Group, 2003), 181.

[7] Ibid., 23.

PART 7

Leading Is Assuming Responsibility, Not Receiving Privileges

The LORD said, "When someone has been given much, much will be required in return; and when someone has been entrusted with much, even more will be required."

—Luke 12:48

Let's clarify upfront when talking about leadership what we mean by the words *responsibility* and *privilege.* Responsibility is having a duty to deal with something or control someone. Privilege is a special right, advantage, or immunity granted or available only to a particular person or group. Looking throughout society, we find two differently motivated kinds of leaders. One looks to serve and the other to be served.

We find those driven by the desire for greater responsibility because they seek to be in a leadership place that allows them to serve and care for larger numbers of people. These are the leaders who want to weed out the organizational bureaucracy that so often stifles the progress of those they lead. These are the leaders who want to make sure those they lead are cared for properly, and the organization's mission is always achieved. Seeking Responsibility orients leaders toward others.

In contrast, some leaders seek to lead because they see positions of leadership as positions that will grant them privileges for their service. These are the leaders that believe they should be entitled to unique advantages others "beneath" them are not allowed to experience. These are the leaders who want the bigger office with the great view, the parking space closer to the business entrance, the secretary to buffer them from others, and what some may believe the "privileged" are "entitled" to. These are the leaders who believe they can come into work at their leisure, show up as they feel for scheduled events, and others should wait for them and serve at their convenience. Seeking Privilege orients a leader toward self.

We do not lead to receive. We lead to give ourselves away!

Examples of Assuming Responsibility in Leadership from God's Word

Jesus says "My purpose is to give them a rich and satisfying life. I am the good shepherd. The good shepherd sacrifices his life for the sheep" (John 10:10–11). (A leader with the correct motivation for leading desires increased responsibility when it corresponds to caring for an increased number of people being led. Leaders at every level should seek to make the lives of those they serve and lead more satisfying. Throughout God's Word, the word *shepherd* represents a leader, and their "flock" is their people. Jesus was a perfect leader who ultimately sacrificed His life for people's sins. Thankfully, no one is asking today's leaders to make this kind of sacrifice for those they serve and lead. Still, Jesus's purpose for leading was in the interest of others. This is what God expects and requires of all leaders. Every leader should have one mind-set for wanting to lead more significant numbers of people. A perspective of the more people you are responsible for, the more people's lives you can make better. Don't seek promotions for titles and prominence; seek them to be provided the privilege of serving more people.)

"***I will appoint responsible shepherds who will care for them, and they will never be afraid again. Not a single one will be lost or missing. I, the LORD, have spoken!"*** (Jeremiah 23:4). (As a method for speaking into the leaders of an organization, I would use my introduction time with others to convey a leadership message. With their leaders present, I would tell everyone, "You deserve leaders who will properly train and care for you and your families' needs. If you are not getting this from your leaders, come and let me know. If I substantiate your claim, I will replace the failing leader and provide you leaders who will properly train and care for you. Your leaders, and I included, exists for you." This may sound blunt, but I wanted everyone to know how I viewed every leader's responsibility for our people's care. If you desire subordinate leaders to adopt and implement your view of being responsible in their leadership role, tell them!)

Work willingly at whatever you do, as though you were working for the LORD rather than for people (Colossians 3:23). (When you are leading, you are working for the LORD. He is the One that has blessed you to lead and allows you to continue leading. God has anointed and appointed you to look after His flock. As a person, it's not what you are doing; it's who you are doing it for. For the Christian, everything we do, regardless of its trivial or grandiose nature, is for the glory of God. For the leader, it's not about doing something for self-projection, but doing something to project the lives of those you are honored to lead. The beautiful and wonderful thing about working for the LORD is that His Word tells us exactly how He would have us lead. Lead according to God's Word and His Truth. His flock will be in great hands, yours!)

If God has given you leadership ability, take the responsibility seriously (Romans 12:8). (Being blessed to lead means God has given you leadership ability. But all the world's leadership ability is meaningless if not driven by the correct motive for leading. Take God's blessing seriously and take measures to maximize your leadership effectiveness. Spend time in God's Word, studying and learning from the numerous examples He provides for becoming a great leader. Seek mentorship from experienced Christian leaders. Pursue higher education goals in Christian Universities. Saturate your life with people of strong Christian character and let your presence represent God's presence in the lives of those you serve and lead. When it comes to leading as God would have you to lead, be all in!)

Yes, each of us will give a personal account to God (Romans 14:12). (Ultimately, everyone will answer to God. In Isaiah 45:23, the LORD says, "***Every knee will bend to me, and every tongue will confess allegiance to me.***" I don't know about you, but I have enough to worry about without adding guilt from not leading God's people His way. Here is a simple remedy for responsibly leading people according to how God wants us to lead, lead according to His Word. Then, when God reviews how you led His people, He will say to you, "***Well done, my good and faithful servant***" (Matthew 25:21).

Get up, for it is your duty to tell us how to proceed in setting things straight. We are behind you, so be strong and take action (Ezra 10:4). (One of the responsibilities in leading is to lead. I have to say the obvious because some leaders don't want to behave like a person in charge when the situation requires them to. A great leader himself, Dr. Martin Luther King, Jr., said, "A genuine leader is not a searcher for consensus, but a molder of consensus." The leader is a doer, an inspirator, motivator, decision-maker, and a pacesetter. Leading is not for those weak in personal courage. Speak up, speak out, take charge, and lead. They need you to be their leader and be responsible for all that the duty of leading requires. Dr. and Pastor Pat Robertson teaches us that "True leaders must not only be in charge; they must also be responsible for what they do."[1] God has placed you here in leadership, now, serve His will for your life, and lead!)

Whatever you do, do well (Ecclesiastes 9:10). (Everything and no matter its significance or insignificance, is a test of your life philosophy. Either you will do just enough to get by, or you will excel and give your best in every situation. I would say to others, "If we are going to do this, then let's do this better than anyone else ever has." I understand that we live in a day and time where competitions award "participant" awards to every participant. We do not want to call or imply anyone is a "loser." But come on, whatever happened to inspire others to try and win? As a leader, give it all you have, hold nothing back, go full throttle in serving those you lead. Sometimes being a participant may be the best a person can give; God Bless them for trying. Unfortunately, this is not an acceptable tolerance when it comes to leading. Remember what Jesus said in Luke 12:48, ***"When someone has been given much, much will be required in return; and when someone has been entrusted with much, even more will be required."*** In other words, leader, DO WELL!)

Keep a close watch on how you live and on your teaching (1 Timothy 4:16). (One of the responsibilities of leading is leading by example. We talked extensively on this subject earlier in this book. Part of the ***"much will be required"*** from the previous verses discussion most definitely applies here. A leader is on display all the time. The way they live their lives, their conduct in and out of the workplace, and what they teach others must be right, always. A leader is never out of the spotlight of judgment and being a role model for others to emulate. Guard yourselves against letting others down, and most importantly, letting God down.)

Responsibility in leadership automatically implies that sacrifices will have to be made by those titled "leader." We see the perfect example of supreme sacrifice in God's Word when Jesus came into this world with the responsibility of saving mankind from our sins through giving his life on the Cross.

In Matthew 20:25–26, ***Jesus said, "You know that the rulers in this world lord it over*** (to act in a way that shows one thinks one is better or more important than someone else) ***their people, and officials flaunt their authority over those under them. But among you it will be different. Whoever wants to be a leader among you, must be your servant.*** Jesus continues with his example in Matthew 20:28, ***"For even the Son of Man came not to be served but to serve others and to give his life as a ransom for many."***

Jesus made sure to point out the requirements associated with the responsibility of serving and leading others. In Luke 12:47, Jesus says, ***"When someone has been given much, much will be required in return; and when someone has been entrusted with much, even more will be required."***

Thankfully, we are not charged with such a tremendous eternal responsibility as Jesus was. However, the responsibility of leadership does impact the quality of people's physical lives. When a person becomes a leader with motives for leading oriented toward responsibility, they commit to personal sacrifices for the organization and those they serve and lead.

Jesus said, "If you cling to your life, you will lose it; but if you give up your life for me, you will find it (Matthew 10:39). If a leader clings to what they seek to achieve for themselves, they serve under the wrong motive. Eventually, their selfish desires will cost them the chance to continue leading or achieve future success. God does not think favorably of leaders that turn to selfish motives in their responsibility of caring for others. The LORD says to the shepherds (leaders),

> ***What sorrow awaits you shepherds who feed yourselves instead of your flocks. Shouldn't shepherds feed their sheep?*** (Ezekiel 34:2).
>
> ***Instead, you have ruled them with harshness and cruelty.*** (Verse 4:)
>
> ***I now consider these shepherds my enemies, and I will hold them responsible for what has happened to my flock. I will take away their right to feed the flock, and I will stop them from feeding themselves. I will rescue my flock from their mouths; the sheep will no longer be their prey.*** (Verse 10)

God's Word warns leaders to place the needs of those they serve and lead first. Leading requires leaders to treat those they are entrusted to serve and lead with gentleness and tenderhearted care. According to God's Truth in leading, any leader who does not lead responsibly will not have the privilege of leading for long. God will not subject people to irresponsible leadership. A leader is like a person's life, only here for a little while. ***Your life is like the morning fog—it's here a little while, then it's gone*** (James 4:14).

Maybe you and I share something in common. We have both had leaders we could not wait for to be like the fog and disappear. I have witnessed the most horrible leaders more than a few times. What made them so horrific? They thought it was our privilege to have them as our leader. They were full of themselves and only cared about seeking benefits from being a leader. Everyone in the organization counted the days until they would be gone while hoping never to see them again. They would not sacrifice for anyone but would make others sacrifice for the privilege of their comfort and luxury. However, if a leader offers themselves for the organization's needs and those they serve and lead, they fulfill their responsibilities.

One of the wrong mind-sets of people when assuming the mantle of leadership is that now they are "in charge," they are entitled to some form of privilege or benefit. Where in the journey of growing in our competencies and experience to gain the title of leader, do we suddenly decide we are entitled to privileges? Have we taken our eye off the prize of making lives better for those we serve and lead and started to look again at the person in the mirror? From the first day, a person becomes a leader, they exist to serve the needs of the organization and others'; this is a form of work. There is not a point in time when leading changes from working to being entitled. The higher in a leadership position, the more responsibility is assumed. That's the truth in leading.

Make no mistake, when a leader grows in greater responsibilities, those greater responsibilities may come with what some naïvely view as privileges. They see the secretary, the private office, the assistant, or the personal aide as leader's privileges. These are not privileges in a sense they become perks, benefits, or entitlements for a leader's enjoyment. These are not privileging at all; these are requirements for a leader with such a vast number of positional responsibilities requiring an accouterment of talented personnel to effectively carry out their office of responsibility.

Every aspect of being an ethical leader is driven by a leader's character, grounded in being a responsible person. A leader is a responsible person who seeks to be accountable for others' care and needs and an organization. Promotions into leadership authority result from the performance proven to be accountable and worthy of being trusted with increased responsibilities. In Matthew 25:21 Jesus says, ***"You have been faithful in handling this small amount, so now I will give you more responsibilities."*** Being responsible for what you have been given responsibility for is the overarching theme of leadership.

Being responsible is an individual requirement for everyone on the team or in the organization. Being responsible, generates individual and organizational success. For the defensive perimeter of a military unit's tactical location, fighting positions are emplaced. Each fighting position is assigned a sector/lane of responsibility in front of their fighting position to observe. The people assigned each position are responsible for watching and, if required, engaging enemy forces entering their designated fighting positions sector/lane. If each lane of responsibility is watched and protected vigilantly, the lanes of responsibility adjacent to it will be protected and safe through the interlocking lanes of responsibility this provides. When each person performs their duties responsibly, the entire organization remains secure and protected. In today's public and private organizations, when leaders display and hold others accountable for their job responsibility, organizations gain efficiencies and are safe from mission failure and protected from economic losses.

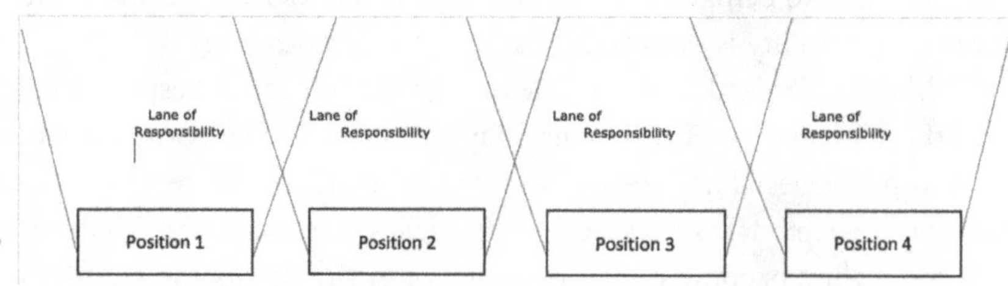

But what about the leader that has taken their eye off of their lane of responsibility? When leaders are not responsible and are not holding others accountable for their responsibility, the people and the organization are doomed for failure and ultimate vicissitude. God's Word warns leaders:

> ***"What sorrow awaits the leaders of my people—the shepherds of my sheep—for they***

> ***have destroyed and scattered the very ones they were expected to care for," says the LORD. Therefore, this is what the LORD, the God of Israel, says to these shepherds: "Instead of caring for my flock and leading them to safety, you have deserted them and driven them to destruction. Now I will pour judgment on you for the evil you have done to them."*** (Jeremiah 23:1–2)

United States President Harry S. Truman kept a sign on his desk in the Oval Office, which read "The Buck Stops Here." President Truman was acknowledging that his leadership office was ultimately responsible for everything, good/bad/right/wrong in the country during his leadership watch. The President's desk sign stated, "I won't pass the blame for failures on to anyone else, I will be responsible, and I am accountable for everything happening while I lead the nation." We see the opposite in leadership today. Especially in politicians' political world they blame everything wrong or failing on opposing political parties and their current/former leaders. Blaming others does not fix things. Assuming responsibility, searching for, and instituting corrective measures is what elected or appointed leaders are expected to do while in office.

The same is true for leaders throughout society. Leaders don't make excuses; they find solutions. Being responsible is assuming ownership of the good and the bad. Leaders don't identify problems and pass blame; leaders identify and present countermeasures to turn difficulties into successful opportunities. Just like a person lifts weights to tear a muscle down to ultimately promote greater strength, leaders tear down issues and failures to identify and implement robust and more successful antidotes. Responsibility in leadership doesn't allow time for the blame game. Responsibility in leadership is about creating success for those being served and led, including the organization.

> ***Because of the privilege and authority God has given me, I give each of you this warning: Don't think you are better than you really***

> ***are. Be honest in your evaluation of yourselves, measuring yourselves by the faith God has given us.*** (Romans 12:3)

One last thing, privilege does have its place in leadership. The only privilege in leadership is the privilege of being trusted by God to lead our fellow man. Being a leader is a blessing and honor granted by God. Maintaining an attitude of thankfulness for the privilege of serving and leading others is essential in knowing our place of responsibility to others and, ultimately, God. Significant responsibility in leadership is balancing the organization's needs with those you serve and lead. I like to refer to this one as "The Challenge." Let's go ahead and get into it; here we go!

Reflection Time

Do you enjoy the responsibility of leading? What parts do you enjoy the most?

Is there a "perk or privilege" associated with your leadership position that leaves you feeling awkward about having it? Would you be willing to give it up for your peace of mind?

Is there any part of the "perks or privileges" that keeps you from knowing and serving those you lead with the attention and diligence others deserve from you? (Private eating area, filters of staff personnel preventing access to you, for example)

---

[1] Pat Robertson, Ten Laws for Success: Keys to Win in Work, Family, and Finance. (Lake Mary: Charisma House, 2020), 75.

PART 8

The Challenge (Achieving a Balance between the Organization's Mission and the Needs of the Those You Serve and Lead)

The LORD demands accurate scales and balances;
he sets the standards for fairness.

—Proverbs 16:11

Walking in the door of a new organization and not knowing "how things are done around here" presents enough challenge for any new person and especially a new leader. Coming in the door as a new leader, you are full of ideas and methods for creating success, heck, that's what prompted them to hire you. But before you can jump right into leading your way, you must take some time to observe and assess what's working and what's not. You need to allow time to learn what you don't know about the people and the organization.

Taking a shortcut and bypassing this essential step will create more havoc than a little tactical patience (allowing the conditions for success to develop) could prevent. ***Good planning and hard work lead to prosperity, but hasty shortcuts lead to poverty*** (Proverbs 21:5). Once you have learned and self-inculcated the organization's mission mind-set, organization's value's, and the organization's unique and individual organizational culture, you are ready to look at what is and what is not working well. Once identified, you now have areas to interject your talents for better chances of creating the successes you are capable of.

As a self-imposed method for doing this, I never made a change for the first ninety days (a different length of time may apply to your situation) of entering a new organization. If I made a knee-jerk change in operational methods or policy before I knew what I didn't know, I might have to revert the policy. This would present an impulsive image that could erode the trust I was seeking to establish within the organization. It is only natural to want to walk in the door and place your leadership stamp on things, but who are you rushing to do this for? Your image and your name? Don't run to failure, remain faithful to the leader God made you be for others, and be patient.

Allow your method of leadership to creep up on the organization and the people. They are already feeling some anxiety about the unknowns about you, the new leader. Don't flash flood your leadership style on them; sprinkle them with your ways, and give them time to absorb your style and intrinsic motivation for them. Let them observe your leadership walk and allow their trust in your methods and reasons to grow naturally. Bring others closer to you and make their lives better by the love your leadership character evokes through your caring nature. In Jeremiah 31:3, the LORD says, ***"With unfailing love, I have drawn you to myself."*** You cannot talk your way into others trusting you. Jesus spent time doing miracles and leading with his walk of love. Once He had people's trust, then they heard His love and care for them in Matthew 11:28–30, ***"Come to me, all of you who are weary and carry heavy burdens, and I will give***

you rest. Take my yoke upon you. Let me teach you, because I am humble and gentle at heart, and you will find rest for your souls. For my yoke is easy to bear, and the burden I give you is light."

Jesus's method of building trust by his walk is one every leader should emulate. But you say, "I am not new to the organization, but I am a newly promoted leader" or a leader that "wants to reorient my leadership method."

You had spent years learning how to be a good follower before others recognized you can be trusted to lead others. Lead according to how the organization "does things" and what is required of everyone that works there.

You know your leaders. You know and understand what is important to them and what matters most. You have learned your boundaries within theirs and the organization's tolerances of behavior and actions. You have learned what amount of authority you hold and your lateral maneuver space to work within your authority and responsibility scope. In other words, you have learned just how much you can push the envelope and impart your ideas and still be in compliance with the organization's standards and policies and the leadership above you.

After years of being a follower and task executor of your job specialty, you became a subject matter expert. Your head is filled with the "work/technical/bureaucratic" components an individual requires before being allowed to lead in the organization. You feel at home and comfortable within the culture and the mission of the organization. You know and understand what needs to get accomplished, how to get it done, and how to improve the organization from your formidable years and preparation.

You have enjoyed and learned from good and even a few times, great leaders along the way. But you have also endured the agony and frustration of perhaps several terrible leaders along the way. From these awful leaders, you have learned exactly how not to lead. It is now your time to do things the right way, for both the organization and those you lead. For the new leader coming into the organization, the leader who has been there a while but wants to reorient their leadership motive and with the newly promoted leader in the organization, you are ready for your greatest leadership challenge. Achieving a balance between the organization's mission success and caring for those you serve and lead.

Let's look at the dilemma facing you, the leader. Your reason for existence in the organization as a leader is to achieve organizational success. To achieve organizational success, you need a group of people committed and loyal to its organization's mission. If the organizational mission fails, organizations and their workforce will suffer potential financial losses. These losses could result in an organization's closure and careers being cut short. Suppose the organization's workforce is not committed and loyal to the organization's mission. In that case, the quality of work could diminish the organization's financial earnings. This could result again in an organization closure and careers being cut short. Both go hand in hand with one another. The organization needs leaders who achieve success for the organization. The workforce needs leaders who are there for their needs. What are both the organization's success and the needs of the workforces saving grace? You, the leader, because you are in this for both of them.

> ***As workers who tend a fig tree are allowed to eat the fruit, so workers who protect their employer's interest will be rewarded*** (Proverbs 27:18).

Achieving a successful balance between the organization's mission and the care of those you lead is like the juggler at the circus keeping all the bowling pins in the air without dropping one. Thankfully, it is a bit easier than this. I can't even juggle a few tennis balls without one bouncing away in the first few seconds. The first and crucial step in balancing these two essential needs is to know the organization and know your people. This is one reason earlier we discussed "Know Those You Lead." As a leader, you want to win on all fronts, organization, and people. But never forget, the mission must be successful. You cannot sacrifice the organization's success to be "liked" by recklessly placing people's needs first.

Even though Jesus came to love and serve before dying on the Cross for all of the people's sins, He still recognized authority's rules. He revealed the balance between answering to man's head of governance and answering to his spiritual needs. In Mark 12:14–17, Jesus is asked by the Pharisees and supporters of Herod,

> ***"Now tell us—is it right to pay taxes to Caesar or not? Should we pay them, or shouldn't we?" Jesus saw through their hypocrisy and said, "Why are you trying to trap me? Show me a Roman coin, and I'll tell you." When they handed it to him, he asked, "Whose picture and title are stamped on it? "Caesar's," they replied. "Well then," Jesus said, "give to Caesar what belongs to Caesar, and give to God what belongs to God." His reply completely amazed them.***

This balance between man's requirements and God's requirements were nonnegotiable. So are the needs of the organization and the needs of those you lead. Both are important for success, peace, and harmony in the organization.

With those you lead, let them know you are focused on the mission and them. When meeting with the people of a new organization I was assigned to lead, I let them know upfront my priorities. I would say to them, "We are going to exceed every standard and succeed at every mission we are assigned; my job is to prepare you for those challenges, but nothing says we can't have a good time doing it. I will be there for you and work hard to take care of you, so when the time comes for the mission to be accomplished, you can be there for the organization's needs."

One of the XVIII Airborne Corps' semiannual requirements is that every soldier successfully conducts a tactical ruck march. The twelve-mile timed event required every soldier wear their tactical gear, a thirty-five-pound rucksack, and assigned weapon. Every soldier must complete twelve miles (walking or running) in less than three hours. Our schedule for conducting this requirement fell on a date that was only a couple of days before Christmas. Usually, the soldiers are on a reduced work schedule during the holiday period to allow extended family time. No one (me included) looked forward to coming in before the sun came up in the cold weather this close to Christmas to train. But a standard is a standard, and the organizational mission readiness required it.

As we finished the ruck march and gathered for personnel and equipment accountability, I had a large military cargo truck pull into our assembled area. Once the driver dismounted and opened the back of the cargo area canvas, it revealed a truck bed covered with six-foot sub sandwiches and beverages. The soldiers had achieved the required standard. Instead of loading up to head back to headquarters, we sat around and ate and drank together. The soldiers spent the time laughing and eating together. Success was achieved, but with some fun (and good food) in the end.

There are going to be plenty of times when the mission dictates over other's needs. When you had displayed a selfless attitude and been there for the needs of those you led when circumstances allowed, those you lead will understand and be there for you and the organization. Loyalty from those you lead is garnered through your commitment in their times of need. Go an inch for them, and they will go a mile for you and the organization. Every organization's mission is different, but when you know the organization, you can then find opportunities within the day-to-day operations tempo to take care of those you lead.

Leadership is not a popularity contest. In the television show *The Office*, the office manager's insecurity about being liked by everyone makes excellent humor. This is only a television show and in no way represents how a leader should lead. A leader is not there to be everyone's friend. A leader is there to make sure the job gets done. However, this does not mean the leader doesn't care. People in the workforce understand this and seek a leader who recognizes the organization's mission and them.

A leader does not have the privilege of having a personal relationship with those they lead. Still, they do have a professional responsibility of caring for those they lead. When a leader enters a personal relationship with a person they are responsible for, they open the door for their authority position in their professional capacity to be compromised. The leader becomes vulnerable to allowing personal feelings to influence their decision making when it comes to the person they are now emotionally attached to. A leader must know their people and understand how "close" they can allow them to who they are as a person.

One of the roles of being a leader is keeping everyone informed. Information dissemination keeps everyone on the same sheet of music and moving in the same direction. But information dissemination is merely the broadcasting of words, words for the masses. Individuals listen to all disseminated information to first understand, "How does this information affect me and my future?" Informing those you lead is very important. It assists in fulfilling the needs of an individual's desire to be accepted and valued.

This is a basic humanistic need of every person. Leaders must create a climate of acceptance and value for each individual they lead. This is achieved by the previously discussed actions to build trust and form genuine caring professional relationships with those you lead. Through your acts of self-sacrifice, self-giving, and making others the center of your focus, you are caring for their needs and helping them feel accepted and valued. Caring for those you lead is established through everyday interaction and communication. Caring is not addressing their needs only if they reach a crisis point. Caring is a continuous process. Caring for those you lead generates synergy toward achieving the organization's mission success. Observers witnessed this caring leadership trait in the inspiring leader, Dr. Billy Graham. "Empathy and wisdom on such occasions, become human building blocks, creating loyalty and trust. When storms strike individuals or organizations, a leader who responds with genuine concern and calm establishes his or her leadership."[1]

John 10:10 Jesus says, **"My purpose is to give them a rich and satisfying life."** (Everyone seeks success. When a leader helps those they serve and lead be successful in their work, people and the organization are both successful. Our families, friends, and close relationships make our lives rich and satisfying to a point. Still, we also need professional success for a rich and satisfying life. Take care of them, and they, in turn, will take care of the organization's needs. You just achieved balance in "The Challenge!")

This is your purpose in leading, to give those you lead "a rich and satisfying life." As a leader, you must achieve the organization's mission, and you must care for the needs of those you lead. Achieving both of these provides riches and satisfaction for the organization and the people. You know the work and what has to be completed for success. You know the people you lead, and you know their needs. Make whatever time is required to achieve success for both. Sacrifice, commit yourself, and give everything you have to those you serve and lead. Create the balance, and neutralize the challenge.

Reflection Time

Which do you enjoy most, the mission or the people? Why?

What can you do today to help your people so that when tomorrow's needs of the organization come, they are ready to serve as needed?

What sacrifices do you need to make today to make those you serve and lead better prepared for tomorrow's organizational challenges?

---

[1] Harold Myra and Marshall Shelley, The Leadership Secrets of Billy Graham (Grand Rapids: Zondervan, 2005), 187.

PART 9

Disciplining Those We Serve and Lead (Never Personal, Always Professional)

You have the authority to correct them when necessary, so don't let anyone disregard what you say.

—Titus 2:15

Leading Is Also Being the Disciplinarian

I know, I know, why do we have to talk about the ugly part of leading? Why do we need to discuss disciplining others? Well, if I could have read through God's Word, and He never mentioned discipline, it would not have been included in becoming a great leader. However, God's Word provides us extensive guidance on disciplining those who have taken the wrong path. Wrong behavior will almost always continue if a person is not held accountable. Disciplinary actions are God's method for man to use in mitigating future wrongful or illegal conduct. God's Word speaks of His love for us as the reason He disciplines us.

And have you forgotten the encouraging words God spoke to you as his children? He said, "My child, don't make light of the Lord's

> ***discipline, and don't give up when he corrects you. For the Lord disciplines those he loves, and he punishes each one he accepts as his child."*** (Hebrews 12:5–6)

Being the disciplinarian at home or in the workplace is no one's favorite responsibility. It is the most unliked part of leading, especially since we only want good things for those we serve and lead. In society, we have law enforcement and a judicial system to enforce society's laws of conduct. In the workplace, we have leaders responsible for the enforcement of the standards of conduct and behavior within the organization by their position of authority. Disciplining those who violate the organization's standards of conduct and behavior is a method leaders use to enforce the standards.

God's Word on Discipline and Practical Application

Why Discipline Is Required

The LORD says, ***Don't do these horrible things that I hate so much. But my people would not listen or turn back from their wicked ways*** (Jeremiah 44:4). (Leaders can want everyone to do the right thing but cannot do what is right for them. Each person is responsible for the choices they make. When people make the wrong choice, there are potential disciplinary consequences. In other words, "Help me help you. Do the right thing, and all is well. Do the wrong thing, and I will do the leader thing no one enjoys. I will provide consequences for the wrongs.")

Jeremiah 30:11 ***says the LORD, "I will discipline you, but with justice; I cannot let you go unpunished."*** (Leaders must let people know they will hold every person accountable appropriately. Everyone is required to adhere to the established standards of work and conduct. When a leader lets others know there will be disciplinary measures applied as needed, they can't say it as a threat. Just as every position within an organization has specific tasks and responsibilities, so does a leader's role. A leader should explain to those they serve and lead, the leader is responsible for enforcing the organization's standards and conduct. With this responsibility comes the authority to discipline others when infractions occur. Just as the leader expects others to do their job entirely, the leader should let others know they will do their job thoroughly and appropriately discipline individuals as required.)

But if you do what is wrong, you will be paid back for the wrong you have done. For God has no favorites (Colossians 3:25). (Maintaining a professional relationship prevents favoritism often incubated by personal relationships. Leaders have no choice, and when a person does wrong, they must be disciplined. Others are watching to see what you will turn a blind eye to. If you look the other way instead of disciplining wrongs, you have set a precedence others will call you on. In disciplining, what is imposed on one person must be applied to others if they violate the same conduct standards.)

To reject the law is to praise the wicked; to obey the law is to fight them (Proverbs 28:4). (Letting misdeeds go unpunished says that you are okay with them. Disciplining misdeeds says you will not tolerate them.)

Those who plant injustice will harvest disaster, and their reign of terror will come to an end (Proverbs 22:8). (A leader who does not discipline today's wrongs will soon have chaos run amok in the workplace. Ultimately, the undisciplined workplace will require a new leader to set things right. When a society adopts passive policing methods, criminals have no fear or respect for law enforcement authorities and continue in crime. Once a new law enforcement authority has been emplaced and implements stricter policing and stronger judicial punishments for convicted criminals are administered by the courts, crime diminishes. President Theodore Roosevelt's foreign policy had it correct, "speak softly and carry a big stick; you will go far." Never look the other way when injustice rears its evil head. Step into it hard, immediately!)

A king detests wrongdoing, for his rule is built on justice (Proverbs 16:12). (Let everyone you serve and lead understand your absolute loathing of inappropriate and wrongful behavior. Let everyone you serve and lead know that appropriate conduct in behavior is everyone's required standard.)

Discipline your children while there is still hope. Otherwise, you will ruin their lives (Proverbs 19:18). (Discipline is a corrective measure a leader takes to alter behaviors to what an organization desires from employees. Changing behaviors to align with acceptable organizational norms early in a person's tenure prevents undeterred minor infractions from escalating into significant offenses. Significant violations can result in decisive disciplinary actions or even employment termination. Disciplinary medicine does not always taste great, but it can prevent minor behavior issues from mutating into untreatable misconduct.)

So there is no justice among us, and we know nothing about right living. We look for light but find only darkness. We look for bright skies but walk in gloom (Isaiah 59:9). (A workplace where chaos runs amok, disciplinary actions don't exist, and no one is held accountable for their corrupt conduct is like a city with no police on the streets. No person wants to live in such a city, and no person wants to work in an organization without justice in place. If they are, it is only out of a desperate need for employment. This would be a sad place to work. Leaders who promote justice and hold people accountable to the standards provide hope. The light of justice in the workplace leaves no dark corners or a dark corridor for injustice to hide. Everyone and everything is saturated in the light of justice, hope, and opportunity. Good lives in the light, evil lives in the darkness. ***Jesus spoke to the people once more and said, "I am the light of the world. If you follow me, you won't have to walk in darkness, because you will have the light that leads to life"*** (John 8:12). Your role in leading gives you the privilege of being a source of light and hope in the dark moments of other's lives. When the light comes on, things that exist in the dark disappear. Justice lives in the light. Turn on the bright light of justice for those you lead by exposing and disciplining those who need to come in out of the dark.)

We look for justice, but it never comes. We look for rescue, but it is far away from us (Isaiah 59:11). (A leader provides what society and the workplace thrive on, security from injustice. Justice rescues a society and the workplace from evil. Corrupt people desire to instill fear, take hope hostage, and prevent people from feeling safe. Justice, hope and safety in the workplace come from the hands of ethical leadership. A leader must be a guardian of justice in the workplace, assuming King David's revealed mind-set in Psalm 101:8, ***My daily task will be to ferret out the wicked and free the city of the LORD from their grip.***)

Our courts oppose the righteous, and justice is nowhere to be found. Truth stumbles in the streets, and honesty has been outlawed. Yes, truth is gone, and anyone who renounces evil is attacked. The LORD looked and was displeased to find there was no justice (Isaiah 59:15–16). (If society feels this way, or the people of an organization feel this way, both the community and the organization will soon cease to exist. Justice must prevail for life, society, and an organization to have a chance at success. When speaking to Moses, God spoke of his stand on establishing justice, saying in Exodus 34:7, "***I lavish unfailing love to a thousand generations. I forgive iniquity, rebellion, and sin. But I do not excuse the guilty.***" Everyone must be held accountable for their actions. There are no free passes where justice resides. Leaders keep justice alive in the workplace by consistently and appropriately disciplining wrongful behavior.)

Leaders Discipline Others Today for Tomorrows Opportunities

Jeremiah 31:20 ***says the LORD, "I often have to punish him, but I still love him. That's why I long for him and surely will have mercy on him."*** (Being a leader at work is no different from being a leader at home. We may find ourselves disciplining those we care for because we want the best for their future. Leaders do not punish out of any motive other than one of love and a desire to see others have a better tomorrow by discontinuing wrongful behavior today.)

Discipline your children, and they will give you peace of mind and will make your heart glad (Proverbs 29:17). (Discipline today deters tomorrow's strife. Peace and harmony have a chance tomorrow, but discipline must start somewhere. In every organization, it must begin with leaders enforcing discipline. Discipline early on, when wrongful behaviors or conduct is first encountered, establishes a foundation of what will not be tolerated. ***And it is good for people to submit at an early age to the yoke of his discipline*** [Lamentations 3:27].)

Disciplining Others Comes from the Heart, Not the Tongue

He will bring justice to the nations. He will not shout or raise his voice in public. He will not crush the weakest reed or put out a flickering candle. He will bring justice to all who have been wronged. He will not falter or lose heart until justice prevails throughout the earth (Isaiah 42:1–4). (Imposing disciplinary measures is not an event filled with yelling and condescending personal remarks. A leader must maintain a professional and normal speaking voice when conducting disciplinary actions. After contemplating all known contributing factors, disciplinary judgment is not meant to belittle or crush the offender's human spirit. State the infraction, state the corrective measures to be administered, and then encourage the offender to overcome wrongful behavior. Let them know you believe in them and want nothing but success in their future. Once disciplinary measures are imposed, the real work for the leader begins. Now, the leader has the responsibility of setting the prior offender up for success, to help them stand back up. Disciplinary actions are not to be continuously held over the offender's head. They made a mistake; they were disciplined and paid the price, don't keep them down. If God did not give us another chance for all of our sins in life, we would all be doomed for eternity. Instead, God forgives, allows sins consequences to work, and lets our offenses go. God wants good things for all of us, even though we let him down over and over in life. God's grace is something every leader should learn to give others after they have paid for their offenses.)

So correct me, LORD, but please be gentle. Do not correct me in anger, for I would die (Jeremiah 10:24). (Emotion is never allowed in discipline! Emotions create physical reactions, voice inflections and make discipline personal, not professional. Very early in my military career, I had a friend responsible for driving our organization's senior leader to official meetings. The senior leader coordinated a pick-up time following one of his appointments for my friend to be there to pick him up and get him to his next scheduled event. My friend made a severe mistake and fell asleep. He awakened up an hour after he was supposed to pick-up the senior leader from the meeting (this was years before cell phones, so no one could locate my friend). He drove like a mad man to where the senior leader was to be picked up. There, on the side of the street, stood the senior leader waiting for him. When the senior leader climbed inside the vehicle, he was not irate and yelling at my friend for being late. He calmly said to my friend, "When a person in my position is scheduled to be somewhere at a given time, people are waiting for me. When you are late doing your job, I can't do my job." When my friend told me this story, he said the senior leader could not have yelled any words that would have hurt him any more than knowing he had let the senior leader down. With a calm tone of voice, the senior leader was heard, loud and clear. My friend no longer drove for the senior leader after his failure. He was moved back to his original duties in the organization. But nothing hurt my friend more than knowing he had let the boss down. This senior leader knew something every leader should be aware of. Your words have a considerable impact on those you lead, especially words of chastisement and admonishment. Harsh comments from leaders leave a mark on those they lead, marks that discourage, not encourage. Marks that create fear, not hope and marks that penetrate a person's spirit of life, that hurts for much longer than the moment at hand. ***The tongue can bring death or life*** (Proverbs 18:21). With a person that cares, your words penetrate their heart, be gentle, even in admonishment. Dr. Pat Robertson provides sound advice stating, "Wise people will use gentleness when dealing with others."[1])

Patiently correct, rebuke, and encourage your people with good teaching (2 Timothy 4:2). (A person honored to serve and lead others has proven their ability to achieve success during their career. But along their career journey, even the best leader never did everything entirely right, every time. We all have needed guidance, corrective criticism, and encouragement to overcome deficiencies. It was through these measures that we grew and eventually found greater success. This is now your role as the leader. Don't be a hypocrite and demand perfection from those you lead. A leader is also a teacher, a preparer, and a developer of tomorrow's leaders. No one wins when we institute a "zero defect" climate in the workplace. Some of the greatest lessons we learn are in our failures. Be patient, be constructively critical, but always be encouraging. No person wants to fail and disappoint others intentionally. Promote a work climate where not only yourself but everyone rallies behind a person struggling to achieve success.)

He made my words of judgment as sharp as a sword (Isaiah 49:2). (A leader's terms of judgment create a significant emotional moment in the life of those being disciplined. Choose your words carefully; don't kill a person's dreams and hopes for the future by slaying them with the sharpness of your tongue. A leader is not a person's final judge of life. Why say words that they will not be able to move past in the future? When religious leaders brought an adulterous woman to Jesus for judgment and stoning, he did not verbally berate the woman after all of her accusers shrunk away as hypocrites. Jesus simply told her in John 8:11, ***"Go and sin no more."*** People who care feel bad enough for their mistakes. They don't need a leader to pile on with sharp demeaning words that will leave emotional scars for days, weeks, and even years to come.)

My child, don't reject the LORD's discipline, and don't be upset when he corrects you. For the LORD corrects those he loves, just as a father corrects a child in whom he delights (Proverbs 3:11–12). (The best method for disciplining others is to do so with a parent's love. Being respectful, stern, and not getting emotional in doing so. Those being disciplined should know you take no joy in carrying out this part of your leadership responsibility. Punishing others as a leader is NEVER personal; it is ALWAYS executed from your professional obligation. You are condemning the wrongful action, not the person. When you criticize the person, you are opening the door for them to become upset and angry with you as a person and as a leader.)

Though he brings grief, he also shows compassion because of the greatness of his unfailing love. For he does not enjoy hurting people or causing them sorrow (Lamentations 3:32–33). (The judgmental decisions a leader makes in imposing disciplinary punishment should be made using a combination of the leader's mind and heart. The mind contemplates factual organizational judicial logic, and the heart considers the impact of punishment on the offender. Out of our love for others, a leader gets no joy from the discipline process. Disciplinary actions are hard enough on the one being disciplined. Having compassion as a leader does not imply the offender goes unpunished. It means a leader carries out their responsibility respectfully and with genuine care for those being disciplined.)

Disciplinary Measures Should Match the Severity of the Offense

For the LORD is a God who gives just punishment; he always repays in full (Jeremiah 51:56). (Disciplinary actions taken should always equate in magnitude to the severity of the infraction and be fully enforced.)

Words alone will not discipline a servant; the words may be understood, but they are not heeded (Proverbs 29:19). (When my friend failed in picking up the senior leader on time, he not only received the gentle verbal admonishment from the senior leader, but he lost his position of being the boss's driver. The job of driving the senior leader implied that the soldier was super squared away and always kept a sharp military appearance. The job was given to soldiers that were considered trustworthy, was technically competent in their career field, and exemplified the Soldier's Creed. The senior leader sent a message that everyone has a responsibility. If they lose his confidence in their abilities to perform as required, there are more significant consequences.)

Those who spare the rod of discipline hate their children. Those who love their children care enough to discipline them

(Proverbs 13:24). (Disciplining those you lead is one of your most substantial methods of stating you care about their current and future chances for success in the workplace and life. When a leader does not discipline offenders, they allow them to continue toward guaranteed future strife and potentially more significant consequences.)

Leaders Discipline Others Based on the Organization's Standards

I can do nothing on my own. I judge as God tells me. Therefore, my judgment is just, because I carry out the will of the one who sent me, not my own will (John 5:30). (A leader never disciplines a person based on their personal beliefs. A leader judges according to the standards and policies of the organization's rules. It is from and by the organization in which the leader has their authority to judge and discipline. It does not matter what the leader personally thinks. They have a positional responsibility as a leader to enforce the organization's rules and standards of conduct.)

O people, the LORD has told you what is good, and this is what he requires of you: to do what is right, to love mercy, and to walk humbly with your God (Micah 6:8). (Every leader should make opportunities to ensure those they lead understand their understanding, interpretation, and tolerances of the standards and rules of the organization. Leave nothing to doubt and allow those you lead to ask for clarification of standards that may leave room for interpretation. Having everyone on the same page of your views of the rules and standards of conduct provides everyone an insight into how you expect them to act and perform. Being upfront with everyone is not a threatening act. It is words that say, "Here is how I expect myself and all of you to professionally conduct ourselves." The leader owes this to everyone as an investment into promoting right and proper behavior.)

Disciplinary Actions Apply to Everyone Equally

Showing partiality is never good (Proverbs 28:21). (What is right and expected of one is acceptable and expected of all. What is tolerated by one must be accepted by all.)

It is wrong to show favoritism when passing judgment. A judge who says to the wicked, "You are innocent," will be cursed by many people and denounced by the nations. But, it will go well for those who convict the guilty; rich blessings will be showered on them (Proverbs 24:23–25). (The only way to keep justice in the workplace is to enforce the organization's disciplinary standards equitably. NEVER shy away from your responsibility of being the organization's disciplinarian in the workplace. This is the method for creating a workplace of adherence to the standards.)

The LORD detests double standards; he is not pleased by dishonest scales (Proverbs 20:23). (What is suitable for one is ideal for all. Like infractions receive like disciplinary measures, for everyone.)

In Revelation 3:19 God says, ***"I correct and discipline everyone I love. So be diligent and turn from your indifference."*** (Everyone should know you are fair and equitable in your disciplinary measures. No one is exempt from receiving the same corrective actions if required. People will understand it is not personal and know that you are doing your job as a leader.)

Discipline Promotes Peace and Harmony

Throw out the mocker, and fighting goes, too. Quarrels and insults will disappear (Proverbs 22:10). (Every workplace has its stressors created by deadlines, external marketplace competitors, and economic challenges in which a leader has very little authority to influence. However, a person creating stressors from their instigation of confrontational situations between co-workers cannot be tolerated. These individuals represent cancer that, if left untreated, will spread into the entire organization. The instigator must be cut out for healing and good organizational health to occur. Let the instigator take their infectious disease elsewhere. Severely disciplining them is the appropriate prescriptive measure for the required peace and harmony in the workplace. A leader has the authority and the responsibility for ridding the workplace of these kinds of foolish people.)

Justice is a joy to the godly, but it terrifies evildoers (Proverbs 21:15). (One of the greatest measures of creating peace and harmony in the workplace while simultaneously sending a message to those contemplating wrongful behaviors is the revelation by leaders that they will impose consequential actions on anyone violating the standards.)

A wise king scatters the wicked like wheat, then runs his threshing wheel over them (Proverbs 20:26). (It is not always the norm, but you will often find as a leader those that want to test the depths of your tolerances for acceptable behaviors and actions. These people want to see how much they can get away with outside acceptable conduct standards. This is a critical moment for any leader. Do you coward away from your responsibility to enforce the standards, or do you do your job?

An example must be made for all to know what you stand for. As a leader entering a new organization, I would leave no doubt in everyone's minds where I stood. I would tell them, "Do not think that I will let you do as you like because I have told you that I am here to take care of you. One of you will test me to see how much you can get away with. And when you do, you will find that I will make an example of you in a way that no one else would dare do the same things in the future." This one lamb sent to the slaughter sends a message to the rest of the flock that their shepherd will not tolerate misbehavior.)

When a crime is not punished quickly, people feel it is safe to do wrong (Ecclesiastes 8:11). (One of the wisest and kindest things a leader can do when disciplining someone for a substantiated wrong is to do it quickly. There are two reasons for this. First, no one receiving discipline wants the action, just lingering and hanging out there with no end in sight. If it is inevitable that they will be disciplined they wish to get it over. They want to pay the price and move forward.

They deserve quick action from the leader. If the person cares and is sincerely remorseful for their wrongdoing, they are already in a self-imposed turmoil. Dragging the disciplinary process only creates more unknown stressors for them and likely those close to them.

Second, everyone else in the workplace aware of the person's offenses is watching to see what disciplinary action you will impose. In Luke 18:8 Jesus says, ***"I tell you, he will grant justice to them quickly."*** If the disciplinary process is long and drawn out, people will soon think no corrective action will occur and assume that the person's wrongdoing will be tolerated. This will only open the door for others to attempt the same misdeeds. As the legendary Deputy Barney Fife once stated, "You have to nip it, nip it in the bud quickly!")

> ***If you punish the mocker, the simple-minded will learn a lesson; if you correct the wise, they will be all the wiser*** (Proverbs 19:25).

If a person is unpleasant in the workplace by using insulting and perverse words, committing insulting actions against co-workers, and breeding bitterness, a leader is wise to discipline their foolish behavior quickly. These people prevent peace and harmony in the workplace by their slandering others' good names. These are the people who question authority's decisions and undermine the leader's efforts to create a climate of trust and positive workplace relationships. As a leader, you cannot afford to have this kind of arrogant and conceited behavior in the workplace. Disciplining their ignorant behavior and calling them out as the bully is the only way to deal with them. Remember, other people will follow insubordinate actions if you don't make a disciplinary example of insubordination. A leader must squelch the voice of those undermining the good the leader is working to promote in the organization's climate and culture. King David warns against allowing mockers to exist and continue in Psalm 101:3–7,

> ***I hate all who deal crookedly; I will have nothing to do with them. I will reject perverse***

> ***ideas and stay away from every evil. I will not tolerate people who slander their neighbors. I will not endure conceit and pride. I will search for faithful people to be my companions. Only those above reproach will be allowed to serve me. I will not allow deceivers to serve in my house, and liars will not stay in my presence.***

Justice in the Workplace

"For I, the LORD, love justice" (Isaiah 61:8). (If the perfect leader of this world loves justice, how can any leader think otherwise?)

This is what the LORD says to the dynasty of David: "Give justice each morning to the people you judge!" (Jeremiah 21:12). (Be on guard at all times and in every place you venture within the workplace against injustices being committed. Ensure that the treatment of everyone you lead is one of respect and consideration. Lead by your example of genuine concern for every individual. Demand the same of everyone with one another, regardless of their position or title.)

Disciplining Others Is Not Our Goal in Leading

In Jeremiah 42:10 God said, "***For I am sorry about all the punishment I have had to bring upon you.***" (No leader should enjoy disciplinary actions on those they lead. Even God hates to discipline us, but He does so because He knows what is best for us in life.)

God said, ***"My child, don't make light of the LORD's discipline, and don't give up when he corrects you. For the LORD disciplines those he loves, and he punishes each one he accepts as his child"*** (Hebrews 12:6). (I learned a long time ago you cannot help someone that will not help themselves. Discipling people who don't care because their motives are based on selfish desires is mostly a futile effort to reorient their wrongful behaviors. However, the people who do care, but they made an honest mistake are worth the corrective disciplinary actions. Through your respectful disciplinary actions, you correct future behaviors and say to them, "I believe in you and know you are better than this. That you have a future here and you are worth more than your mistake." Society sees being disciplined as a punishment. Still, as a leader, we must see disciplinary measures as an action to promote the right behaviors in the future. No one wins when discipline is used only to punish and keep someone down. On the contrary, when a leader disciplines someone, they say you are worth helping get corrected and back on a path to success.)

No discipline is enjoyable while it is happening—it's painful! But afterward there will be a peaceful harvest of right living for those who are trained in this way (Hebrews 12:11). (There is no joy in discipline for the leader disciplining someone, as much as there is no joy for the person being disciplined. I can still remember looking up at my dad when he was about to discipline me (always deserved) and hearing him say, "This hurts for me to do, as much it is going to hurt you." At that moment, I was thinking, "Well, save yourself the hurt and mine too, and just let me go on my way (wishful thinking)." But if he had let me go undisciplined, I would have indeed gone and done the same adolescent shenanigans again. Instead, after receiving my deserved discipline, I never wanted to let him down by doing what caused us both pain. The people you lead, the one's that care, they don't want to let you down again either. Through discipline, future acceptable actions can be emphasized, and peace and harmony can once again exist in the workplace.)

Every person is obligated to respect the authorities appointed over our lives. Authorities are obligated to enforce the laws and standards of conduct within societies. In this same sense, leaders are obligated to enforce the standards of acceptable behavior in the workplace. As a result, organizations empower leaders to discipline those that violate the organization's standards of allowable conduct. Some former Chief Executive Officer did not dream this up; God's Word instructs leaders to use discipline to enforce acceptable behaviors. ***For the Lord's sake, respect all human authority—whether the king or head of state, or the officials he has appointed. For the king has sent them to punish those who do wrong and to honor those who do right*** (1 Peter 2:13–14).

Learn Both Sides of the Story Before Passing Judgment

"Is it legal to convict a man before he is given a hearing?" (John 7:51). (These are the words the religious leader Nicodemus spoke to the Pharisees who were determined to kill Jesus.)

As a leader, we discussed the value of surrounding yourself with great people and listening to their insights and information to help you in your decision-making. This is another way of saying, surround yourself with the truth about what is the reality of the situation or circumstances at hand. Making decisions and judgments for the good of the organization is a task you take seriously. You understand that your actions will impact the organization's future. So then, shouldn't a leader apply the same truth-finding methodology when weighing the judgment of someone being considered for disciplinary actions against them?

The truth is a beautiful thing, and one wishes truth was the norm in society, but sadly it's not always. When someone's career is in jeopardy, it is easy to alter the truth a bit. The offender tells those doing the judging what they think will sway the leader to a decision in their favor. Without courtroom drama, it only comes down to leaders making sure they have looked at all sides of the issue before rendering their punitive judgment. We have discussed God's Word and His view on discipline in our lives. Still, God also said we are to make informed judgments when contemplating disciplinary actions on others.

Let us review the situation together, and you can present your case to prove your innocence (Isaiah 43:26). (Allowing a person pending your judgment to be heard represents an open-minded leader willing to weigh and consider all information before deciding innocence or guilt. How would you like it if you were the one being judged, and when you walked into the boss's office, they had already made up their mind of your guilt before hearing your side of the story? We spoke earlier of being considerate and compassionate when fulfilling your responsibility of administering disciplinary measures against those you serve and lead. Reviewing the matter together and hearing their information are acts of consideration and compassion. Through your discussion, you gain a better understanding of the situation and facts from both sides. You deserve to know the truth, and they deserve to be heard.)

A truly wise person uses few words; a person with understanding is even tempered (Proverbs 17:27). (Allowing both sides of the story to be heard requires that while one person is talking, the other person is listening. Let your words be few, but to the point. Take the emotion out of your judgment and remember you are fulfilling your professional obligation for the organization. The person being judged will have enough feeling already in play. There is no need to add the fuel of your emotion to an already challenging moment for them.)

The first to speak in court sounds right—until the cross-examination begins (Proverbs 18:17). (Be open-minded and neutral until you know everything from both sides before contemplating your punitive judgment. Until everyone has had their say, you don't know what you don't know.)

Spouting off before listening to the facts is both shameful and foolish (Proverbs 18:13). (Nothing makes a leader seem more biased as a judge than launching into a verbal tirade of guilty accusations before hearing the other person's story. Present the charges and ask the person to tell you their side of the story. Show fairness, open-mindedness, and refrain from any words that would imply a prejudgment of the person before you.)

When a king sits in judgment, he weighs all the evidence, distinguishing the bad from the good (Proverbs 20:8). (Absolutely!)

False weights and unequal measures—the LORD detests double standards of every kind (Proverbs 20:10). (There will be times when an infraction involves multiple people being party to the offense. Regardless of a person's position or how long they have been with the organization, all are judged to the same organizational standards of conduct. Wrong is wrong, and equal justice must be applied to all guilty parties.)

The LORD says, ***"But this is what you must do: Tell the truth to each other. Render verdicts in your courts that are just and lead to peace"*** (Zechariah 8:16). (The goal in every disciplinary action is to determine the truth and decide the appropriate justice that will promote continued peace and harmony in the workplace. Just like we see in society, injustice leads to more significant societal turmoil. Your task as a disciplinarian is to do right by the organization and those you serve and lead. This promotes justice in the workplace.)

This is what the LORD says: "Be just and fair to all. Do what is right and good" (Isaiah 56:1). (Being just and fair to everyone is not only a rule for leading; it is a rule for life.)

Let God weigh me on the scales of justice, for he knows my integrity (Job 31:6). (Doing the right thing means being fair and judging others as you would like to be judged, as in Matthew 7:2, ***For you will be treated as you treat others. The standard you use in judging is the standard by which you will be judged.***)

This is what the LORD says: "Be fair-minded and just. Do what is right! (Jeremiah 22:3). (If the LORD says it, it is not a suggestion, it is His command. Everyone deserves a chance for success in life and the workplace. A fair-minded leader levels the playing field by removing biases, dishonest motives, and injustice from the workplace. This is the right thing to do!)

And the LORD says, "But he was just and right in all his dealings. That is why God blessed him. He gave justice and help to the poor and needy, and everything went well for him. Isn't that

what it means to know me?" says the LORD (Jeremiah 22:15–16). (Being just and right as a leader when judging others not only sits well with those you lead, but it establishes your Christ-like character as a person and as a leader. Leaders don't lead for what is right and just for themselves; leaders lead for others, their needs, care, and justice.)

Having to discipline someone we care about is hard on everyone involved. In a perfect world, everyone would always do what is right, and discipline would not be required. However, that ideal world ended in the Garden of Eden long ago. Today we continue in man's struggle between good and evil, and right and wrong. Nothing has changed in man's behavior since the beginning of humanity. While everything around man has continuously evolved through inventions and technological advancements, man's natural and humanistic nature has remained the same. Unfortunately, this includes wrongful motives and actions by people at times.

Being accountable to others means we answer to them when we have committed an offense against them. When those you serve and lead commit an offense against the organizations's standards of conduct, they answer to you, their leader. As a leader and as a person we are all accountable to God. ***Nothing in all creation is hidden from God. Everything is naked and exposed before his eyes, and he is the one to whom we are accountable*** (Hebrews 4:13). God's Word teaches us that He disciplines those he loves, which is all of us.

Along with God's discipline, which He intends for our greater good, His Word tells us we are to discipline those within our relational responsibility. We are not told to enjoy disciplining those we care about, but we are told to discipline with love. Since leadership is an act of love through caring for those we serve and lead, we discipline others with love as our root motive for correcting improper behaviors and conduct. While leading others is an honor, it is more responsibility. Disciplining those we serve and lead is a responsibility which great leaders accomplish with love, compassion, and respect. After all, You Work for Them!

Reflection Time

How lenient are you in adherence to the standards of conduct in the workplace? Is a little wrong still okay?

What parts of the disciplining process do you dislike the most? Are you letting your personal feelings play in the process?

Are you allowing both sides of the story always to be heard and considered before making your judgment? Are you listening to both sides or forming opinions as information is provided instead of waiting until all information has been heard?

---

[1] Pat Robertson, Ten Laws for Success: Keys to Win in Work, Family, and Finance. (Lake Mary: Charisma House, 2020), 27.

PART 10

Newsflash! You Work for Them

Don't be concerned for your own good but for the good of others.

—1 Corinthians 10:24

What do you expect from those you serve and lead? More than likely, you expect them to be available when you need them. You expect them to listen to what you have to say, to listen to what you need from them. You expect them to act on issues and requirements important to you as soon as possible. You expect them to provide feedback on their efforts in meeting the tasks you have presented to them. And you expect them to care about what you care about.

HELLO, this is exactly what those you serve and lead deserve and expect from you, their leader. Since, in reality, you are only a leader if there is someone to lead, you owe your position in leadership to their needs. Fulfilling the needs of those you serve and lead, says, I work for them.

> ***Then they began to argue among themselves about who would be the greatest among them. Jesus told them, "In this world the kings and great men lord it over their people, yet they are called 'friends of the people.' But among you***

> ***it will be different. Those who are the greatest among you should take the lowest rank, and the leader should be like a servant. Who is more important, the one who sits at the table or the one who serves? The one who sits at the table, of course. But not here! For I am among you as one who serves."*** (Luke 22:24–27)

(Wow, here is the King of King's, LORD of Lords, and the only perfect leader to ever walk this earth, and He says, "***I am among you as one who serves.***" There was no arrogance, pride, or self-seeking glory in Jesus Christ. His humility, kindness, and reason for leading were all for one purpose, serving others.)

In the military, the Thanksgiving meal in military dining facilities is a special time. The men and women who work in the dining facilities work long and hard days, every day of the year. They are trained culinary specialist that spend all year adhering to some pretty bland meal plans. But come Thanksgiving, these men and women lay out a meal second to none. They decorate the dining facilities and fill them with incredible culinary displays that you can't wait to devour.

Still, perhaps the very best part of Thanksgiving in a military dining facility is the act of service displayed by leadership. It has long been a tradition that on Thanksgiving Day, the senior leaders of each military organization put on their fanciest military attire, cover it with an apron, place serving gloves on their hands, and a paper hat on their head. The senior leaders stand behind the serving trays of delicious Thanksgiving entrée's and serve each military person eating with them that day. Every leader gets a chance to not only serve those they lead but to tell them how thankful they are for them. This was one of my favorite days as a leader because humility was the main entrée being served for those we led. If I had it to do all over again, I would have added the Chick-Fil-A twist to serving and told everyone, "My pleasure." Don't worry about how others see you when you lead by serving. They may not understand that your proudest claim to success is that you are honored, appointed, and anointed by our Creator to work for them.)

If you are protesting this leadership mind-set, I would ask you to set aside your self-importance pride and realize that you would have no one to lead without them to work for. Yes, those you lead are accountable to you as their leader, but you, as their leader, are just as much accountable to those you lead. Everyone who leads is working for those they lead. The President or Prime Minister of a nation-state serves the people of that nation. Even holding the highest political office appoints one to serve others' needs. So does every leadership position in every organization.

Observe an organization with a low personnel retention rate, also known as a high turnover rate. Look at an organization with a significant number of employees routinely calling out sick, and you will discover an organization where leaders lead as if everyone works for them. However, look at an organization with a loyal workforce, a low turnover rate, and a high percentage of daily workforce availability. You will observe an organization where the people feel led by leaders working for their success and best interests. Before we can discuss the impact a leader's approach in leading has on those they lead, let's look at what God says concerning the concept of "You Work for Them."

In Mark 10:45 Jesus said, ***"For even the Son of Man came not to be served but to serve others and to give his life as a ransom for many."*** (The King above of all kings, and the greatest and most powerful leader to ever walk this earth, came to ***"serve others and give."*** Jesus Christ established the perfect example for all leaders to emulate by coming into this world to lead by serving.)

After all, what gives us hope and joy, and what will be our proud reward and crown as we stand before our Lord Jesus when he returns? It is you! Yes, you are our pride and joy (1 Thessalonians 2:19–20). (You know that look of pride and joy you see on a parent's smiling face as they watch their child complete a race, score a goal, score a touchdown, or finally make contact hitting a ball for the first time? That child is their parent's pride and joy. Seeing their child find success is the greatest treasure a parent could ever have. It should be no different as a leader. When a leader sees those they lead achieving success, going the extra step to help a workmate in need, or receiving an award for outstanding performance, the leader should be beaming with pride and joy. The success of those you lead is your success. This indicates you have encouraged them, afforded them opportunities for greater self-development, or provided them with opportunities to show their stuff. Seeing those you serve and lead achieve success reveals nurturing their professional growth and looking out for their careers. When those you serve and lead are recognized for their achievements, you are proud of them. You can also take pride in the fact that you have done right by them. Who doesn't want to be associated with successful people? Keep others first as you work for them, and everyone will find success.)

I will brighten the darkness before them and smooth out the road ahead of them (Isaiah 42:16). (The future is full of unknowns and challenges. If everything is going okay right now, wait a minute, and something is sure to go wrong up ahead. In John 16:33, Jesus said, ***"Here on earth you will have many trials and sorrows."*** A leader represents so much more than someone in charge. A leader represents hope, help, and light when the darkness of a challenging time appears. When those you serve and lead know that their leader is "in this for them," they know that no matter what difficulties may come in the workplace or their life, they have a helper in you. They know they have someone filled with empathy for their challenges, compassion for their needs, and a desire to make things better for them. It is no sign of weakness for a leader to say, "I work for you." On the contrary, it is a sign of a leader's courage and priority motive in leading.)

And without question, the person who has the power to give a blessing is greater than the one who is blessed (Hebrews 7:7). (Throughout this book, you have read the words "those you serve and lead" more than a few times. The term *serve* scares some leaders. These are leaders who believe, saying they "serve" others minimize their stature as a leader. To say, as a leader that you "serve" those you lead is not to place yourself in a subordinate position to them. It is to say that your labor is done so on their behalf. Your labor of work is empowered with the positional authority to invoke divine care into the lives of those you serve and lead. This is the honor of leading, to have the power to make the workplace a place people look forward to serving in. The most incredible privilege of being a leader is the entrustment given for the care of and service to our fellow man.)

Do not withhold good from those who deserve it when it's in your power to help them (Proverbs 3:27). (This verse comes from the wisest man to ever live, King Solomon. He charges leaders to continuously and selflessly exert their power of influence toward the needs of those they lead. This is one of the very best parts of being allowed to lead others! Don't flaunt power; use it for making the lives of those you serve and lead better!)

They do not fear bad news; they confidently trust the LORD to care for them (Psalm 112:7). (Confidence in a leader's abilities and motives promotes feelings of safety and encouragement for those being led. No matter what obstacles and challenges arise, everything will be okay because their leadership always takes care of them. Leaders should let those they serve and lead know that they will be there for everyone when the times get tough. Leaders encourage others to believe that together they will overcome whatever challenge or difficulty comes their way. Just as God told Joshua through Moses before leading the people of Israel into many tough and fearful times in Deuteronomy 31:8, "***Do not be afraid or discouraged, for the LORD will personally go ahead of you. He will be with you; he will neither fail you nor abandon you.***")

Know the state of your flocks and put your heart into caring for your herds (Proverbs 27:23). (This relates to the importance of "Know Those You Lead." Knowing them opens the door to identifying their needs and concerns. Once you know their concerns and needs, give everything you have in addressing and helping them.)

In John 10:10–14, Jesus teaches,

> ***The thief's purpose is to steal and kill and destroy. My purpose is to give them a rich and satisfying life. I am the good shepherd. The good shepherd sacrifices his life for his sheep. A***

> ***hired hand will run when he sees a wolf coming. He will abandon the sheep because they don't belong to him, and he isn't their shepherd. And so the wolf attacks them and scatters the flock. The hired hand runs away because he's working only for money and doesn't really care about the sheep. I am the good shepherd; I know my own sheep, and they know me.***

(Just as a shepherd cares for the safety and well-being of their sheep, a leader counts those they serve and lead as their own. The leader is willing to do whatever is required for their safety and well-being. People rejoice in feeling and being safe. Knowing they have a leader who will protect their interests, job, and wages provides them with a sense of peace and calm. ***I know the LORD is always with me. I will not be shaken, for he is right beside me. No wonder my heart is glad, and I rejoice. My body rests in safety*** (Psalm 16:8–9). When a leader's motive is "them" and not "self," and that they will always remain by their side when troubling times and circumstances attack, people feel safe and encouraged to succeed. Providing a safe and peaceful environment for those you serve and lead is another task for you, their leader, as you work for them.)

Their work is to watch over your souls, and they are accountable to God (Hebrews 13:17). (Every leader is charged with the responsibility of watching over their people's work lives. To whom much is given, much is also required. Since God ultimately appoints every leader, every leader is accountable to God for how well they watch over and care for those they serve and lead. Now that gets my attention, and it should get yours too!)

Whoever wants to be a leader among you must be your servant (Matthew 20:26). (Becoming a leader, at any and every level of leadership, a person must be willing to serve others. President Thomas Jefferson warned against leaders that were into leading for their gain and not that of serving others when stating, "*Whenever a man has cast a longing eye on offices, a rottenness begins in his conduct.*" Motives for wanting to lead must be centered on a desire to serve others. Do not get hung up on the term "servant." Secular society has tainted the true meaning of being a servant to those we lead. To provide an example of the secular world's view of the term "servant," the Google search engine defines a "servant" as "a person who performs duties for others, especially a person employed in a house on domestic duties or as a personal attendant." However, we are seeking to lead according to God's Truth in leadership. According to God's Word, being a servant is a quality and characteristic found even in Kings, as in a king's position concerning his people. In 1 Kings 12, King Rehoboam sought the counsel of those that had advised and provided counsel to his father, King Solomon. The wise and older counselors reviewed a request from leaders within the country sent to King Rehoboam. They advised the King in 1 Kings 12:7: ***If you are willing to be a servant to these people today and give them a favorable answer, they will always be your loyal subjects.*** Unfortunately, King Rehoboam disregarded the wise counsel he was given. His entire reign as King was one of injustice and chaos in the kingdom. His desire to lead for selfish and greedy gains instead of one as a servant to those he led brought suffering on everyone. We lead to serve others. God's Word says so.)

Now these are the gifts Christ gave to the Church: the apostles, the prophets, the evangelists, and the pastors and teachers. Their responsibility is to equip God's people to do his work and build up the Church, the body of Christ (Ephesians 4:11–12). (Just as those anointed and appointed to lead the Church were to lead, they also were given the responsibility of serving God's people by equipping them for their work. Being a leader in any and every calling of life must be synonymous with helping others. When a leader provides training, resources, and professional development of those they lead, they serve others' needs. Like it or not, and no matter how secular society paints it, leading is serving or working for others.)

"He must become greater and greater, and I must become less and less" (John 3:30). (These are words John the Baptist spoke when Jesus entered into His ministry. This is also the mentality a leader must take when serving those they lead. As you work for them, you are seeking to increase their value within the organization. Part of "working for them" is placing the spotlight on their accomplishments and achievements. As a leader, you are grooming and developing tomorrow's leaders. Like it or not, there comes an end to everyone's role as a leader in an organization. The real test of a leader's worth is not what they did for themselves, but their willingness and efforts to make others more extraordinary.)

He cared for them with a true heart and led them with skillful hands (Psalm 78:72). (A true heart in leading represents one in which those being led come first. Use your gifted talents and authority to make their lives full and rewarding.)

Don't be selfish; don't try to impress others. Be humble, thinking of others as better than yourselves. Don't look out only for your own interests, but take an interest in others too (Philippians 2:2–4). (A leader must get past themselves and stop worrying about how others see them. Let your walk be one of humility, honoring God's way of leading others, and trust that His ways are perfect and right; they are! Keep your intentions oriented toward the interest of those you serve and lead. You take care of God's people (that is all of us), and God will take good care of you!)

Don't just pretend to love others. Really love them. Hate what is wrong. Hold tightly to what is good. Love each other with genuine affection and take delight in honoring each other (Romans 12:9). (You cannot fake love. Every one of us must pursue growing in our love for others. Love is the key ingredient to building relationships. Love as a motive when leading others is right in life and the workplace. A genuine nature of loving others is revealed in our walk and talk as a leader. Love lifts others, where hate tears others and the workplace down.)

Have you ever worked in a place where the organizational climate and the organizational culture were ones that every workday you dreaded having to go there? Or have you ever cringed at the thought that you may encounter a particular leader at work? So much so, you spent your time doing whatever it took to avoid being in their presence. One of the reasons God's Word leaves nothing unsaid about how a leader is to lead is that when God appoints someone to lead, he assigns them to take care of his children in the workplace. Leaders create and maintain a workplace culture that can either be a positive one or dread for the workforce.

Do you recognize as a leader, how you lead impacts the physical health of those you serve and lead? A person's emotions produce most of their physical disease. A person's inner thoughts are connected to their physical health. Anytime I feel emotional stress, my entire back begins to tighten up to the point I have to lay on a hard surface and practice proper breathing techniques to make the tightness and associated pain reside. This type of reaction is called an Emotional-Induced Illness (EII). Many years ago, Dr. John A. Schindler, MD of the Ochsner Clinic in New Orleans, presented his findings to the medical community in a published paper. Dr. Schindler stated, "74 percent of 500 consecutive patients admitted to the department handling gastro-intestinal diseases were found to be suffering from E.I.I."[1] His findings were later supported by a report from Yale University's Out-Patient Medical Department who reported, "76 percent of patients coming to the Clinic were suffering from E.I.I.!"[2]

When physical symptoms of an illness begin, people rarely realize that many began as mental symptoms created by emotional sources internalized over a long period. Dr. Schindler made "a partial list of the hundreds of symptoms this disease can produce. The percentage number after each symptom indicates how often its occurrence is due to emotionally induced illness.

Complaint	**Percentage**
Pain in the back or neck	75
Lump in the throat	90
Ulcer-like pain	50
Gall bladder-like pain	50
Gas	99
Dizziness	80
Headaches	80
Constipation	70
Tiredness/fatigue	90[3]

An organization's climate and culture serve as a constant source of either a positive or negative emotional energy source. The organization's workforce internalizes these emotional energies. Dr. Schindler points out that "most cases of emotionally induced illness are the result of a monotonous drip, drip of seemingly unimportant yet nevertheless unpleasant emotions. The everyday run of anxieties, fears, discouragements, and longings."[4] This signifies how influential leaders are in the overall health of those they lead. Remember, a leader who "works for them" creates and promotes an environment or a climate that lifts others, providing a safe, encouraging, and fulfilling workplace. People may present a brave and impenetrable demeanor. Still, Dr. Schindler points out, "A person may have an outwardly genial manner and yet have a set of fundamental mental emotions that are doing him no good."[5]

Think about it this way, a person goes to work for a third or more of their time four to six days a week and will do this for three to four decades of life. They are under stress to perform a task while at work. They are expected to meet established productivity requirements and sustain their needed value in the organization. Peek outside their workplace requirements. The person is raising a family, nurturing personal relationships, attending classes for self-improvement, and maintaining their living residence. And let's not forget the emotional stressors many people endure just in their commute to and from work. In other words, people already have a lot of stressors banging at their emotional stability every day.

Why would a leader that cares about them want to add to their emotional load by being anything but encouraging and supportive of them? When a leader approaches leading as "working for them," they make at least a third of a person's daily life more emotionally bearable. I always sought to establish a work climate of one that people looked forward to coming to. I set out to establish a work climate that, while at work, people knew they were in a place where they were valued, cared for, and appreciated. It never diminished my authority as a leader when I told them, "I work for you. Please allow me to use my position of authority to help you when needed."

No one is any better than any other person. We are all equals as people. When a person serves in a leadership position, they are in a role to accomplish the organization's mission and influence others to achieve that mission. The best way to influence others is through working to meet their needs. Establish and require full adherence to a leadership climate and culture where the workforce's emotions are uplifted and encouraged. Work for them by your walk, not just your talk.

The last thing I would like to leave you with as we discuss your role as a leader regarding EII is Dr. Schindler's list of every person's six basic needs. I would ask you to take a moment as a leader after reading this list and ask yourself, "How well in my service to those I lead, do I meet their needs?"

Basic Needs

1. The Need for Love: Receiving such affection makes us feel important and valuable; it makes us feel that we have a place in the order of people and things.
2. The Need for Security: People know you will help them through a deal of trouble.
3. The Need for Creative Expression: No one, including you and me, has fundamental happiness if he is not being constructive either in his leisure hours or in his work.
4. The Need for Recognition: Everyone needs to be regarded by someone as being of some importance and doing something that is of some good.
5. The Need for New Experiences: A human being cannot be kept in a dull, monotonous routine without developing a monotonous repetition of unpleasant emotions and functional disease with it.
6. The Need of Self-Esteem: In spite of disappointments, in spite of the little or big personal failures that a person experiences through life, most everyone, nevertheless, manages to think sufficiently well of himself to be encouraged to go ahead.[6]

Just as each person should be comforted by God's assurances stated in Isaiah 41:10, ***"Don't be afraid, for I am with you. Don't be discouraged, for I am your God. I will strengthen you and help you."*** And again, when God says in Isaiah 41:13, ***"Don't be afraid. I am here to help you."*** So should those you lead feel needed, safe, and encouraged in the workplace. Those you serve and lead should remain confident that your leading motive is oriented toward theirs and the organization's beneficial interests. It is not necessarily what a person physically ingests that always makes them sick. There are many instances where the emotional aspects of anger, guilt, shame, anxiety, stress, and despair are eating away and leading to physical illness. Please don't be a catalyst of EII for those you serve and lead. Know and understand the impact your leadership has on the lives of those you serve and lead. It does matter how others feel.

If a leader stops caring about how their leadership impacts others' lives, they should not be allowed to lead. The best way to ensure leaders care is by making sure they understand why they exist. You know, those people they work for! We are told in Luke 1:79 that Jesus came into this world ***to give light to those who sit in the darkness.*** As a leader, you exist to do the same for those God has blessed you with the honor of serving and working for. Leaders shine a light of hope and joy into the workplace and the lives of those they serve and lead.

Would you be a little timid of asking those you serve and lead, "Who do you see when you see me?" Maybe, more importantly, let me ask you something which requires brutal honesty on your part, "Who Do You See in the Mirror?"

Reflection Time

Does the phrase "You work for them" bother you? If so, why?

Do you feel like you answer to those you serve and lead? I mean, if you work for someone, don't you have to answer to them? Do you see yourself accountable to those you serve and lead? Should you be?

Would you be okay if your job evaluation allowed those you serve and lead to having a place on it to rate your service to them and the organization from their vantage point? Why?

---

[1] John A. Schindler, M.D., How To Live 365 Days a Year (Revised Edition) (Philadelphia: Running Press Book Publishers, 2003), 35.

[2] Ibid., 35.

[3] Ibid., 38.

[4] Ibid., 42.

[5] Ibid., 79.

[6] Ibid., 183-193.

PART 11

Who Do You See in the Mirror?

Jesus says, "Outwardly you look like righteous people, but inwardly your hearts are filled with hypocrisy and lawlessness."

—Matthew 23:28

Please allow me to say something you may or may not be aware of. Those you serve and lead recognize you for who you are on the inside, not your outward appearance. When you look in the mirror, do you look to see past your reflected outward appearance? Do you look to know who you are as a person and a leader on the inside? Whenever our leading efforts fail to check all of the ethical blocks, the person in the mirror knows the truth. Have you ever looked in the mirror and could not recognize the person looking back at you? It is a sad place to find oneself. The person looking back at you is unrecognizable due to behaving in ways that you never thought you were capable of. Sometimes we find ourselves disgusted with who we see in the mirror, and we wonder if others see us the same way?

There are quick failures, but there are no quick fixes for the things that make us dislike the person we see in the mirror. When we take our eyes off of those we serve and lead for an extended period, we are at risk of jeopardizing all the opportunities we have for helping others in the future. Suppose you are more concerned with how your exterior appears to others. In that case, your interior motives may begin finding ways to discredit and ultimately disgrace you. Yet we should seek to respect the person in the mirror before we should expect others to respect us.

Have you ever seen a classic sports car on display that looked as perfect as the day it was originally built? In your mind, you picture this beautiful car heading out across the highways and backcountry roads effortlessly, bringing enjoyment and creating memories. You move in a little closer to admire the classic car's beauty, and you can't wait to get under the hood to check out the engine. Surely it must be as pristine as the exterior. But when you lift the hood, you are brought crashing back to reality as you see an engine as old as the car itself. It has seen its last days of revving up and cruising down any road or highway. Under the hood, the engine reflects the car's incapability. The exterior is only a mirage of the vehicle's actual value.

Looking sleek, looking concerned, looking the part, looking, looking, looking, is that all we care about in society today? Society makes people seen on television and in movies into "celebrities." These are people who are pretending to be someone else in a role they are playing. They are showing you an edited version of what they want you to see of "who" they are. People and today's social media make others into a "celebrity." A person's actions (not acting) of selflessness without regard for personal safety make a hero. In other words, a "celebrity" is created and celebrated by people for what is seen outwardly. A hero is made by selfless actions for others from what is inside them, who they are. This is true in being a leader as well.

The multibillion-dollar cosmetics, skincare, and cosmetic surgical procedures industries are supported by people desiring to look their best on the exterior. There is nothing wrong with those pursuits. However, when it comes to leading, if we are alluring on the surface, but we are appalling on the inside, we are simply a deplorable leader. Os Guinness tells it like it is, "Everyone sees what you seem to be, few experiences what you really are."[1] As a leader, you should want others to look past your title and position and look at the person you are. When others experience what you are, a leader who cares, you are making their lives better.

In leading, it is about what's inside us that counts. With your leadership, others should get what everyone deserves. A leader who is selfless, kind, caring, patient, gentle, loyal—you know, all those characteristics and attributes associated with being a great leader. All that "stuff" that a mirror does not reflect, but others see in your walk and hear in your talk. God's Word warns the leader's not to be fooled by the sophisticated image they see in the mirror.

If you think you are too important to help someone, you are only fooling yourself. You are not that important (Galatians 6:3). (These are some very sobering words, but oh so true in reality. Look back across history at the names of larger-than-life leaders; where are they now? For only a second in time, they were considered "important." While some of their legacies may live on, the person themselves, like everyone, will eventually be no more. First Chronicles 29:15 reminds everyone, ***We are here for only a moment, visitors and strangers in the land as our ancestors were before us. Our days on earth are like a passing shadow, gone so soon without a trace.*** A leader should never look in the mirror and tell themselves they have "arrived" and are now an "important" person. Vanity is a selfish attitude. As discussed earlier, selfishness and leadership cannot coexist in anyone desiring to be a great leader.

Leaders should realize that they are not that important in the grander scheme of things. Living a life of service to others is essential, not the person doing the serving. A person's leadership position, along with a $1.50, can get them a beverage from a vending machine. The vending machine does not care about the "leader" putting the $1.50 in. What is essential to the vending machine is $1.50. Just like the vending machine identifies money as necessary in the transaction, those you serve and lead see your actions on theirs and the organization's behalf as necessary, not you. Congratulations on being a leader. Now do the critical stuff leaders do while you can. And remember, when you look in the mirror and think you are all that and a bag of chips, the only person you are fooling, is the one in the mirror!)

In quietness and confidence is your strength (Isaiah 30:15). (Have faith in your abilities, not arrogance. Let your walk reveal your strengths in good character and creating value in the lives of those you serve and lead. Talking a good game and looking good can be used to deceive. Humble actions of genuine care and service reveal your power in character and leading.)

If you listen to constructive criticism, you will be at home among the wise (Proverbs 15:31). (While a mirror can help a leader see what they want others to see visually, the truth of what others see will set you free to become a better leader. No one desires criticism, but let's be honest with ourselves, not a single one of us gets everything we set out to do right. Our first reaction to being criticized by others is to take it as an insult. Still, King Solomon tells us in Proverbs 12:16, ***A fool shows his annoyance at once, but a prudent man overlooks an insult.*** A sensible person looks for the truth in what others are saying to them. Dawson Trotman, the Navigators Ministry Founder, stated, "There is a kernel of truth in every criticism. Look for it, and when you find it, rejoice in its value."

For over thirty-five years as a leader in the military and the private sector, I have received my fair share of criticism. In retrospect, most of it was warranted. As an Adjunct College Professor, at the end of each class, students surveyed are provided the opportunity to assess my performance. If given, denying their criticism limits my ability to become more of what they need me to be in meeting their educational goals. If what they are saying is offered to help me become a better teacher, I will assess their criticism as a tool to help me grow into what they need from me as a professor. Constructive criticism is given to reveal where we need growth. We all know that we have yet to arrive at perfection in all that we do, especially in leading. "You never win the gold without hurting. Likewise, every leader has to develop a plan for handling criticism because criticism will come in any dynamic organization."[2])

Let everyone see that you are considerate in all you do (Philippians 4:5). (The mirror reflects your physical appearance. Still, what matters most is what they see in your actions. Let them see your care, genuine concern, and willingness to be of service to their needs. Their spirit for work and life is a reflection of your consideration and kindness to them.)

We are careful to be honorable before the Lord, but we also want everyone else to see that we are honorable (2 Corinthians 8:21). (God sees and knows the motives of our heart. ***People may be pure in their own eyes, but the LORD examines their motives*** (Proverbs 16:2). When leading, everyone recognizes leader's motives. It matters if they see you as being trustworthy or being unscrupulous. It matters if they see you as a person with integrity. When you look in the mirror, you know what lays behind the reflection looking back at you. You know if the person you see is selfless or selfish. You know if the person you see is leading for others or themselves. Ensure the person behind the reflection can not only look themselves in the eye, but those they serve and lead with their head held high. Suppose you look at your reflection and cannot respect yourself. In that case, eventually, no one else will respect the person looking back at you either. Get right with God and seek His character for how you live and lead. Then you can get right and stay right in the eyes of others.)

Because of the privilege and authority God has given me, I give each of you this warning: Don't think you are better than you really are. Be honest in your evaluation of yourselves, measuring yourselves by the faith God has given us (Romans 12:3). (When a person or a leader receives a work promotion, they often catch themselves taking a glimpse at the things represented by their rise in responsibility. It is only natural to take a second to celebrate their advancement. When a Colonel is promoted to Brigadier General (One-Star) in the Army, they become what is called a "Flag Officer." A Red Flag represents this with an appropriate number of large General Star(s) commensurate to their new rank. The newly-promoted Brigadier General will receive their Flag from the Department of the Army by mail. I had a friend who received his Flag in the mail. He tied the red Flag around his neck and allowed the Flag to hang like a cape on his back. He ran wildly around his home like a superhero celebrating his huge accomplishment. In the private sector, a person may take a moment to look at their name on a sign outside their new office. They pause to see their name and new position stenciled on the entry into their new work accommodation. These actions are warranted, as these leaders have worked hard for many years to achieve their recognized success. Everyone should celebrate their professional and personal achievements, even leaders. But the moment of celebration quickly evaporates as the reality of increased responsibility must become the focus moving forward. At this point, they still have not arrived. There is still much improvement to be made in one's self. Continue to seek self-improvement. Continue to seek mentors, advisors, and people that will speak the truth about how you can continue to grow as a leader. Every day when you look in the mirror, see yourself for where you need to improve and remember much more is expected of you today than yesterday. The great and remarkable leader, Dr. Billy Graham, reminds us, "When we come to the end of ourselves, we come to the beginning of God.")

One last thought and experience I would like to share with you regarding who you see in the mirror. After putting on the uniform every morning, I would always step in front of the mirror to check that I looked like a squared-away soldier. I was responsible for enforcing the Army's standards in our organization; therefore, I looked at the reflection in the mirror to see who they would see when they looked at me. This practice was merely a superficial attempt to look like a standards bearer. I was looking beyond the obvious reflection of a uniform and a haircut to be honest with you. I was looking at the man under it all. Many times, I did not like the person I saw. I wondered if they saw through my exterior façade of looking the part and saw the uncertainty, vulnerability, and weaknesses I possessed as a man.

On a day in which everything seemed to be going wrong, my frustrations grew to the point of anger. I was working out of my home study, and there was no one else around except my beautiful wife Jenny in the next room. Out of my mouth (which reflects my heart) came a loud release of words that painted a very colorful and graphic portrait of my anger. ***So get rid of all evil behavior. Be done with all deceit, hypocrisy, jealousy, and all unkind speech*** (1 Peter 2:1). This was not a moment I am proud of, but it allowed me a wonderful teaching moment.

A voice filled with love asked me a question that hit me like a freight train from the next room. Beautiful Jenny asked me, "How are you supposed to be a wonderful Christian leader out in the world if that is not who you are in our home?" ***Human anger does not produce the righteousness God desires*** (James 1:20). I sat in silence; I had no reply. She was unquestionably correct. I was ashamed that I let the one person I wanted to see the best in me see the worst. This reminded me, it is not about who we see in the mirror as much as it is about how others see who we indeed are. People spend hours looking in a mirror trying to perfect the image they want to convey to others about what they must be like as a person. "If I look beautiful or handsome on the outside, they may believe I am just as beautiful or handsome on the inside." If you ever looked at an attractive person and then experienced their personality to find out they are not attractive on the inside, you know what I mean.

If you want to see the real person in the mirror, then your mirror must be the faces of those you lead. Those faces have ears and eyes that absorb everything you do and speak. They see the motives of your heart and hear them in your words. Their actions and emotions reflect the nature of your character as their leader. Their smile, their eagerness to do well, their enjoyment of life while at work in your leadership presence is all a reflection of who you are. This is how important leadership is. It is not about the person in the mirror. It is about the life of the one standing in front of you, reflecting who you are to them.

Social media has provided a platform for self-exposure. People snap selfie after selfie to capture an image they want to post online for others to see. Social media serves as a highlight reel showing the high points in a person's life. Still, we all know the highlights never capture the reality and hidden images of struggles and challenges in a person's life. Life's truth is not what we show others. Life's truth is how we feel underneath the fake exterior we show others.

What if social media showed how a person feels on the inside? Their fears, insecurities, shame, guilt, remorse, pride, deviousness, good intentions, bad intentions, motives, hopes, desires, needs, hurts, cares, and sometimes their emptiness. We are all guilty of wearing a mask, concealing who we are and how we feel on the inside. A lot of days during my military career presented significant physical risks.

I would be lying if I did not admit that many times what we were doing (airborne operations, live-fire exercises, or combat operations) scared the heck out of me. But do you think I would ever show that fear or admit to it? No, because that's not what we do. We offer others what we think they need to see to make ourselves seem something that is not true.

Leaders are afraid to show weakness. Leaders want to appear invincible. Leaders are afraid to reveal any kink in their emotional or faculty armor. Armor used to shield others from seeing our insecurities. Being vulnerable scares most people, myself included. But there is one person we can be susceptible to, one person that does not judge our weaknesses but loves us unconditionally, God. As a leader, my hope is that you see the same person that those you serve and lead need and deserve to see when you look in the mirror. A leader who does not judge their weaknesses but sees their potential. A leader who genuinely cares for them unconditionally and a leader who is in this game of life for them. They need you to see yourself as they see you. This is the truth that will set you free to be everything God intends you to be. God has anointed your life with the honor of leading others, now that's a privilege beyond compare.

Reflection Time

When you are getting ready for the day, do you see past the reflected exterior to the person underneath, or are you a surface only person? What do you see?

Aesthetics only go so far. What do those you serve and lead see in your character underneath your polished exterior?

What would you describe as the differences between who you are in the mirror and who you are on the inside? Would it surprise or disappoint those you serve and lead?

---

1 Os Guinness, When No One Sees: The Importance of Character in an Age of Image (Colorado Springs: NAVPRESS, 2000), 64.

2 Harold Myra and Marshall Shelley, The Leadership Secrets of Billy Graham (Grand Rapids: Zondervan, 2005), 85.

PART 12

PAUSEX!

When the godly are in authority, the people rejoice.
But when the wicked are in power they groan.

—Proverbs 29:2

Spell-check went crazy with the title of this last chapter. I could have titled it "Conclusion," "That's a Wrap," or simply "Last Words." However, in keeping with my brain-washed use of terms from the military, I thought the term "PAUSEX" best suited where we are in becoming the leader God's Word teaches us to be. In the military, people regularly train to fight the wars of our nation. When a person in the military is not deployed in combat operations, they are always training and preparing for future deployments. During many Major Training Exercises, there is an opposing force (OPFOR) of military members. The OPFOR is dressed, equipped, and fight like potential enemies of future combat operations. Their mission is to replicate the tactics our enemies will use on the battlefield.

These Major Training Exercises are very intense, fast-paced, and extremely challenging by design, lasting several weeks. They are designed to push the US forces to their physical and mental limits. At pre-scheduled points in the Major Training Exercise, there are Pauses in the Exercise (PAUSEX) to allow the Exercise Evaluators to sit with the US forces leadership and review their performance in the Exercise to that point. They use this time to inform the US forces leadership of their assessment of their organization's performance. The leadership can then reassess their operational tactics if needed and make adjustments once the Exercise resumes.

This is where you are now. You are at a PAUSEX in your way of leading. During this PAUSEX, I ask you to self-evaluate your performance as a leader. You should spend time assessing your standards and motives of operating as a leader against the way God intends leaders to serve and lead. While this book did not and could not address every challenge encountered in leadership, its goal was to orient you to the authority that addresses every challenge you will face, the authority of God's Word.

At the age of ninety and after more than six decades as a Pastor, Dr. Pat Robertson (Founder of the Christian Broadcast Network, Founder of Regent University, and a former Marine Corps Officer) wrote a recent article *The Power of the Name of the Lord.* Dr. Robertson began his article by stating.

> *The more I study Scripture, the more treasure I find. The Bible never runs dry. We can never plumb the depths of it! I have read the Bible over and over again, and I have taught it for many years. But I still find truths that I've never seen before. God continues to open my eyes to gems of wisdom, understanding, discernment, discretion, encouragement, and power I didn't know were there.*[1]

Dr. Robertson's life of serving God and studying His Word still reveals new things as he reads it after all these years. For my lifetime, I have felt a passion for making the lives of others better. Little did I realize that these natural feelings I had to serve others were aligned with how God would have me to lead as a leader. As I began to explore God's Word, I discovered that God had already described the methods and characteristics required for each of us to become great leaders. As you spend time reading and absorbing God's Word, He reveals His Truth in how you are to live your life, lead your family, and lead others in the workplace.

The purpose of my instruction is that all believers would be filled with love that comes from a pure heart, a clear conscience, and genuine faith (1 Timothy 1:5).

Maybe you have noticed, I never provided a "one size fits all" definition of leadership. Having served a lifetime as a leader in the military and acquiring a post-graduate degree in leadership, I know man's "definition of leadership." I do not need to offer another wordy description or introduce some overly complicated explanation of the subject. Enough is enough already. Identifying oneself as a leader sounds like they may be someone important. In actuality, they say, "I work for others, and I am responsible for theirs and our organizations' ability to be successful."

Being a leader is just what Jesus says we are to do, serve people who can do nothing for us in return. This is what we do in leading, we give, we care, we serve, and we love one another as Christ did in his ministry, all the way to the Cross. If you are going to lead, you will sometimes fall short of your expectations; just don't fall short of others' needs. Fail while trying; not watching. Don't let the pressures of the secular world to conform to "their way" sway you from where Jesus wants to take you as a person and as a leader. ***It is better to take refuge in the LORD than to trust in people*** (Psalm 118:8).

So my dear brothers and sisters, be strong and immovable. Always work enthusiastically for the Lord, for you know that nothing you do for the Lord is ever useless (1 Corinthians 15:58).

Bob Goff warns us, "Aligning with love will earn us weird looks and find us in more than a few tricky circumstances. A glance at the lives of anybody who has followed Jesus can prove this world just doesn't quite get it."[2] But you do, and now you know and understand that the honor of leading is that you are allowed the privilege of entering into meaningful relationships with others. Others who God has placed under your authority of care, to **love** and **serve** them. This is the secret to great leadership. Jesus commands us in John 15:17, ***"Love each other."***

As a person, when we spend time in God's Word and prayer with Him, we gain closeness to God. Through this closeness, God transforms us more and more into the person He designed us to be. My prayer for each of us is that by knowing God's Truth, we will continue to evolve and transform into the leader He would have us to be for others. ***For the Lord is the Spirit, and wherever the Spirit of the Lord is, there is freedom. So all of us who have had that veil removed can see and reflect the glory of the Lord. And the Lord—who is the Spirit—makes us more and more like him as we are changed into his glorious image*** (2 Corinthians 3:17–18). Those you serve and lead are worth your efforts and commitment to becoming a great leader, according to God's Truth in leading!

As a leader, you hold a position of great responsibility. When you lead according to God's Truth in leading, you impact the lives of those you serve and lead in the way God would have you impact their lives. You are helping a more significant cause than fulfilling a person's workplace needs. Your walk and words are God's way of speaking through you into the lives of those He seeks to be in a relationship with. Your leadership establishes in others' how we are to lead, and we lead as God's Word reveals. Once God's way of leading takes root, Ephesians 4:14–15 says, ***Then we will no longer be immature like children. We won't be tossed and blown about by every wind of new teaching. We will not be influenced when people try to trick us with lies so clever they sound like the truth. Instead, we will speak the truth in love, growing in every way more and more like Christ.***

Don't give in to this world's examples of leadership. Keep your eyes focused on God's Words for leading. Have faith and be confident that leading God's way is the way people want to be led. After all, God created us, not man. This world tells us it's way to lead. God has told us His way to lead. God's Word and Truth for leading is the very best example of leading. So much so, God's Word warns us in Hebrews 12:25, ***Be careful that you do not refuse to listen to the One who is speaking.*** Why can these ways seem so different? Because one is man's attempt to figure things out, and the other is God's Word. By the way, God doesn't have to "figure things out," He knows everything. Don't follow the world's practices, be different, be GREAT, lead according to God's Truth.

PAUSEX is over. It's time to get back to leading as God would have you to lead. God has given you His command in Joshua 1:9–10, ***"This is my command—be strong and courageous! Do not be afraid or discouraged. For the LORD, your God is with you wherever you go."***

Remember, it is not who you used to be. It is who you are becoming that matters! Stay in the fight, Be Strong and Courageous, Glory to God!

> ***Oh that you would bless me and expand my territory! Please be with me in all that I do and keep me from trouble and pain!*** (1 Chronicles 4:10)

> ***So we must listen very carefully to the truth we have heard, or we may drift away from it.*** (Hebrews 2:1)

> ***For I am the LORD! If I say it, it will happen.*** (Ezekiel 12:25)

> ***Now all Glory to God, who is able, through his mighty power at work within us, to accomplish infinitely more than we might ask or think.*** (Ephesians 3:20)

---

[1] Pat Robertson, "The Path to Greatness," Miracle Living Today (Virginia Beach: The Christian Broadcasting Network, Inc., Summer 2020), 7.

[2] Bob Goff, Live in Grace, Walk in Love, A 365-Day Journey (Nashville: Nelson Books, 2019), 282.

BIBLIOGRAPHY (FOR FURTHER READING)

Ciulla, Joanne B. ed. *Ethics, the Heart of Leadership* (Santa Barbara: ABC-CLIO, LLC, 2014), 16.

Evans, Tony. *Your Comeback: Your Past Doesn't Have To Determine Your Future* (Eugene: Harvest House, 2018), 18–19.

Evans, Tony. *Time to Get Serious: Daily Devotions to Keep You Close to God* (Wheaton: Crossway, 1995), 309.

Goff, Bob. *Live in Grace, Walk in Love, A 365-Day Journey* (Nashville: Nelson Books, 2019), 238.

Graham, Billy. "A Return to Integrity in the Boardroom and Beyond," *San Diego Business Journal* 24, no. 19 (2003): A2.

Guinness, Os. *The Call: Finding and Fulfilling the Central purpose of Your Life* (Nashville: W Publishing Group, 2003), 85.

Guinness, Os. *When No One Sees: The Importance of Character in an Age of Image* (Colorado Springs: NAVPRESS, 2000), 64.

Holladay, Tom. *The Relationship Principles of Jesus* (Grand Rapids: Zondervan, 2008), 29.

Johnson, Carrie. "Ebber's Gets 25 Year Sentence for Role in WorldCom Fraud," *Washington Post.* July 14, 2005, B2.

Karabell, Shellie. "Corruption 101: The Dark Side of Leadership," *Forbes.com.* 19 June 2015, https://www.forbes.com/sites/shellie karabell/ 2015/06/19/corruption-101-the-dark-side-of-leader-ship/ #3989a4a039a8.

Kahn, Roomy. "White-Collar Crime—Motivation and Triggers," *Forbes.com.* 22 February 2018, https://www.forbes.com/sites/

roomykhan/2018/02/22/white-collar-crimes-motivations-and-triggers/#1cd656bd 1219.

Marsh and McLennan Companies. "*The Global Risks Report 2018*," 16 June 2018, https://www.marsh.com/nz/Insights/research/the-global-risks-report.html.

Myra, Harold, and Marshall Shelley. *The Leadership Secrets of Billy Graham* (Grand Rapids: Zondervan, 2005), 58.

Patterson, Kathleen, and Bruce Winston. "An Integrative Definition of Leadership," *International Journal of Leadership Studies, 1, no. 2 (2006): 6–66.*

Robertson, Pat. *Ten Laws for Success: Keys to Win in Work, Family, and Finance.* (Lake Mary: Charisma House, 2020), 75.

Robertson, Pat. "The Path to Greatness," *Miracle Living Today (Virginia* Beach: The Christian Broadcasting Network, Inc., Summer 2020), 7.

Rogers, Adrian. *Mastering Your Emotions (*Memphis: Love Worth Finding Ministries, 2012), 56.

Schindler, John A., MD. *How To Live 365 Days a Year (Revised Edition)* (Philadelphia: Running Press Book Publishers, 2003), 35.

United States Congress, Office of Compliance. *Compliance.gov,* https:www.compliance.gov/2017-annual-report

Yukl, Gary. *Leadership in Organizations: Sixth Edition* (Upper Saddle River: Prentice Hall, 2006), 422.

ABOUT THE AUTHOR

Roger Kingston holds a Doctorate in Strategic Leadership from Regent University (Christian Leadership to Change the World). Educated and extremely experienced in leadership, he has led at every leadership level within numerous organizations in complex and stressful environments. Roger retired from the US Army as a Command Sergeant Major after thirty-two years of active-duty service. He has led thousands of soldiers in peacetime and multiple combat operations in the 101st Airborne Division, 82nd Airborne Division, and the 25th Infantry Division. He also served as the Commandant of a US Army Leadership Academy. He has instructed leadership development in federal agencies, lead the business operations of a healthcare facility, and currently serves as an Adjunct College Professor teaching leadership. He serves as a Board Member for the Fellowship of Christian Athletes local Chapter, developing and implementing leadership-focused curriculums. He serves as an advising consultant for the leadership development of Christian business leaders.

CPSIA information can be obtained
at www.ICGtesting.com
Printed in the USA
BVHW091939060122
625623BV00011B/62